Varieties of Writing

A wider range of reading and writing for English 16–19

Varieties of Writing

A wider range of reading and writing for English 16-19

John Brown and David Jackson

Macmillan Education

First published 1984
Reprinted 1985

Published by
MACMILLAN EDUCATION LTD
Houndmills, Basingstoke, Hampshire RG21 2XS
and London
Companies and representatives
throughout the world

Printed in Hong Kong

British Library Cataloguing in Publication Data
Brown, John
    Varieties of writing.
    1. English language—Composition and exercises
    I. Title   II. Jackson, David
    808'.042   PE1413
    ISBN 0-333-32169-3

Contents

Introduction   1

1 AUTOBIOGRAPHY

Introduction   7

A   *Personal history and public events*

B   *The process of remembering*

Introduction

The need for change

Only 4% of students taking A level English Literature at 18 will go on to read English at university. This is a startling statistic, when you consider how closely the current A level syllabus is related to university demands. It is for the sake of the other 96% that we have devised this collection of writing, drawn from a more varied range of sources than is usually admitted to the A level syllabus.

This book is offered not only as a way of widening the current range of English Literature courses at 16–19, but also as a diverse collection of spoken and written experiences that will motivate a wide range of purposeful language activities at different levels from 16+ through to 19. The extracts are therefore intended to encourage students to become more confident and effective language users in the outside world as well as being part of a fresh approach to the A level English Literature course and syllabus.

Viewpoint

There is no such thing as a neutral anthology. A selection like this always implies a subjective viewpoint. In this particular case we have the clear intention of making the main, organising principle of this collection a 'view from below'. The underdog's perspective is there primarily because it is a neglected one. The official literary establishment often ignores voices like Dot Starn, Robert Roberts, Bert Fielder and Jeremy Seabrook's presentation of some of the Sunderland unemployed, Linton Kwesi Johnson and Keith Waterhouse's *Daily Mirror* tone. So these unheard, other voices, are included here, alongside the better-known ones (who are still very fully represented) in an attempt to redress something of a lost variety, reach and balance.

Breaking away from the classic text

Varieties of Writing brings together a broad range and variety of genres and different ways of telling. It is put forward as the first stage of a challenge to the established canon in English Literature courses (where the First Division league table of prescribed texts*—Chaucer, Hardy, Dickens, Austen, Milton, Pope, Charlotte Brontë, George Eliot—have a cyclical predictability) and to the view of literature as a received and predetermined, mono-ethnic National Cultural Heritage with a limited number of classic texts. This sense of settled, established literary terrain does a great injustice to the rich diversity of literature available for study, especially from the last hundred years.

That is not to say that we do not wish students to encounter Shakespeare, Chaucer or George Eliot, but we want to promote a much wider spread of choices and possibilities, and a greater variety of different voices from different backgrounds. That is why we would agree with Anthony Adams and Ted Hopkin when they comment:**

> The selection of books appears to be determined more often by that which will be useful to the student of literature later on in his studies rather than what is likely to engage his interest now—even though only 4% will actually go on in their studies in this area. This perhaps explains the regularity of the appearance of works that one might feel to be too maturely demanding for the average A level student at this age without a great deal of prior literary experience which just cannot be taken for granted.

Confirming diversity

Since we all live in a multi-racial society, we have tried to include material of quality that respects and confirms a flexible range of ways of speaking, life-styles, perceptions and viewpoints. We have therefore selected poems of Edward Brathwaite and Linton Kwesi Johnson, letters from George Jackson and James Baldwin and autobiography by Richard Wright.

We have also taken special note of some of the lively initiatives being taken in oral and social history, local publishing and community-organised adult literacy groups.

It was our conscious policy to represent some of the frequently neglected areas of experience alongside the more familiar. For example, you will find pieces from *Working Lives* collected by Centerprise, and Robert Roberts' *A Ragged Schooling,* rather than the over-used products of the rural nostalgia industry.

New forms

More complex pressures in society over the last hundred years, bringing with them fresh cross-currents of experience, have given rise to new forms of expression. (Just consider the way that changing patterns of communication, and particularly the

---

* *Journal of literature teaching politics:* No. 1 1982 c/o Andrew Belsey, Dept. of Philosophy, University College, Cardiff, pp. 5—6.
** *Sixth Sense: English: A Case Study* ed. Adams and Hopkin, Blackie.

rise of television, have emphasised the 'prompt verifiability'* of information, and perhaps have given rise to a new emphasis on documentary reporting where the selected appearance of actuality seems to be just as important as an overtly fictional re-construction.) We have tried to recognise these new forms of writing which are just as worthy of study as the conventional genres, in our selection.

New relationships between spoken and written language have emerged (look at the further references suggestions on 'Spoken histories'), and have produced the vitality of the oral history, people's autobiographies and History Workshop** movements. We have tried to represent some of the flavour and tone of voice of this more informal language.

In some ways these new forms are a response to an increasingly bewildering variety of daily experience, and therefore use a hybrid, dislocated mode of organisation to keep faith with the complex nature of the experience. As such they also tend to accord more readily with students' habitual way of looking at themselves and the outside world. Two examples will illustrate this point.

John Berger, who with Jean Mohr has been pioneering new relationships between image and text in *A Fortunate Man* and *The Seventh Man,* includes a combination of poems, short stories, an historical essay, description, explanation and even a novelette in *Pig Earth* in order to represent the diversity of the collective life and memory of a French peasant community. It is as if only new fusions of different kinds of writing will allow him to do justice to the subtle unfolding of the experience.

Similarly W.H. Auden and Louis MacNeice in *Letters from Iceland* build up a kaleidoscopic collage of letters, poems, questionnaire, travel guide statistics, an anthology, a diary, gossipy eavesdroppings, a list of proverbs and a map to create an appropriate form for the flickering, whirling impressions of travelling.

Period studies

Another innovation in the construction of syllabuses and courses is the possibility of period studies playing a greater part in the work that can be done between 16 and 19. There have been movements towards an organisation by period in the past, but mainly in terms of exclusively literary texts and rather loosely categorised chronological periods.

The need to place writing in a wider context (the need to 'look at literary texts as a product of specific societies at specific historical moments'***) becomes evident when we consider the instance of Steinbeck's *The Grapes of Wrath* being taught as a hermetically sealed object for practical criticism/discrimination purposes alone. The student can only understand the real meaning of the book if it is placed into some kind of economic/social/historical background.

---

* See the essay, 'The Storyteller' from Walter Benjamin's *Illuminations* Fontana, p. 89.
** See *People's History and Socialist Theory* ed. Raphael Samuel, History Workshop Series, Routledge and Kegan Paul.
***Carole Snee, 'Period studies and the place of criticism', *Re-reading English,* ed. P Widdowson, Methuen.

We have not the space in this book to develop complete syllabuses based on these lines, but we would like to suggest how one sample period could be treated, breaking down the boundaries between literary and non-literary texts, in the interests of giving the student an overall understanding of the period. Here is a sample sequence of varied sources on Britain in the 1930s:

(i) Documentary films, e.g. Edgar Anstey's *Housing Problems,* (1935); Ralph Bond's *Today We Live* (1936–7); *Workers' Newsreel, Jubilee* (1935)

(ii) A study of the popular press

(iii) A study of the photographs from *Picture Post* and *Shadow of Light* (Bill Brandt)

(iv) Working people's writing, e.g. *These Poor Hands* (B.L. Coombes), *Means Test Man* (Walter Brierley), *We Live* (Lewis Jones, George Garrett, Jim Phelan)

(v) Oral history, e.g. *Unemployment* (ed. Jeremy Seabrook); *Hooligans or Rebels: An Oral History of Working Class Childhood and Youth 1889– 1939* (Stephen Humphries); *The Hungry Years 1918–1940* from *The Long March of Everyman (1750–1960)* ed. Theo Barker.

(vi) Prose literature, e.g. *Journey to a War* (Auden and Isherwood); *Letters from Iceland* (Auden and MacNeice); *The Road to Wigan Pier* (George Orwell); *Journey Without Maps* (Graham Greene); *Autumn Journal* (Louis MacNeice); *Mr Norris Changes Trains/Goodbye to Berlin* (Christopher Isherwood)

(vii) The poetry of W.H. Auden in the 1930s

(viii) The collected essays, journalism and letters of George Orwell: Volume 1, *An Age Like This, 1920–1940* (ed. Sonia Orwell and Ian Angus) *Worktown People: Photographs from Northern England 1937–8* (Humphrey Spender) *Mass Observation* (Charles Madge and Tom Harrison)

Expanding response

Allied to our attempt to modify the traditional content of 16–19 English courses is our concern to expand the student's response away from any sense that there is an officially approved, single-track way of approaching English studies.

One way of doing this is to question the effectiveness of a didactic/transmission teaching style in helping the student to make up his/her own mind in reacting to what he/she reads. As an alternative the 'Ways of Working' sections suggest a series of preliminary responses (like jotting down first impressions in a reading log, discussing in small groups and thinking about a text through diagrams, etc.) as ways of making the reading experience the student's own.

We have included a whole section on 'Response', not only responses to reading but to films, architecture, and other experiences, in the hope of awakening more adventurous ways of approaching any text.*

---

* See my 'Dealing with a set book in literature at 16+ (*Great Expectations*—Charles Dickens)' from *English in Education:* Spring 1982: Volume 16 No. 1.

Organisation of the book

The sections

These have been chosen not as definitive categories of writing but as a first step towards broadening the established base of present A level English Literature studies.

Each section includes particular, concrete examples of that genre of writing, with tangential commentaries as well, which will assist the reader in considering the significances of that type of writing.

The sections can be expanded, condensed or tailored to suit the needs of the particular school/college/institution using them.

Section introductions

There are brief, introductory comments before each section. These aim to illuminate some of the possible ways of thinking about the writing contained in each section, and they usually include references to particular examples.

Ways of working

Instead of instructions or information being dictated by the teacher or by the book, the implied student/teacher relationship is a more open one, inviting initiatives from both sides. Work stimulated by this book will be more effective if it has been talked over (often in small groups), argued and negotiated, so that students' and teacher's perceptions, enthusiasms and preoccupations have been recognised in the setting-up of the task.

We have therefore made the 'Ways of working' a series of non-prescriptive suggestions, classroom techniques, possibilities for extension and a framework of options, simply to define the method of approach more precisely both for student and teacher. But the reader is welcome to discard these suggestions and work out individual routes to suit individual needs.

Other reading suggestions

We have also provided suggestions for further reading at the end of each section of the book, in order to give flexibility to what is read in the English classroom. The suggestions are there to widen the knowledge of resources available, and to encourage the student in an independent choice of further study.

1
Autobiography

INTRODUCTION

> 'My childhood is built into the everyday life of today . . . .'
> *Norman Nicholson*

We all carry our past around with us in our heads and it shapes the way we look at ourselves and the outside world. That is why autobiography is so important, because it tries to sort out what has formed our present consciousness, or, as Penelope Lively says, it tries to make sense of 'the things that have never stopped happening, because they are there always, in your head . . . .'

It is language that helps us to do the sorting-out. Through chewing the past over in talk, or through the process of writing it down on paper, we are able to dredge up and salvage some of our memories. And this process often involves an increase in understanding as we get it out of ourselves and inspect what we have come up with, as in Anna Leitrim's sense of moving from a conforming girl to an angry woman (see 'Me and my history').

Why record the past?

There are many possible explanations; Stuart Hood and Laurie Lee suggest that we deal with the obsessive tug of the past through setting it down on paper. It can be a 'laying to rest of ghosts', or a 'purging of the past'.

It can also be seen as a way of regularising the sheer fragmentariness of experience. In selecting, organising and processing these random moments we are 'ordering the mind'. Another way of looking at the reasons is the need to break out of the silence of unnoticed experiences* trapped by neglected backgrounds and sometimes limiting contexts. In Charles Forman's oral history of St Helens in the 1920s we catch working people's voices wanting to share a way of working and relaxing that is often just carried to the grave and forgotten. 'We too have our place,' agrees Douglas Dunn, 'who were not photographed/So much and then only in multitudes . . . .'

---

* See Ken Worpole (ed.) *The Republic of Letters,* Pluto Press; and Sheila Rowbotham *Hidden from History,* Pluto Press

As well as listing 'exposure, confession, apologia and revenge' as other possible explanations, Laurie Lee also goes on to view autobiography as 'an attempt to hoard (life's) sensations'. 'Any bits of warm life' recorded through writing, he says, 'are trophies snatched from the dark.'

Selecting memories

Autobiographies are always selective and heightened versions of the past ('Some things we choose to forget': Stuart Hood). As writers and talkers we choose to record resonant moments, things, places, 'odds and ends', that seem to sum up, with arresting clarity, whole areas of our lives.

Tom Paulin, in *Deceased effects,* draws attention to the importance of 'things that people once belonged to', like the other pieces that deal with family photographs, an ancestor's hat, a clock, a piano, a telephone number. Places can also carry this same kind of voltage, like the river in the crossing keeper's son's memory.

These moments of illumination Laurie Lee chooses to call 'flashpoints'. 'Seizing these flares and flashes became a way of writing, episodic and momentarily revealing, to be used as small beacons to mark the peaks of the story. . . .' We find the same kind of memorable incidents in the 'telling lies' episode, Dot Starn's pierced ears story and the 'stealing dolls' episode from 'Me and my history'. In Richard Wright's autobiographical sketch this idea of the shaping moment of illumination is used as a method of organisation.

Fact and fiction in autobiography

Autobiographies are never transparently true in a factual sense, a detailed recording of past happenings in the actual world. They are always made or created as works of art. Or as Georges Gusdorf comments, 'Autobiography reconstructs the unity of a life across time.'*

So autobiography is not really about literal truthfulness (total recall of the past in terms of things seen and things said is an impossibility) but about catching the flavour and spirit of the original happening, or series of happenings, through an act of imaginative fleshing-out. And this reconstruction of the past obeys the current world-view and self-image of the speaker or writer. So certain moments are left out or lightly sketched in and others are dwelt on and emphasised to conform with the point of view held by the autobiographer.

Personal testimony/public chronicle

Arthur Koestler's article 'The pitfalls of autobiography' points up the difference between the autobiography that is closer to external events (the public chronicle) and that which mainly follows internal events (personal testimony). So whereas 'St Helens in the 1920s' veers towards chronicle, so 'Boo to a goose' is much nearer personal testimony.

---

* 'Conditions and limits of autobiography', Georges Gusdorf in James Olney (ed.) *Autobiography,* Princeton University

Perhaps the most richly textured autobiography is the one that starts from particular, personal incidents and then tries to fit them into a wider, more general frame of public reference. It is a blend of the personal and the public and both levels work together, subtly interweaving with each other, as in Anna Leitrim's 'Me and my history', which combines personal autobiography with general argument and reflection, and Richard Wright's 'Autobiographical sketch' where the general conditions of social injustice and racism in the Southern states of America are sharply conveyed to the reader through the power of specific, snapshot incidents.

Tony Wailey's account of the 1966 seamen's strike (included in the documentary section) is instructive in this context. He speaks out energetically and clearly, through his own sense of what happened, using his own conversational rhythms and words. But it is not just isolated, personal testimony; it also speaks for a wider, collective experience of the seamen's strike, so that testimony and chronicle reinforce and strengthen each other. Nadezhda Mandelstam's autobiography, Robert Roberts's, Pablo Neruda's, B.L. Coombes's, Stuart Hood's and Ron Barnes's make especially interesting reading if seen against this general background.

Oral history and spoken vernacular

Spoken, tape-recorded autobiographies are just as important as written ones. The tape recorder allows otherwise neglected voices to come through on to the page in all their spontaneous immediacy without literary paraphernalia weighing them down and getting in the way: George Ewart Evans showing the terrified but fascinated gaze of a young child seeing cockroaches for the first time, '. . . and you saw these wriggling—they all had their legs in the air. . .'; and Ronald Blythe's crossing keeper's son registering the shocking, cold surprise of river water to a sixteen-year-old, 'We just took our jacket off and jumped in and you'd feel the river ride up your legs cold to the crotch.'

This vernacular voice is included here not just because of its directness and vitality, but also because of its perspective. Oral history gives the view of events from below, rather than from on high, and that allows many people to make the hsitory of their own lives in their own words. Even when 'going public' the best examples stay loyal to the way things are said at home and in their local area rather than trying to imitate a metropolitan literary establishment. As Dave Douglass comments, this oral history is a 'history as carried in stories, in memories, in old arguments'; there are, he says, miners who 'carry a history of coal work as old as time in [their] bones'.*

Autobiographical style

We have deliberately included a wide variety of styles within this section, ranging from the honest, open piece on telling lies through to the much more patterned

---

* Dave Douglass, 'Worms of the earth: the Miners' own story', in Ralph Samuel (ed.) *People's History and Socialist Theory*, Routledge and Kegan Paul

and composed writing of Robert Roberts, Tom Paulin and the perhaps over-wrought piece by Sylvia Plath: which is not to suggest that there is a hierarchy of value from spoken/raw through to written/shaped. Rather there is a fluid continuum linking different arrangements and forms.

There is a need for self-discipline and control in writing autobiography, to avoid the 'poeticised shimmer' of the sentimental autobiography. This patterned control is clearly at work in the Robert Roberts piano episode from *A Ragged Schooling,* where the humour comes from the organised contrast between the domestic, down-to-earth details associated with the mother and the elevated airs and graces of the father, and Colleano. The energetic precision of the language, as in the Collison's 'Sweetone' grinning at them 'like an old mare', is there to sharpen up the structural tensions within the book as a whole. And as such it 'bodies out our personality (and, yes, our background too)', as Richard Hoggart has put it.

The bond with the reader

We have ended the autobiographical section with two short extracts from Stuart Hood's *Pebbles from my Skull,* because they bring up the question of audience in a startlingly original way.

Although autobiographies are records of subjective experience, they can strengthen the reader's grip on her own sense of her life. 'They are reassurances that others face or have faced the same difficulties, problems, choices.' They can offer a common meeting-ground for isolated individuals exchanging shared experiences. We can all take some kind of comfort from an internalised reader who is tunnelling 'through the same dark'; and start to escape the locked-up privacy of being alone with ourselves in our skulls.

(A) PERSONAL HISTORY AND PUBLIC EVENTS

SCHOOL DAYS

We're out in the schoolyard drilling, and it was hips bend and all. Well, somebody at the back of me give me a shove. Of course, I half fell down and I shoved some-body in front of me. He's seen me. He says, 'Get inside! Get inside!' And, of course, I had to go inside. They came back in school and he says, 'Come out the front here, Maddison.' He says, 'Undo your trousers and get your trousers down.' He said, 'I'm making an example of you.' I says, 'Look, Mr Herman,' I says, 'my father's never told me yet to get my trousers down,' I says, 'and don't think you're going to get my trousers down because I'm telling you you're not.' He says, 'Do you know who you are speaking to?' I says, 'Certainly, sir, I'm speaking to my teacher.' I says, 'And do you know what my teacher's told me?' I says. 'My teacher's telling me to do something my own parents don't do.' He says, 'Come out here. I'll take them down.' So I was a big lad when I was at school and I went out the front. But he was the first on the floor—I had him down easy. The lads thought it was great, this. 'Yippee! Go on, Maddison!' they were shouting. Just then Mr Carter next door, he heard. He came in, and I had to go and see the headmaster, Mr Philipson, and he says, 'What happened?' And I told him. But he says, 'You've got to learn discipline.' I says, 'That's not a case of discipline to me.' I says, 'In school you get a cane and it's either on your hand or else it's across your bottom but never a bare bottom.' I says, 'That's the difference with me.' 'Well,' he says, "will you take a punishment from me?' I said, 'That all depends what it's going to be, sir,' I says, 'the hands or I'll lie across a desk, but not me trousers down.' 'Well,' he says, 'I'll give you the normal cane on your hands.' And I got, I think, six off him and it never worried me. So I went back to me class. 'Maddison, out, out of this school,' he says. 'Don't come back here any more.' So I went out. Next morning I came back—on a Friday morning. I just came and sat at me desk. He said, 'I thought I told you to leave school?' I says, 'You have no authority to tell me to leave school sir. You're only my teacher.' I says, 'My headmaster hasn't told me to leave school and I don't finish school until tonight.' I was fourteen. I says, 'I finish tonight. I won't be back on Monday.' 'Well,' he says, 'I'm not having you in this class today.' 'Well,' I says, 'that be up to you and the headmaster, but my education doesn't finish, not unless the headmaster sends me home.' 'Well,' he says, 'I'm not going to have you. I'll give you a job.' And he give us all insurance cards for the teachers, every school in South Shields. And I had to go round giving the new insurance cards out. Aye.

Stephen Humphries
Hooligans or Rebels? (Basil Blackwell)

ANCESTORS

Every Friday morning my grandfather
left his farm of canefields, chickens, cows,
and rattled in his trap down to the harbour town,
to sell his meat. He was a butcher.
Six-foot-three and very neat: high collar,
winged, a grey cravat, a waistcoat, watch-
chain just above the belt, thin narrow-
bottomed trousers, and the shoes his wife
would polish every night. He drove the trap
himself: slap of the leather reins
along the horse's back and he'd be off
with a top-hatted homburg on his head:
black English country gentleman.

Now he is dead. The meat shop burned,
his property divided. A doctor bought
the horse. His mad alsatians killed it.
The wooden trap was chipped and chopped
by friends and neighbours and used to stop-
gap fences and for firewood. One yellow
wheel was rolled across the former cowpen gate.
Only his hat is left. I 'borrowed' it.
I used to try it on and hear the night wind
man go battering through the canes, cocks waking up and thinking
it was dawn through the clinking country night.
Great caterpillar tractors clatter down
the broken highway now; a diesel engine grunts
where pigs once hunted garbage.
A thin asthmatic cow shares the untrashed garage.

Edward Brathwaite
The Arrivants (OUP)

FAMILY PHOTOGRAPH
(ON AUNT NELL'S LAP)

Squinting against the glare
of my own shyness
in a passed down Joseph coat.
I fiddled with a button,
wavering between tears
and the start of an expected smile.
Knowing that these knees
were Aunty Nell's from Manchester
but not knowing the hand that gripped me.

David Jackson
(the one on the left)

TELLING LIES

We never had to tell lies, and we never had to give cheek. As easy-going as my
dad was with us, I'd have never dreamed of answering him back, even to just
before he died. He always used to say to us 'If you tell me the truth, no matter
how bad, I won't punish you. But if you tell me lies, and I find out . . .'

12

After the butchers, my eldest brother went to work in an engineering firm. He used to say he got tips, and he'd bring back a couple of chops, or a pound of sausages—always food. My mother couldn't understand it, but she couldn't say 'You're not getting tips.' Then one day this big posh car comes up to the door, with our Bob in it and the boss of his works. The boss said he'd been helping himself from the petty cash box. 'I'll kill him, I'll kill him, I will!' my dad said, then he turns on Bob: 'Now get up to bed and I'll deal with you later.'

He goes on so much that the boss starts saying 'Now, don't be too hard on him. It's the first time, and boys go through this stage . . .'

'If we pay you back, will that be the last of it?' my dad says. 'I promise he'll be punished.'

'Fair enough,' the boss says and goes out. When he's gone, my dad sits down and pulls out a cigarette. All the time he's sat there smoking it I'm going on, 'Don't hit him, dad. Don't hit him.' And my mother says, 'Now you're not going to take your belt to him; you've never done it before, and you're not doing it now. He needs a good hiding, but not too hard.'

Then my father finishes his cigarette and goes to the bottom of the stairs. 'Bob, come along and get your tea,' he shouts. Bob came down and my dad talked to him. Bob was crying, really crying. Then dad said 'I'm not going to mention it any more.' That was that, and that was my dad all through.

Lifetimes 1: A Couple from Manchester

BOO TO A GOOSE

'You couldn't say *Boo* to a goose', my grandmother said
When I skittered howling in from the back street—my head
With a bump the size of a conker from a stick that someone threw,
Or my eyes rubbed red
From fists stuffed in to plug the blubbing. 'Not *Boo* to a goose,' she said,
But coddled me into the kitchen, gave me bread
Spread with brown sugar—her forehead,
Beneath a slashed, ash-grey bark of hair,
Puckered in puzzle at this old-fashioned child
Bright enough at eight to read the ears off
His five unlettered uncles, yet afraid
Of every giggling breeze that blew.
'There's nowt to be scared about,' she said,
'A big lad like you!'

But not as big as a goose—or not the geese I knew,
Free-walkers of Slagbank Green.
From morning-lesson bell to supper-time

13

They claimed lop-sided common-rights between
Tag-ends of sawn-off, two-up-two-down streets
And the creeping screes of slag.
They plucked their acres clean
Of all but barley-grass and mud. Domesticated but never tamed,
They peeked down on you from their high
Spiked periscopes. No dog would sniff within a hundred yards
Of their wing-menaced ground.
At the first sound
Of a bicycle ring they'd tighten ranks,
Necks angled like bayonets, throttles sizzling,
And skein for the bare knees and the cranking shanks.
They were guarded like Crown Jewels. If any man were seen
To point a finger to a feather
He'd end up with boot-leather for his dinner.
They harried girls in dreams—and my lean
Spinning-wheel legs were whittled even thinner
From trundling round the green's extremest hem
To keep wide of their way.
No use daring me to say
Boo to them.

The girls grew up and the streets fell down;
Gravel and green went under the slag; the town
Was eroded into the past. But half a century later
Three geese—two wild, streaked brown-grey-brown
As the bog-cottoned peat, and one white farm-yard fly-off—
Held sentry astride a Shetland lochan. The crumbled granite
Tumbled down brae and voe-side to the tide's
Constricted entry; the red-throated diver jerked its clown-
striped neck, ducked, disappeared and perked up from the water
A fly-cast further on. The three geese took no notice.
But the moment I stepped from the hide of the car
The white one stiffened, swivelled, lowered its trajectory,
And threatened towards me. Then,
Under the outer arctic's summer arc of blue,
With a quick blink that blacked out fifty years
And a forgotten fear repeating in my stomach,
I found myself staring, level-along and through,
The eyes of that same slagbank braggart
I couldn't say *Boo* to.

Norman Nicholson
A Local Habitation (Faber)

EARRINGS

After our sumptuous meal, we went to the forest nearby. There were gypsies selling little ornaments, flowers made of paper, some of wood, all looking like chrysanthemums. I was with a girl and we saw a pair of black earrings for a penny. She bought them. I said:

'Why did you buy them? You will have to have your ears pierced to wear them.'

'Could you do it?' she asked me.

'I don't know — it will hurt you. It will have to be done with a needle.'

'You do it', she said. 'I want to wear them.'

After a struggle I managed to push a piece of wire through both ears. She never murmured and she was so proud of them. Apparently when she got up next morning her ears were all red and swollen and when her grandmother, who she lived with, saw the ears and the earrings she clouted her on both sides of her face. Poor little soul; I thought she had been punished enough. I must admit, I have pierced many ears since then, but never like that.

One day my sister May said:

'Why don't you let me pierce your ears? When you get some money you can get some nice earrings at Woolworths for sixpence.'

That night Mum said:

'I'm off to bed. Hurry up and turn out the gas.'

May said:

'I'll do them now.'

I threaded the needle with strong white cotton — real cotton, not like the rubbish we have to buy today. I held a cork at the back of the ear lobe. She did one.

'Oh!' I said.

'Do you want the other one done?' said May.

'Of course I do'.

'Well that's it then', she said. 'Pride feels no pain, does it?'

'No', I said very meekly. 'Not much.'

In the morning my ears felt a bit sore, so I rubbed some Vaseline on, pulling the cotton earrings so they wouldn't stick. When 'sharp-eyes' Mum saw the ears she said:

'You have improved yourself, I must say.'

'Well, mum,' I said, 'the Queen wears earrings.'

With a haughty look she replied:

'Well, maybe she does, but you are *not* the Queen.'

Anyway, that got smoothed out and eventually I had a small pair of earrings. I've worn earrings ever since. One day, looking through a magazine someone had lent me to look at, I saw a picture of a titled lady in a sleeveless dress. She had a large anchor tattooed on her arm just above her elbow.

'Oh, mum, look! I'm going to save up and have an anchor tattooed on my arm.'
'You will do no such thing. Drat the child, what next?'
She used that phrase a lot although I never knew what it meant.

Dot Starn
When I was a Child
(Centerprise)

ME AND MY HISTORY

This is an account of my life so far, my childhood, my school-life, my family background and what I'm doing now. I first started writing about myself two years ago and as I look back on it, some of the things I've written about my childhood and school seem very irrelevant now – but they were important to me at that age and therefore those memories are an important part of me and my history.

Since I first started writing my autobiography I've changed radically; I think this is very obvious as one reads through it. There are many reasons why I've changed. Society – the male-dominated society in which we live – has changed me from a conforming girl to an angry womin. (I've spelt womin this way because I'm not a WO'MAN – this is just one small example of how sexist our language is.) I used to be religious until I began to realise the hypocrisy and contradiction behind the Catholic Church. It oppresses me as a womin. The family oppresses me, school oppresses me, its only function is to train young people like robots for jobs in industry and wimmin to be inferior to men. The whole education system needs to be changed radically so that a school is a place where young people 'want' to go, where they will be extending their knowledge in a non-competitive way.

Anyway back to the autobiography. At times it seems mixed-up, maybe irrelevant, but that's because I was very mixed-up myself at the time. I was going through enormous pressures at home and school. I could have written about myself much more critically because now I am learning how to analyse myself, my thoughts and actions. It hurts sometimes but I'm very good at coping. I had to be when I lived at home.

The first part of the autobiography is about my childhood, the second part about school and the third about work. The fourth part is about my family and I am now writing the fifth about what I'm doing now that I've left school.

My first memories

The thing that sticks in my mind most from when I was very young is the first time I stole something; I was about two years old at the time. My mother and I were visiting friends who had some older children who had practically every toy under the sun because they had rich relatives who spoilt them. Anyway, even at such an early age I wondered why they could have so many lovely toys when all I had was a few cars, a teddy bear and a bedraggled old doll. So I decided that I would have some of their toys. I remember picking out the things that would not be missed, and I stuffed them behind the pillow in my pram which was very easy to climb into. When it was time to go home, my mum told me to get into the pram, but I refused. So I walked home. When we got home I started taking the toys out. My mum was very angry and brought me back with the toys. I had to say sorry, and I remember feeling very resentful because I thought it just was not fair – they had everything they wanted, and I didn't.

I was, and still am, up to a point, very close to my father. He was not soft with me as a child. He was always firm but fair. If he thought I needed a good slap then I'd get one or two but he would never ever over-do it. Every weekend he would bring home a large bag of sweets to my brother and myself if we were good. He said he had a horse-friend and a squirrel who spied on us when he was at work, to see we were behaving ourselves. Then they would meet him on his way home and give him the report. My brother and myself always wondered how he knew what we had done that day. We really believed he did have a horse and a squirrel friend. We did not realise that it was our mum who was the horse and squirrel. But if we fought we knew we need not expect any sweets.

As a child I was terribly jealous of my brother. Ever since Mum first brought him home I hated him. Mum left me with the friends I have already mentioned. She was a long time in hospital because she had to have a special operation for John to be born (Caesarian). Anyway I did not remember her after such a long time and I was calling the lady I was staying with, Mummy, instead. I was really shocked when I was brought home again to find someone else had 'taken my place'. As soon as I saw John I scratched him across his face and every chance I got afterwards I hit him with all my strength.

I was never really all that much interested in doll's houses and mini-ironing boards and cookers and silly things like dressing up in wimmin's clothes and high heels and all the things that most little girls are conditioned to do. My mother did not really believe in putting me into frilly frocks and snow white socks. I nearly always wore trousers and 'boys'' clothes. My brother laughs when he sees me in these clothes in old photos but I don't see anything 'wrong' or funny about girls wearing 'boys'' clothes.

Religion played quite a big role in my childhood. As we are a Roman Catholic family we went to church every Sunday morning. My parents taught John and myself to say our prayers every night before we went to bed. They encouraged us to believe that God was very important and that he was to be thought of with the highest respect. As a child I always wondered what God looked like.

When my grandmother and grandfather died (my mother's parents) I knew I should feel sad but I didn't. I must have been too young to realise. I remember my mother was very sad especially as they died within 10 months of each other. I did not know my grandparents very well as they lived in Ireland even though we went to visit them almost every year.

I remember my granny as a fat woman with a nice kind face. She always wore a blue dress with red flowers in it. My grandad was tall and thin and very strict.

When my grandparents died my mother went to both their funerals. Dad took over whilst she was away; John and I were always hoping that she would not come back for a long time because Dad gave us nice things to eat and ice-cream every day after school, which we would not normally have with Mum.

We did not have our own house when I was young. We lived in a flat which was in a house over a sweet-shop. The place was owned by some rich businessman who would hardly even bother looking at our rent, he was so rich. Nevertheless my mum walked from West Hampstead to Finchley Road every week with the rent. I wouldn't say we were poor. It was just that my parents were saving up to buy our own home that we could call 'ours'. I was very sad when I had to leave the flat. After all I had spent eight years of my life there. I had had many happy memories there and now I had to leave all those memories behind me.

I started school when I was five years old. I went to a Catholic School. It was a new school in Kilburn called Mason's. We said prayers every morning and also went to Church once a week on either a Friday or a Monday.

I remember my first day. I was very shy and found it hard to make friends straight away. I 'fell in love' with one of the boys. I felt sorry for him because he did not want to leave his mum at the classroom door. I was not sad leaving my mum but she was sad leaving me!

My teacher was a nun called Sister John. She was quite nice but I was really scared of her. She once made me stand on the table in front of everyone and pulled down my socks and slapped me on the legs for something. I can't quite remember what for.

I did not find the lessons difficult. But I could never find a style of writing. It was either minute or gigantic.

My first report was very good. So were most of them. I was hardly ever absent and I don't think I was late for school more than twice.

I remember when I was about six and a half I pretended to my mum that I had a stomach ache because I did not want to go to school because of a certain lesson. I think I did have a pain but I exaggerated it and in the end my mum brought me to the doctor who sent me to the hospital because he thought I had appendix trouble. But the time I reached the hospital the pain had gone. I did not tell my mum. Lots of doctors examined me, I had blood tests taken and was given lots of injections but they found nothing. I felt really ashamed and guilty afterwards for dragging my mum around London on a hot summer's day all for nothing.

When we were younger, my brother and myself always had our baths together. We were not embarrassed in front of each other or our parents but if friends came in we would feel ashamed.

But if we asked where we came from, our parents never told us the truth. They said they chose us from lots of other babies at the hospital. I think that if they had told us the truth then it would have saved my embarrassment at the mention of the word 'sex' on the television or in the papers. I was about 11 when I got over this embarrassment.

When I was 7, I made my first confession. I was very frightened about telling all my 'dreadful' sins. I thought that the priest would hit me for being so naughty.

So I did not confess everything. I felt awfully guilty afterwards and kept thinking God would strike me down dead.

After my first confession I took my first Holy Communion. It was a very important event in my life. I had all the trimmings – white dress, veil, socks, sandals, rosary beads and prayer book. All in white. I think white is meant to be pure and honest and virginal. Anyway I don't remember feeling any different.

When I first started school there were two black girls in the juniors. I think they were the first people I saw that had brown skin and I was very puzzled as to how this could be. I must have made them feel very embarrassed in front of their friends because I kept on asking them why they were dark and I was light. They never did, nor could they give me an answer.

My love of football started in this school when I was goalkeeper for the boys in the football matches at playtimes.

Mainly school

As we were very young we were not expected to work hard. So we were allowed to play with toys, playhouse or wendy house, a tank of water and a sandpit. When I did start writing and reading I had a habit of writing too large and then I would go to the opposite extreme. My teacher got very angry at this and I was very worried because I could not write medium sized and I was afraid she would hit me. She would also shout at me loudly for the least little thing and I hated her from fear.

Every morning we had to say prayers and sing a hymn which did not have much meaning for me because no one had ever told me 'why' I had to pray to God and 'why' I had to respect and love this God. I could not understand why I had to adore somebody that I had never seen. We had lessons on religion but not other religions such as Hinduism or Judaism; it was just the one religion, Roman Catholicism. And that was what we had to do every single day for six years.

Once a year we had a Christmas party. They were the usual slap-happy affairs when school uniform was left off and everybody got a free paper hat and they could do as they pleased for the day. But nobody thought about the real meaning of Christmas, even after all the religious instruction that was pressed through their brains, which just goes to show what a waste of time it was and still is.

We had all our lessons in the one room except for maths and PE. We had the same teacher for all subjects and by the end of the day I'm sure he/she was sick of the sight of us all.

We were all given the same chances of learning and got sufficient help from the teachers. But in the last year we had a bad teacher, Mr Gordon, and he was always helping the clever ones and the children that bought him presents at Christmas. This was a terrible thing. Every Christmas some of the children gave the teachers presents – some even got bottles of whisky and cigarette lighters. I wanted to get a present for my teacher one year, but my mother would not hear of it and said she did not want me crawling up to the teachers. I was glad afterwards that I did not get them a present. But if you gave your teacher a present you were their special pet for the rest of the year.

In this school the cane was used on anybody that misbehaved. I never got it myself but my brother did and I saw other people getting it. My brother got it because he punched a girl and according to the headmaster boys weren't supposed to hit poor, weak defenceless little girls! My brother was not allowed to give his side of the story (he was not all to blame) it was just the fact that he had hit a girl and so he had to be punished for it. I was so angry when I saw his face with tear stains and dirt and two large welts on both his hands, which were trembling.

Our headmaster was very small and thin and my mum and others like her thought that he should have been changed and someone very big, muscular and fierce-looking put in his place, so that all the children would respect him and look up to him. But even so, the headmaster we had was respected or in my case, feared. I did not respect him but I was very frightened of him; even when he spoke to me, I would tremble.

Sometimes if I was going past the headmaster's office I would hear screams of agony and I hated that headmaster more and more. He once hit me on the legs twenty times with a ruler for pinching someone. I heard him say one time to a teacher, 'If their parents won't put any manners in them, then I will'.

Once a week we had to go to mass in the church next door to the school, where the fear of God was put in us all with the threats that we would go to hell if we misbehaved, but if we were all good little children we would all become beautiful little angels, floating around in heaven with our divine father, God. I never questioned the fact that there was a God because I was too afraid.

I remember that this school was very sexist, as everything else is in society. I did not realise it at the time but now as I look back on it I realise just how sexist it was as I'm sure many other schools were and still are. The boys for example did all the masculine things like football, rugby and crafts. We girls had to do all the feminine things such as needlework, netball and drawing, which was not very fair. It was the same when we first started school. The girls played with dolls and prams and kitchens, and the boys played as 'daddies' and cowboys, the very masculine things. I think this is why people accept the roles that society gives them because they are learning their roles from a very early age. The sooner this kind of thing is changed the better because then young children can enjoy all kinds of activities without being called names and being thought odd or different.

Although I was not very bright or clever at this school I noticed that in the last few years of my time there, the brainy children were helped and encouraged more than people like myself who had certain difficulties in learning. The children who had potential for grammar school were given extra guidance and encouragement whilst we had to battle along by ourselves. I had a 'friend' and I hated her, not because she was more clever than me but because my mother was (and still does) always comparing me to her. She, according to my mother was the one that was brainy enough to get into grammar school and not me (not that I care whether I got into such a school). She was the one who always did everything properly and right but not me. She was a perfect little angel and I wasn't. This constant comparing made me feel very inferior and dejected. I felt as if I was a failure through and through. So for many years I went about my life in an insecure way. I had no confidence, nothing to live or hope for because I knew I would fail everything I tried to do. There were times when I really wanted to die and I honestly tried to kill myself when I was about ten years old, because I could not stand the continual comparing from my mother. I could not face up to each day knowing that I was going to be told I was a failure, that I was no good at anything. I had no one to talk to and all I wanted was to die and then she'd be sorry.

In this school, especially in the lower years, we were encouraged to behave ourselves by being awarded stars. At the end of the term whoever had the most stars for doing 'good' things like working hard, running errands, helping the teacher and so on, was given a 'special' prize which was something like a bar of chocolate. I don't think anyone bothered about the size of the bar, they enjoyed competing with one another; it nearly always ended in a fight after school because the children who did not win got the feeling that they were not good enough and once they got that feeling they didn't bother anymore because it was always the clever children that won and not them. I think this was a wrong system to use because it made children believe that every time they did something 'good' they would get a reward and every time they did something bad they would be punished. It also encouraged them to believe that the only way to get success is through competition which is not true.

When a young child is compared with others and made to feel a useless 'object', it can be very, very damaging to them; mentally and physically. It makes them insecure and often leads to social problems (mine was eating, which explains my size today). That is why I think schools and parents should adopt a different attitude in the way children are taught. Instead of turning them into insecure unhappy people because they have not lived up to a certain standard they should be encouraged to work hard to their own standards and at the things they enjoy and are good at.

My family

My mother and father were born into farming families in County Leitrim in Ireland. My father was the youngest of eleven children, his mother died when he was eight years old and his father when he was thirteen. I think my grandma must have died from having so many children, there was so such thing as contraceptives in those days and even now in Ireland contraception is almost non-existent. This is due to the Catholic Church and the hypocrites that run it.

My other grandma and grandpa are also dead. I don't really remember them much although when I was younger, myself and my family spent holidays with them. My mother was the youngest of eight children.

They all had a very cruel and hard childhood, working on the farm before they went to school and again when they came home until they went to bed and their father beat them a lot with anything he could lay his hands on, be it a hammer or a stone. He didn't care, he just wouldn't stand any laziness, noise or disruption or answering back. He was a cruel man, but he had to keep his farm going, it was all he had. He used to keep the children back from school to help him on the farm, bringing in the turf from the bog, reaping the hay, milking the cows, feeding the hens, walking miles in their bare feet to the town with a sack of turf on their backs to sell. I don't think he meant to be so cruel, but he had to earn money to exist.

Sometimes when my parents are in a good mood they tell me about the good times they had. They said even though they had no money to have fun, they made their own fun.

My parents came to England to work and get married. My grandpa begged my mum not to go but she was fed up of working on the farm and so was my dad. They were attracted to England by the thought of earning 'big money', but when they arrived they must have been pretty disillusioned when they found the streets weren't paved in gold. My mother landed a job as a live-in maid with a rich family in St John's Wood, and my father got just as scabby a job on a building site and lived in crummy rotten 'digs'. When they saved some money they got married and lived in a rented room. My mother worked in places like Sainsbury's. One night they came home to find all their belongings on the street – the landlord had found out that I was on the way.

Since coming to England, my parents seem to have rejected their Irish nationality and culture. They have become very 'Englishified' so to speak. The only thing they live for is their house. They believe that until you have your own house, your flash roof, fitted aluminium windows, telephone, telly and your car outside the door, you can't be happy or successful. Well they have all these things but they still don't seem any happier. They go to English Clubs, have lots of English friends; they hardly even talk about their own country, they have rejected their country and have conformed to the 'English' way of life and it makes me very sad.

Even though I was born here, I feel that I am Irish, Ireland is part of me, and that's something that I will never forget or reject as long as I live. I really look forward to going to Ireland – my home. We stay in my mother's house with my two uncles. They are her only family left there. They have been in a mental hospital for about twenty years – even though there wasn't much wrong with them. I think my grandpa drove them there with his cruelty and obsession with money. I really love my two uncles, they are so thoughtful and honest. They even feed the rats, that's how kind they are. My mum hates going to Ireland, she's become so used to the English way of life that she feels alienated in her own home! When we go to the local parish church I feel ashamed of her because she shows off, wearing sun-glasses and sticking her nose up in the air, looking down on everyone. She thinks she's a 'Somebody' just because she comes from England. And another thing, when she answers the phone or talks to people she puts on an English accent, it's really quite unbelievable.

My parents are both Roman Catholics and attend church every Sunday and pretend to pray. It's just a duty to them – go to mass, say your prayers, receive communion, praise God and thank him and fear him – then straight into their English Club across the road.

I hardly talk to them anyway. I find I have nothing to say to them and they find it an embarrassment to make conversation with me because they still want me to be a good, religious, conforming little girl and because I'm not that, they hate me.

I've made up my mind that I'll have to get out of this situation before they turn me into a cabbage. So as soon as I can I'll leave home and then I won't be such an embarrassment to them in front of the neighbours.

My brother's name is John and he is seventeen months younger. I feel sorry for him because he's so mixed up. I think my parents have already turned him into an unthinking cabbage. It's a cruel thing to say about my own brother, but it's the truth and that's something too many people are afraid of.

So that's my immediate family – my parents and my brother. My other relations I hardly know, they nearly all live in America and have done very well for themselves according to their infrequent letters. I don't regard these people as my 'family' because they seem unimportant, they don't know me and I don't know them so I guess we're just strangers and not a family at all – just like my immediate family, we don't know or understand each other – we're just like strangers.

Secondary school

The night before I was to become a pupil at secondary school I cried and cried because I was frightened and friendless. I was on the verge of entering a big, new strange world which I knew nothing about. What made things worse, though, was the fact that I had no one to talk to about the problem that was facing me. My parents would just have said, 'There, there, you have nothing to worry about.' I had no friends to talk to because I had left them all behind me in the cosy world of primary school, or they had gone their separate ways. I wondered if they had the same fears as I had. I doubted it though, because I was always the shy, awkward fatty that was always left out of things because I was fat. Nobody wanted to know me just because I looked different. And that's just what it was like for the whole of my first year and most of my second year. People picked on me, called me 'Fatso'. In PE I was always the last to be chosen when teams were picked. I made no friends, I was confused with so much homework, the vast modern building, the students, the teachers. I cried every night when I was in the safety of my bed. It was just like being a new-born baby, coming into the big, wide world.

It was only during my second year here that I began to feel settled into any kind of routine. I still felt very isolated. It was as if I was just another body with legs and arms and eyes and ears except that I had no feelings, no character, no personality, all these things had been quenched within me. I was beginning to feel like a robot as I went from one lesson on to the next lesson. Day in, day out, year in, year out. We were treated like robots too, knowledge was pressed through our brains, but found its way out through our ears, or else got lost on the way to our brains. We were told what to do, what not to do, mechanically. Every assembly we sat on the floor and pretended to be listening to the Senior Master reading stories from the Bible. Then we all bowed our heads mechanically, then pretended to listen to the Headmaster ranting and raving about the image of the school, but really our minds were on the problems of homework – have I done my maths homework? Have I written that essay for history?

It wasn't until the fourth year that I began to feel any purpose in school. The only reason being that we were starting exam courses which were supposed to be so very, very important. So that when we left school we could all fit into the capitalist system. Everything seemed to start happening in the fourth year. We started having careers lessons with speakers coming in, funnily enough, though, more people missed these lessons than those who attended them. The fourth year were given special assemblies where the importance of exams was drilled into us weekly. In the fourth year a couple of us got interested in sticking up for our rights and set up an NUSS branch which was condemned from the very beginning by the headmaster and all his old cronies who did everything in their power to stop any activity that might arouse interest in the other pupils.

Things got much better in the fifth year. For example, a group of us decided that we weren't going to be oppressed by wearing skirts so we came in one day wearing trousers. We were locked into a room for the whole day with a teacher to guard over us. We were only let out to go to the bog and even then were accompanied by a teacher. However, when the head heard that all wimmin would wear trousers the next day he got scared and said if all girls came in skirts the next day he would discuss the matter with us. We agreed and a group of us sat ourselves down in his plush office the following morning. He gave us a long wordy lecture about him wanting girls to be able to wear trousers all along but that the girls should've asked him instead of taking the law into their own hands. Anyway, he agreed to girls wearing trousers especially when I mentioned the Sex Discrimination Act.

The teachers in this school are very ordinary and boring except for about three or four who are really great people who understand what it's like to be young and oppressed. I really enjoy their lessons, or if they don't teach me, I always feel close enough to them to tell them whatever is on my mind, and that's really great because you don't feel so isolated in such an oppressive education system.

One of my favourite 'experiences' in this school was the time the head caught me in the boys' bogs. At the time I was really scared, but when I look back it seems really funny. It was like this; me and a couple of friends couldn't bear the thought of sitting through a boring lesson of RE so we decided to bunk it, but all the girls' toilets were locked all the time (to cut down on bunking!). So we went into the boys' bogs thinking we were really safe there. So there we all were smoking, laughing and mucking around when we suddenly heard the head's voice. We girls stood up on the urinal trough, as we called it, which was behind a wall. He came in and looked around three or four times complaining to some boys about the fag ends and smoke, but he didn't see us. Just when we thought he was going, he came in again and saw us. Well, my heart jumped a mile. He went white with shock and said in a shaky voice, 'What the hell are you doing in here?' We were speechless and let ourselves be marched down to the senior master who smelt our breath and told us a letter would be sent home to our parents. I went weak at the knees. The next morning I got up at 6 to look out for the postman so that I could nab the letter before my mum did, but the thing never arrived. But we weren't going to get away with it that easily; we were given an hour's detention and, even worse, extra special lectures for a whole hour. I thought he'd never quit talking. Whenever I remember the look on the head's face when he saw us I just die laughing.

At the moment, school is just one big boring drag. I haven't long to go though. Just as soon as I've finished my last exam I'm finished forever. I can't believe it, I've been coming and going like a robot for the last five years and to think I've only got a few more weeks is just too much. I'm desperate to get out. This school has done nothing for me and I'm sure that applies to most young people in most schools, especially if you're working-class and a womin. Right now I'm just living from day to day waiting for those bits of paper that will tell me whether or not I'm a failure, because that's what it all boils down to in the end, whether or not you are capable of remembering dates and numbers and facts. And if you can't, well then you're done for for the rest of your life. That's why the whole education system needs to be changed, so that young people can feel involved, and have a say in the things they learn.

Work

As I have not left school yet I have not got a proper full-time job. However I have got a part-time job on Saturdays. I work as a shampooist and general dogs-body in a hairdressers.

Where I work now is in a very 'well-to-do' area of London – St John's Wood. I have worked there for two years and it has really opened my eyes to how we live in a very unfair and unequal world. It makes my blood boil when I see millionaires' wives coming to the hairdressers in Rolls-Royces, fur coats, the latest fashions straight from Paris, having their hair done at 'sky high' prices just to play Bridge at a friend's house. And to think that those wimmin have never had to go so low as to work a day in their whole lives. They spend the money that their capitalist husbands squeezed out of working-class people like my parents. They can't any of them say they worked hard to get where they are; they must have exploited someone to be able to afford Rolls-Royces and fur coats, and to me that seems very unfair and wrong when there are people, even here in this country, struggling to pay for the next meal.

So in certain aspects I am grateful to this job for helping me realise some of the terrible things that are wrong with this society. And I'm hoping that my future job will enable me to be involved in changing this unequal society in which some people are struggling to survive while others are 'buying' their way through it (with money that is not really theirs).

I hate going to work – not that I'm afraid of working – it's just that everyone takes the piss out of me because I'm a punk. All the hairdressers think I'm abnormal just because I have my hair short, don't wear 'fashionable' clothes, because I wear badges and a man's rain coat. They call me Trotsky and Sid Vicious. I hate them. I'm always having arguments with the boss about Capitalism and Communism. He always ends up just walking out of the staffroom. There's one womin in particular who is always running me down because of the way I speak. She says to me 'you're not in Cricklewood now, you're in St John's Wood' or she says I'm lazy because I don't pronounce my t's and h's, the ignorant moron. I hate her.

The thing I hate most is the first call of 'Anna' on Saturday morning because it means the beginning of another day of slaving, carrying, fetching, washing smelly heads of hair, handing up rollers, taking them out, making 'madam' a coffee, getting 'madam' a magazine, asking 'madam' if there is anything she requires. It's an awful strain trying not to pour scalding hot coffee over 'madam' or strangling her.

Some of the wimmin are very nice, but most of them babble on about their grandchildren or rotten pet budgies, or going hunting. I get no mental stimulation on a Saturday. Even though these wimmin look important on the outside with their sapphires, minks and gold, they're as thick as two planks when it comes to conversation. They usually expect the shampooist to talk about their boy-friends and weddings and stuff like that. You should see the surprise on their faces when I bring up things like education, politics or religion.

I'm a fool really, to be working there for a wage of £3.50, for the whole day from 8 a.m. till 6.30 p.m., but there is one advantage to it. It's making me more and more aware of the unfairness of the society I'm living in.

My hopes for the future

Obviously I would be very silly if I started drawing up great big plans for the future because through past experiences I have found out that when you plan something it never really happens the way you want it to. However there is no real harm in 'hoping' things for the future.

The first thing I'll be hoping for is to get a good education. I'd like to think that in a just society all young people will have the right to further education and training with a full grant, where there was a fully democratic education system, where there was no sexual discrimination against wommin and gay people, where there were decent facilities in which to enjoy our culture and leisure time, where there was no imperialism and oppression, no threats of nuclear war, where young people would have complete control of all areas of our lives in our work, education, leisure time and personal relationships. To win this means ending the grip of the big companies, politicians and bureaucrats, who try to run our lives for us. I want to live in a socialist society where the mass of the people have control of the wealth and power.

Anna Leitrim
Our Lives: Young People's Autobiography
(ILEA English Centre)

AN AUTOBIOGRAPHICAL SKETCH

My first lesson in how to live as a Negro came when I was quite small. We were living in Arkansas. Our house stood behind the railroad tracks. Its skimpy yard was paved with black cinders. Nothing green ever grew in that yard. The only touch of green we could see was far away, beyond the tracks, over where the white folks lived. But cinders were good enough for me and I never missed the green growing things. And anyhow cinders were fine weapons. You could always have a nice hot war with huge black cinders. All you had to do was crouch behind the brick pillars of a house with your hands full of gritty ammunition. And the first woolly black head you saw pop out from behind another row of pillars was your target. You tried your very best to knock it off. It was great fun.

I never fully realized the appalling disadvantages of a cinder environment till one day the gang to which I belonged found itself engaged in a war with the white boys who lived beyond the tracks. As usual we laid down our cinder barrage, thinking that this would wipe the white boys out. But they replied with a steady bombardment of broken bottles. We doubled our cinder barrage, but they hid behind trees, hedges, and the sloping embankments of their lawns. Having no such fortifications, we retreated to the brick pillars of our homes. During the retreat a broken milk bottle caught me behind the ear, opening a deep gash which bled profusely. The sight of blood pouring over my face completely demoralized our ranks. My fellow-combatants left me standing paralyzed in the center of the yard, and scurried for their homes. A kind neighbor saw me and rushed me to a doctor, who took three stitches in my neck.

I sat brooding on my front steps, nursing my wound and waiting for my mother to come from work. I felt that a grave injustice had been done me. It was all right to throw cinders. The greatest harm a cinder could do was leave a bruise. But broken bottles were dangerous; they left you cut, bleeding, and helpless.

When night fell, my mother came from the white folks' kitchen. I raced down the street to meet her. I could just feel in my bones that she would understand. I knew she would tell me exactly what to do next time. I grabbed her hand and babbled out the whole story. She examined my wound, then slapped me.

'How come yuh didn't hide?' she asked me. 'How come yuh awways fightin'?'

I was outraged, and bawled. Between sobs I told her that I didn't have any trees or hedges to hide behind. There wasn't a thing I could have used as a trench. And you couldn't throw very far when you were hiding behind the brick pillars of a house. She grabbed a barrel stave, dragged me home, stripped me naked, and beat me till I had a fever of one hundred and two. She would smack my rump with the stave, and, while the skin was still smarting, impart to me gems of Jim Crow wisdom. I was never to throw cinders any more. I was never to fight any more wars. I was never, never, under any conditions, to fight *white* folks again. And they were absolutely right in clouting me with the broken milk bottle. Didn't I know she was working hard every day in the hot kitchens of the white folks to make money to take care of me? When was I ever going to learn to be a good boy? She couldn't be bothered with my fights. She finished by telling me that

I ought to be thankful to God as long as I lived that they didn't kill me.

All that night I was delirious and could not sleep. Each time I closed my eyes I saw monstrous white faces suspended from the ceiling, leering at me.

From that time on, the charm of my cinder yard was gone. The green trees, the trimmed hedges, the cropped lawns grew very meaningful, became a symbol. Even today when I think of white folks, the hard, sharp outlines of white houses surrounded by trees, lawns, and hedges are present somewhere in the background of my mind. Through the years they grew into an overreaching symbol of fear.

It was a long time before I came in close contact with white folks again. We moved from Arkansas to Mississippi. Here we had the good fortune not to live behind the railroad tracks, or close to white neighborhoods. We lived in the very heart of the local Black Belt. There were black churches and black preachers; there were black schools and black teachers; black groceries and black clerks. In fact, everything was so solidly black that for a long time I did not even think of white folks, save in remote and vague terms. But this could not last forever. As one grows older one eats more. One's clothing costs more. When I finished grammar school I had to go to work. My mother could no longer feed and clothe me on her cooking job.

There is but one place where a black boy who knows no trade can get a job, and that's where the houses and faces are white, where the trees, lawns, and hedges are green. My first job was with an optical company in Jackson, Mississippi. The morning I applied I stood straight and neat before the boss, answering all his questions with sharp yessirs and nosirs, I was very careful to pronounce my *sirs* distinctly, in order that he might know that I was polite, that I knew where I was, and that I knew he was a *white* man. I wanted that job badly.

He looked me over as though he were examining a prize poodle. He questioned me closely about my schooling, being particularly insistent about how much mathematics I had had. He seemed very pleased when I told him I had had two years of algebra.

'Boy, how would you like to try to learn something around here?' he asked me.

'I'd like it fine, sir,' I said, happy. I had visions of 'working my way up.' Even Negroes have those visions.

'All right,' he said, 'Come on.'

I followed him to the small factory.

'Pease,' he said to a white man of about thirty-five, 'this is Richard. He's going to work for us.'

Pease looked at me and nodded.

I was then taken to a white boy of about seventeen.

'Morrie, this is Richard, who's going to work for us.'

'Whut yuh sayin' there, boy!' Morrie boomed at me.

'Fine!' I answered.

The boss instructed these two to help me, teach me, give me jobs to do, and let me learn what I could in my spare time.

My wages were five dollars a week.

I worked hard, trying to please. For the first month I got along OK. Both Pease and Morrie seemed to like me. But one thing was missing. And I kept thinking about it. I was not learning anything and nobody was volunteering to help me. Thinking they had forgotten that I was to learn something about the mechanics of grinding lenses, I asked Morrie one day to tell me about the work. He grew red.

'Whut yuh tryin' t' do, nigger, get smart?' he asked.

'Naw; I ain' tryin' t' git smart,' I said.

'Well, don't, if yuh know whut's good for yuh!'

I was puzzled. Maybe he just doesn't want to help me, I thought. I went to Pease.

'Say, are yuh crazy, you black bastard?' Pease asked me, his gray eyes growing hard.

I spoke out, reminding him that the boss had said I was to be given a chance to learn something.

'Nigger, you think you're *white*, don't you?'

'Naw, sir!'

'Well, you're acting mighty like it!'

'But, Mr Pease, the boss said . . .'

Pease shook his fist in my face.

'This is a *white* man's work around here, and you better watch yourself!'

From then on they changed toward me. They said good-morning no more. When I was just a bit slow in performing some duty, I was called a lazy black son-of-a-bitch.

Once I thought of reporting all this to the boss. But the mere idea of what would happen to me if Pease and Morrie should learn that I had 'snitched' stopped me. And after all the boss was a white man, too. What was the use?

The climax came at noon one summer day. Pease called me to his work-bench. To get to him I had to go between two narrow benches and stand with my back against a wall.

'Yes, sir,' I said.

'Richard, I want to ask you something,' Pease began pleasantly, not looking up from his work.

'Yes, sir,' I said again.

Morrie came over, blocking the narrow passage between the benches. He folded his arms, staring at me solemnly.

I looked from one to the other, sensing that something was coming.

'Yes, sir,' I said for the third time.

Pease looked up and spoke very slowly.

'Richard, *Mr* Morrie here tells me you called me *Pease*.'

I stiffened. A void seemed to open up in me. I knew this was the show-down.

He meant that I had failed to call him Mr Pease. I looked at Morrie. He was gripping a steel bar in his hands. I opened my mouth to speak, to protest, to assure Pease that I had never called him simply *Pease*, and that I had never had any intentions of doing so, when Morrie grabbed me by the collar, ramming my head against the wall.

'Now, be careful, nigger!' snarled Morrie, baring his teeth. '*I* heard yuh call 'im *Pease*! 'N' if yuh say yuh didn't, yuh're callin' me a *lie*, see?' He waved the steel bar threateningly.

If I had said: No, sir, Mr Pease, I never called you *Pease*, I would have been automatically calling Morrie a liar. And if I had said: Yes, sir, Mr Pease, I called you *Pease*, I would have been pleading guilty to having uttered the worst insult that a Negro can utter to a southern white man. I stood hesitating, trying to frame a neutral reply.

'Richard, I asked you a question!' said Pease. Anger was creeping into his voice.

'I don't remember calling you *Pease*, Mr Pease,' I said cautiously. 'And if I did, I sure didn't mean . . .'

'You black son-of-a-bitch! You called me *Pease*, then!' he spat, slapping me till I bent sideways over a bench. Morrie was on top of me, demanding:

'Didn't yuh call 'im *Pease*? If yuh say yuh didn't, I'll rip yo' gut string loose with this bar, yuh black granny dodger! Yuh can't call a white man a lie 'n' git erway with it, you black son-of-a-bitch!'

I wilted. I begged them not to bother me. I knew what they wanted. They wanted me to leave.

'I'll leave,' I promised. 'I'll leave right *now*.'

They gave me a minute to get out of the factory. I was warned not to show up again, or tell the boss.

I went.

When I told the folks at home what had happened, they called me a fool. They told me that I must never again attempt to exceed my boundaries. When you are working for white folks, they said, you got to 'stay in your place' if you want to keep working.

Richard Wright
Uncle Tom's Children
(New English Library)

PORTRAIT PHOTOGRAPH, 1915

We too have our place, who were not photographed
So much and then only in multitudes
Rising from holes in the ground to fall into smoke
Or is it newsreel beyond newsreel
But I do not know and I have lost my name
And my face and as for dignity
I never had it in any case, except once,
I think, in the High Street, before we left
For troopships and the farewell pipers,
When it was my turn in the queue
In Anderson's Photographic Arcade and Salon,
In my uniform, and I was not a tall man
Although for a moment I had a sense
Of posterity in the eyes of descendants,

Of my own face in a frame on a small table
Over which her eyes would go, and my sons',
And that I would persist, in day and night,
Fading a little as they say they do.

Douglas Dunn
Barbarians (Faber)

DIG FOR VICTORY (THE PIG MUCK)

During the war we had a 'Dig for Victory' campaign; this was to encourage people to grow their own food to help out the meagre food rations, and every plot of available land was put to good use, and at our School, each class had their own bit. We were all very keen; we grew potatoes and vegetables. All the waste from the school kitchens was taken to the 'Pig Woman' as we called her, who lived in a house near school and in return she gave us the pig manure for our gardens. This had to be fetched in a wheelbarrow from the farms over Carlton Hill, a distance of about two miles, and the girls at school had to take it in turns to volunteer and go to fetch it back. One day, feeling very patriotic, my friend Lily and I said we would go; really we only wanted to get out of arithmetic lessons. We set off and took turns to push the wheelbarrow, a few stops on the way and we eventually reached First Avenue. At the bottom of the road was a large stretch of open fields. We had a good walk then down another avenue of trees. We knew we were getting close to the 'Piggery' because we could smell it. There was no one in sight anywhere so we went to find the pigs. We'd never seen pigs that close up before — great fat, pink, ugly-looking things they were. We got some sticks that were lying around and poked 'em; they didn't like that and grunted and ran about squealing and squeaking. Then this man come up and told us off for poking at the pigs and he said 'Come on wi' me and get yer barrer filled up then.' Well, when we saw what was going in that barrow and got a whiff of it, we wished we'd never bothered. There's not a smell in the world like 'pig muck' — it could only come from pigs! We set off back up the avenue; nearly full to the top, the barrer was. We saw some large dock leaves by the side of the road so we covered it up as if it helped the smell and the look of the contents of our load. We turned up the rather steep road with nice private houses on either side, and, as we reached the bend, over went the barrer. Lily and me, well we just looked at each other and wished we'd never come. 'What shall we do?' said Lily. 'I'll go and ask at this house for a dustpan and we'll gerr it up.' I opened the gate and went up to the front door. Just then this woman come from the back, 'Can I borrow your dustpan missus to clean the mess up?' I said. 'The barrer's tipped up.' She came down the path and looked over the gate. Well, when she saw it she went berserk and no wonder; it looked worse out the barrer. So, I said 'Well, if not, we'll have to leave it here and it's for our Dig for Victory as well.' She didn't look very happy and said 'Alright, but you can wash my dustpan at the garden tap and get a bucket of water to clean that up.' Well, eventually, pig manure scraped up and back in the barrer, we set off back. We did get some funny looks from people when they passed and got a whiff and saw what was in the barrer. I wished we carried a barrer saying 'IT'S THE PIG MUCK AS STINKS, NOT US'. Thought we'd never get back to school with it. How the other girls laughed and jeered at us when we reached the playground. 'It's alright for you lot' I said, 'We've done our bit for Dig for Victory' and I never forgot it either.

Kathleen Price
Nottingham Community, Publishing Project
(Your Own Stuff Press)

WORKING LIFE – ST HELENS IN THE 1920s

Glassblower at Nuttalls Bottleworks, born c. 1892

I was a bound apprentice at Nuttalls – you had to be bound to get a job. If you tried to leave, it was quite possible to be put in jail. You signed on a red dot until you were 21. You couldn't leave or nothing – you were a slave kind of thing till you were 21. Putting your finger on the red dot was to make it legal; your father had to be there. You worked for very little wages till you became 21. You learned your trade. It went in stages in the bottleworks. You started off as a spare lad. On night turn, they started work for half past five until five o'clock the next morning. You worked for 3¾ hours, then you got ¾ hour for supper; you worked 2½ hours more and then you had to stay on till five in the morning. Then you had breakfast. That was Mondays, Tuesdays, Wednesdays and Thursdays. On Friday, you finished at two o'clock on Saturday morning.

In the shop where I was apprenticed, there were ten holes, each with a gatherer, blower, wetter-off, finisher and taker-in. The gatherer took metal [molten glass] from the tank, the blower blew the bottle. The wetter-off just wet the flange (the piece of glass which joined the bottle to the pipe). That made it easier for the finisher to break it off and put the ring round the top.

The taker-in used to carry the bottles on his shoulder in a forceps to the arch where they were placed in tiers. Each man would have an apprentice so there would be fifty boys running about the shop. It would make a wonderful film. The blower used to swing the metal over his shoulder. You had a knack of keeping it on the pipe without it falling off. The metal was flying about. We'd always sing the turn through.

When the blower had manipulated the metal and got the right amount of it on the end of the pipe, he put it into a mould which was the shape of a bottle. It was in two halves. The bottom half was fixed, and when you'd put the metal in, you had a treadle to shut the top over it. When you blew the bottle you'd see this faint mark down the side from the mould. If it was too pronounced,

32

they'd throw it away. (Antique bottles won't have a line down the side, as they'd have been blown without a mould.) You'd give it to a finisher, who had what was called a tune to put on the rings. I'd blow with a tobacco pipe in my mouth as well.

Normally, the gatherer had to guess exactly how much metal to pick up on the pipe from the tank. That's where the skill came in. The blower would feel it. 'That's a bit light, fetch a bit more,' or 'That's a bit too heavy.' The blower would have two pipes, one he was blowing, and one in his other hand. The gatherer would be running to get another one – we were on piecework, you see. That was Nuttall's bottleworks. It became United Glass.

The bottles were taken and put in the arch and sealed up. It was an annealing kiln. They stayed in the arch two or three days. This was heated and slowly cooled down – otherwise, if the bottles had just been left, they'd have shattered. When they took the bottles out, there'd be anything up to fifty gross, or thereabouts. They'd be put into trucks and taken to where they were sorted into sizes. You'd have two types. One was a whisky bottle shape, and that held a quart. Then there was a smaller one.

You had to do pretty well in reckoning up, because you reckoned all your own money. They sent you word in of how many gross you'd done. You had so many pipes which you put by when you'd finished with them, and you had a tally pipe. When you had done twenty you put the tally pipe at the end of the row. When you finished work, you counted up how many twenties you had done. The bad ones they used to call the cocks. You reckoned on two or three dozen cocks in a day. If you had only a couple of dozen, you were all right. Each bottle had to be a certain weight. If it was under 14 ounces, it was too light; if it was over 16 ounces, it was too heavy. Come Friday night or Saturday morning, you used to get paid. The finisher used to go down to the office and receive the wages for all the workers. It came in a packet – we used to get down on the floor or some other convenient place and reckon all this money up, so much for him and so much for him. You were all paid definite rates. The taker-in got 7s 6d (his was the least) and a penny a gross overwork. The wetter-off got twopence overwork, and the gatherer tenpence a gross. The blower's overwork was 1s 4d.

Some made it to be blowers and some didn't. At the end of each turn, if you were an apprentice, you had some practice. When you got a bit proficient and someone left, you'd get in. The same group of men always kept together. After each stop, you'd practise. It was then we made quart bottles that held a lot more. How did we do it? You'd use less metal to fill out the same mould – they'd be no good to sell, as they were too light, but we could get them filled up with beer. There was one man who must have lost hundreds of gallons before he found out what was happening to him. In those days, they had no measures on the taps – it just ran out of the barrel.

When you went to the Glass Bottle works, you paid 3s 6d into a works fund. You paid 3s 6d when you came out of your time and when you went from gatherer to blower. This was collected by the steward. When the summer came, they'd have a meeting: 'All right, lads, where are we going this year?'

'Southport in a wagonette.'

It was always 'Southport in a wagonette' every year. The pubs were open all day, we had a good dinner and a good tea. We used to knock about a bit, go to the lake and the funfair and the bowling green. You could count the teetotallers on one hand. The horse knew when to stop. The first stop was the Millhouse on the right, just as you're going into Rainford. One of the first going into Southport was the Morris Dance. We stopped at four places at least going there, and it was the same coming back. You'd have 12 pints inside you by the time you got there. There was no water there, except the Marine Lake — you'd have to go as far as Blackpool to get a swim.

Charles Forman
Work and Play in St Helens in the 1920s (Paladin)

WORKING LIFE – FORD'S ASSEMBLY LINE

Phil Stallings

He is a spot welder at the Ford assembly plant on the far South Side of Chicago. He is twenty-seven years old; recently married. He works the third shift: 3:30 p.m. to midnight.

'I start the automobile, the first welds. From there it goes to another line, where the floor's put on, the roof, the trunk hood, the doors. Then it's put on a frame. There is hundreds of lines.

'The welding gun's got a square handle, with a button on the top for high voltage and a button on the button for low. The first is to clamp the metal together. The second is to fuse it.

'The gun hangs from a ceiling, over tables that ride on a track. It travels in a circle, oblong, like an egg. You stand on a cement platform, maybe six inches from the ground.'

I stand in one spot, about two- or three-feet area, all night. The only time a person stops is when the line stops. We do about thirty-two jobs per car, per unit. Forty-eight units an hour, eight hours a day. Thirty-two times forty-eight times eight. Figure it out. That's how many times I push that button.

The noise, oh it's tremendous. You open your mouth and you're liable to get a mouthful of sparks. (Shows his arms) That's a burn, these are burns. You don't compete against the noise. You go to yell and at the same time you're straining to maneuver the gun to where you have to weld.

You got some guys that are uptight, and they're not sociable. It's too rough. You pretty much stay to yourself. You get involved with yourself. You dream, you think of things you've done. I drift back continuously to when I was a kid and what me and my brothers did. The things you love most are the things you drift back into.

Lots of times I worked from the time I started to the time of the break and

34

I never realized I had even worked. When you dream, you reduce the chances of friction with the foreman or with the next guy.

It don't stop. It just goes and goes and goes. I bet there's men who have lived and died out there, never seen the end of that line. And they never will – because it's endless. It's like a serpent. It's just all body, no tail. It can do things to you . . . (Laughs.)

Studs Terkel
Working (Penguin)

THE BEETLES

That brings me to – the mentioning of the beetles. I must tell you about the beetles. Nearly everybody had beetles in their kitchens in those days; ours were dreadful. We also had crickets. But every night they used to sprinkle Keating's Powder all round the edges of the kitchen and all over the kitchen table. And then the greatest treat was one day when Maudie said:

'Well, you've been a very good little girl for helping me; and I'll tell what I'll do. Don't you let anybody know! I'm going to wake you up in the morning, and you can come down with me and see me sweeping up the beetles.'

So she got me dressed, and she took me down; and she said:

'You stand there while I get the Keating's Powder off the kitchen-table.'

It was a cold morning, and she went to the oven and pulled out a hot brick, wrapped it up in a piece of flannel and let me nurse it. (Bricks were put in the bottom of the oven of the kitchener-stove in the winter after the cooking was done, for anyone to take one upstairs to bed, rolled up in flannel.) Oh! and there were beetles everywhere. Well, she sat me in the middle of the kitchen-table; and she put a piece of dust-sheet round me so that I shouldn't get all spoiled; and she went round with the dust-pan and brush; and you saw these wriggling – they all had their legs in the air – and she swept up dust-pans of these awful beetles. And she put them on the side, and she said:

'Now in a minute I'll get the kitchener going.'

So she got the paper and sticks, and she put some coal on and she started it going; and then she shot all the beetles from the pan into the grate before she hooked the kettle on the great big hook over it to boil the water for the early morning tea. Oh, it was a wonderful time. But how she did that every day I don't know!

George Ewart Evans
The Days that we Have Seen (Faber)

THE CROSSING KEEPER'S SON
(A seventy-nine year old man looks back)

It all comes back to me — when we were boys, y'know. How we used to get in the river to goo tradin' [treading] — things like that. There we'd all be, clear as clear, just as we were. We'd have an ol' hamper, a clothes hamper, and there'd be four or five on us jump in the river with it, and then we'd trade all through the weed, an' where the water pushed through we'd howd our skep. It was like beatin' for birds, except yew done it in the river. We'd trade ivery foot o' the weed an' all the eels and pike, like, used to leap in this hare skep. It'd nearly knock yew over when a grut ol' pike come in. We'd throw the fish on the bank and goo on tradin'. Stampin' the weeds and laughin'. I'd-a bin about sixteen about the last time I done it. We didn't strip. We just took our jacket off and jumped in and you'd feel the river ride up your legs cold to the crotch. Our trousers soon got dry. You couldn't goo in where the mud was deep. Afterwards we'd set and skin the eels, cuttin' round the heads fust. We'd take 'em hoom, boil 'em, then fry 'em. But we didn't eat the ol' pike — no fear! There'd be Harry and Ainger and several more. All clear as clear.

But father loved a pike. So I'd snare him one with a leather bootlace. I'd see a pike lay in the river and I'd take this long ol' leather lace and make it into a loop. Then I'd hang it from a pole and gradually, *gradually,* hold me breath, I'd lower it down right in front of him, this still, still pike. Inter the slip-knot he'd goo and out on the bank he'd come! I caught hundreds o' pike like that — hundreds! They'd be that riled!

It seems that I'm by that river a lot now. I'm a boy and I'm by that river, an' we're all there like we used to be. I can hear our talk plain as plain. 'Let's goo babbin' — things like that. Before we went babbin' we'd goo into the yard and dig up a tinful of worms. Big worms. Then we'd worry mother to give us a bit of worsted and har big ol' darnin' needle, and then we'd thread all these worms in a string. Then we'd wind this worm string round and round our hand till that was a ball o' worms. Then we'd tie an ol' ston' or nut on for a sinker, fix the whol' thing onto a line and take it to the river. All yew had to do was jist touch bottom with it — then *zink!* — an eel's teeth were stuck in the worsted! Yew marn't take the eel off the bait in the long grass. He'd be away in a flash. Away he'd be! What we liked to hev handy was an ol' gig umprella upside-down in the reeds and chuck the catch into that. Then you'd got 'em! *Then* you'd got 'em, my boy!

I'd pass along the river at night with shepherd. There was proper hunger about — it's the Fourteen War now. And I've seen shepherd git hold o' a lovely lamb an' put his knife in the back of that's ear, an' in ten minutes that's skin was off, an' he'd hev half and we'd hev half, and that's the truth. Lamb, nice lamb. Mother salted it down; it'd last a long while. Mind you, they was hard times. Yew wouldn't credit how hard. You'd cheat on rat-tails then, let alone a lamb.

A chap I knew would git a penny a rat-tail, penny a rat-tail. And so'd I. We used to git a packet o' tin-tacks, which cost about a farden, and him and me we'd nail all our rat-tails up on the barn in sets o' dozens. All in order of length, like organpipes. Jist the same. There were millions of rats then, millions! You'd see the runs they made when they went down to the river to drink, and you'd snare these hare runs. About four o'clock in the afternoon, down to the river they'd goo, and do yew know what I see once? I see a rat in the snare and another rat coming back to help it by bitin' the string to let him out. Trew.

It was the schulemaster who was givin' a penny for a rat-tail. Yew niver took the rat to schule, yew took his tail. Yew chopped his tail off by layin' the rat across an ol' scythe and comin' down on him against the blade with a hulk o' wood. Flew off, they did.

Well, come night-time, I'd slip along and git half a dizen o' these tails off the barn door, cut off the bit where the tin-tack went through, take 'em to the schule-master and git a tanner. 'Yew goo and bury them, boy,' schulemaster would say. But I didn't. I used 'em several times and they bro'ght me in several pennies. Several. Penny was a lot then, y'know.

In the winter weather I'd stay at home and see few. If I could git a-hold o' a ol' tea-chest I counted meself happy. I used to rub it all down and make it smooth, and I'd fix a paper pattern on from *Hobbies.* Then I'd cut all round it. Used to take hours. And all in the same room with mother and the dust flying everywhere. Yew drilled your hole and threaded your saw through, an' cut an' cut. Cut careful.

Twenty year ago I started making these hare brass things, ploughs, churches, furniture and the like. At fust I'd make 'em and give 'em away but now I keep everything. And I used anything. Rubbish. Odds and ends. Weldin' wire, ol' fardens, bits of switches, handles, brass buttons, copper bolts, any mortal thing. I don't copy anything, I make what I remember. I tarn wood. I paint the fields. As I say, I've niver bin so happy in my whol' life and I only hope I last out. I've bin a bit of a lad and when I'm workin' I see it all so clear, so clear. I can smell that river and I can see us all so clear.

Ronald Blythe (ed.)
The View in Winter (Allen Lane/Penguin)

THE PIANO

Three men brought it on a handcart, heaved and struggled over the counter and dropped it in the kitchen. The next scene passed into our archives! Father, still panting after giving assistance, went and ripped off the sack-and-straw covering. 'There!' he announced at last. 'The Collison's "Sweetone"! Parlour Model!' A wreck of an 'upright' leaned against the wall.

We gathered in an arc and stared, shocked with disappointment. No one spoke. 'It's a Collison's "Sweetone"!' he said again, as if we hadn't heard the first time, '– all rosewood throughout!' and he turned back the keyboard lid. The instrument suddenly grinned at us like an old mare. He struck a note; nothing happened;

and another. We heard a distinct thud. Bits of straw now began to detach themselves from the carcass. A green baize underbelly gaped open, and again more litter. And the talk, as we remembered, went something like this.

'Has someone been keeping hens in it?' my mother asked.

'It's been in storage,' the Old Man explained. 'Customers in the Boilermakers' ill-used the woodwork. A damn shame! Look at them pint-pot rings on the top! Harry's had it packed away in the stable a while.'

Mother sniffed. 'It smells of beer!'

'What wouldn't, after thirty years in an alehouse! But a bloke that really knows pianos says — old she is, but sound enough in wind and limb! Once done up and tuned — I've a man coming — we'll get a lifetime's pleasure out of it.'

We children went on gazing. Mother stepped forward and felt above the music stand at an object which protruded like a horizontal udder. 'What's this?'

'Ornament!' the Old Man said. 'There've been two others — one at each end, see — but they've fallen off.' He turned to Janie. 'Run and tell Mr Murphy!'

Aloysius came in and, catching sight of the instrument, 'Holy Jesus!' he said, not quite sober, and went over and fondled its wooden bub. 'Sure, an' it's the one-titted wonder you've got! If I can't play it, I'll milk it!' Then he shot back his cuffs and without even a preliminary scale ran into a version of the 'Fairyland Waltz'. The strains which issued reached us etherialized, not, it seemed, from the piano we saw, but rather from a second, ghostlier instrument deep within. Aloysius stopped. Father waited judgement. 'A mellow tone, to be sure. "Refined", I would say.'

'What's wrong with the bass end?' my mother asked. 'You could have got nearly as much sound out of the dresser!'

The lower registers, Mr Murphy agreed, were unresponsive. Certain keys, once down, stayed down, whilst others . . . he hit several with his thumb. They resisted, rock-like.

'Could it be the damp?' my father asked.

'It *could* be the damp,' said Aloysius. He then 'loosened her up' with practice runs, opened the top flap and launched into a powerful rendition of the 'Blue Danube'. Half-way through, a faint cloud began to form about the lid and along the baize chest, like smoke. Aloysius started to sneeze. 'Bigod, an' she's on fire now!' But it was only dust rising.

Father looked inside. 'All this instrument wants is a real good goin' over, inside and out.'

And that's what it got. Grandma's boyfriend, the cabinetmaker, 'came to scoff', Mother said, 'and remained to scoff,' but he put a rich polish on it, leaving not a beer ring behind. Father re-covered the chest and belly, washed the keys with lemon juice and refurbished the 'gold' candlesticks beautifully — that being in his line. Then a repairer came and worked, head down, for hours, giving it finally as his professional opinion that the instrument was 'buggered really', but one could 'knock a tune out of it now,' and it was 'all right for children to learn on'. He played 'The Bluebells of Scotland' and left. Mother thought it still sounded 'refined', but her husband was happy with the result, so happy, in fact, that soon after he made an awful error of judgement.

Mr Murphy brought us the news first, knowing, as he did, what was what in the hotel world. 'Val Colleano and Partner! – on at the Prince of Wales!' Val was married, as Aloysius had been told several times, to Father's niece. He and Cousin Frances played two evenings a week in the Italian restaurant at the Great Northern, where Murphy used to wait on. He came hurrying into the kitchen one evening, Mother remembered. 'Your Val and his missis! – appearing with all the London stars at the "Wales"! Mayor's Charity Show! How's that!' Father swelled with pride. For long he had looked upon his relatives as one of the finest duos in the north and had indeed bragged of them in many a Salford pub. Genius, he felt, was to be recognized at last! London stars! The greatest charity show of the year! And all in a theatre not one hundred yards from his own doorstep!

For the mayor's annual effort prices, except in the gallery, rose steeply to keep out our local *hoi polloi*. This angered Father, who refused to attend on conscientious grounds; the cost of his usual seat in the pit he considered far too high and the company on the 'top shelf' much too low. Cabs and even motor cars outside the theatre on the great night made it clear that all the cream of Salford was bestowing its patronage. After all the boasting Father seemed a little abashed when his wife found it difficult to find the Colleanos' name on a bill which Janie brought in; but in was there, all right – next to the bottom. The 'London stars' turned out something of a disappointment too: 'top of the bill' was an artiste who had not headed any other for many a long year, and the rest were run-of-the-mill performers of no more than regional note. Still, Mr Murphy, pianist himself, stood by and praised the Old Man's relations with loyal enthusiasm. He considered Val 'after the style of the great Paderewski' and thought more would be heard of him.

Father returned home one evening from a visit to his eldest sister (mother to Frances) looking immensely pleased with himself, and, hardly waiting to take off his coat, 'Val and his wife will be calling after the show!' he announced. Mother got up, shocked. 'However could you! Look at the state of us! Holes in the lino, no decent rugs, couch split, wallpaper peeling – years old! And you invite middle-class folk in and put *us* on show!'

'They must take us as they find us,' he said. 'Frances told me – and quite right too – "Uncle," she said, "we wouldn't come to the end of the street and not drop in for a minute!" '

For the next fortnight, when visitors called, Father bragged insufferably. 'He's got letters, you know! "Val Colleano, A.L.C.M.!" Cap 'n' gown! He's reckoned one of the finest players in the city!'

'Classical, of course,' said Uncle Sam.

'Every time! None o' this beerhouse ragtime stuff! Mozart and Verdi and Wagner and that lot! He has a studio in town, you know – gives lessons – "Val Colleano! A.L.C.M.! Piano and organ – four shillings an hour!" '

'Four shillings! Phooh!'

'Brumby's his real name,' Mother said, '– Freddie Brumby!'

'Is he related to that family,' asked Uncle Sam, 'that kept the cookshop off Greengate?'

'*He* was the grandfather, I understand.' Mother told him.

'Brumby or not,' the Old Man snorted, pointing at the piano, 'when he comes he'll make that talk!'

'Lord help us!' said my mother. 'You're not going to ask him to play, are you?'

'What's the use of inviting 'em if they don't give us a duet!'

'But the piano!'

'It's in good fettle now,' he told her, and in fact he had just had it tuned again.

On the great day Father, out of work at the time, strolled about the shop whistling snatches of this and that and trying to decide just what items he would choose to hear in their brief recital. The whole house was agog. Mother scrubbed the kitchen floor and brought down the only bedroom carpet to cover larger holes in the oilcloth. Janie helped after school, cleaning, dusting and polishing. But not the piano! Father saw to that and noticed to his dismay that several keys in the lower octaves had started to stick again. That would never do. Opening the base, he inserted a lighted candle and a holder somewhere in its bowels and closed it again. I watched it all, fascinated. 'Just a little warm air!'

Then Father decreed, as we feared he might, that all children except Janie should go to bed before the 'stars' arrived. I can feel the shock of disappointment yet. Ada, all hopes dashed, began to weep quietly. 'I did so want to see them play!'

Mother looked round at us. 'That's all very well – "everybody in bed!"; but look at that sofa! I've got to have somebody on there to cover up that great tear in the leather. Ellie and Ada, you must both settle on it before they arrive, and stay settled. Understand?' They wriggled with pleasure. 'The rest of you, as Father says, are too young to be up so late.' That left me, as senior, free for the peepholes on the stairs. And all was ready at last. This was to be the night of our young lives, and indeed none of us forgot it.

The visitors were late in coming, and I must have dozed at my post, a shirt wrapped round cold legs. Voices raised in welcome stirred me. They had arrived – the Colleanos! I glued my eyes to the spy holes and followed the scene with an interest almost hypnotic. Val! He stood in the middle of the kitchen, deep in his overcoat, with an astrakhan collar buttoned up to the face, fat and unsmiling. Shortish he was, about up to the mantelpiece. A disappointment, this; I had imagined him towering even over Father. He possessed the 'lion's mane' just as Mr Murphy had told us, flowing over his collar, but an upturned nose gave him the air of a peevish pug dog. And our honoured guest looked clearly unhappy. He nodded round, put his wife's fiddle case on the sofa, where the girls sat stiff as idols, unbuttoned his collar and accepted a glass of beer from Father. Cousin Frances, whom I had never seen before, was plump and pink, and all the time she talked, breathless, gabbling things like 'Ever so nice, really! Place packed to the doors! Yes, Mother said we should call. Of course! Only too glad, I said. Go to the top of the street and not drop in! I said to Freddie – Val! I said, didn't I? I said *that* wouldn't do at all!'

Flushed and beaming, Father asked her how the show had gone. It seemed to have passed off very well; but they appeared second on the programme, and it *did* take time for an audience to warm up! 'One encore. Quite nice.' Mr Murphy came in, spruced and sober, and Val lifted fingers in recognition. The conversation then took a direction too intellectual for me; but Janie remembered it years afterwards. Val's solo, it turned out, the Moonlight Sonata, had, unfortunately, not been full-bodied enough for some of his audience. This had caused a disturbance on the 'top shelf' and cries of 'Play up, lad!' Father and Mr Murphy looked disgusted; but my mother remarked she'd heard before how poor that gallery was for sound, whereupon Cousin Frances told her, lips pursed, 'When Beethoven says *pianissimo*, Auntie, it has to be *pianissimo*, no matter what they hear up in the gallery!'

About this time a low but imperative tapping made itself heard on the kitchen window. Father's boasting had had its effect; a little knot of music-loving neighbours had gathered outside and were growing impatient for the free performance. He rose angrily. The impudence of it! But Mr Murphy got up before him. 'It's for me!' he lied diplomatically, and went out, to return in a couple of minutes. 'All right now!'

There was some talk then about which of the children was going to learn the piano, and Cousin Frances asked what about the very pretty one, and Janie said she would be taking lessons as soon as Mother could afford the ninepence. Mr Colleano enquired who in the world taught piano for ninepence, and Father explained it was a lady in a row of houses on the main street, near the gasworks, who had the same letters behind her name as Val. Soon after, they got up, the gentleman making a splendid display of looking at the watch on his wrist, a gesture new to me. (The wrist watch for males, just then on its way in, was damned by many as 'effeminate'.) Father rose at the same time. This was it! He went over to the piano and patted it like a horse. Val stepped forward a pace or two and peered at the keyboard. Father pulled out the stool invitingly; our visitor ignored it, but leant forward and struck somewhere in the middle. Vibrant the 'Sweetone' rang out. Val recoiled as if stung. There was a clatter inside. 'Something's – fallen off it!' he said.

'It's only a candlestick!' Father was desperate now. 'Come on, Val! Give us a tune. Frances! Just one duet before you go!'

My mother sat silent, but Aloysius rowed in, wheedling. 'Just one, now, for the children!'

Our cousin hesitated, but not Mr Colleano! 'Oh dear, no! No!' he said. 'No, it's too late – far too late! Another time, perhaps. Come along, Frannie, let's be off!'

Father didn't see his guests out, but went and sat again, his face like thunder. Mother escorted them through the shop, Mr Murphy leaving at the same time. I heard the front door bang, and they were gone. The three girls still sat bolt upright along the sofa. Father went over and crashed down the piano lid. A faint chord trembled protest across the kitchen. He strutted back to his chair and buried his face deep in a quart jug, then he looked over the rim and saw the girls. 'You still here? To bed! To bed!' I flew upstairs just before them.

Robert Roberts
A Ragged Schooling
(Fontana/Collins)

DECEASED EFFECTS

We go to auctions now and bid for things
That people once belonged to. They've shed their lives
And kept a dust that never quite scrubs off.
Unfaithful survivors, they fall to scruffy dealers,
The poor, or the ambitious young. Quaint now,
The functional metal beds the dead once woke in
When sirens went at five and mills clanked all night.

Those little bits of china that were fixed
To mantelshelves in neat front rooms, the chairs
They sat in, all the odds and ends they lived among,
Parts of a pattern that only seemed to fit,
Tell us nothing and never go for much –
Though last week there was one lot that told
Its own sparse story: a pile of photographs,
The wedding sometime, plain, unfashionable,
Six fresh-faced children behind dusty glass,
The couple older on an anniversary, and then,
Almost too pat, a mountain of wreaths on a grave,
Knocked down to someone for the frames.

Tom Paulin
A State of Justice (Faber)

OCEAN 1212–W

My childhood landscape was not land but the end of the land – the cold, salt, running hills of the Atlantic. I sometimes think my vision of the sea is the clearest thing I own. I pick it up, exile that I am, like the purple 'lucky stones' I used to collect with a white ring all the way round, or the shell of a blue mussel with its rainbowy angel's fingernail interior; and in one wash of memory the colors deepen and gleam, the early world draws breath.

Breath, that is the first thing. Something is breathing. My own breath? The breath of my mother? No, something else, something larger, farther, more serious, more weary. So behind shut lids I float awhile; – I'm a small sea captain, tasting the day's weather – battering rams at the seawall, a spray of grapeshot on my mother's brave geraniums, or the lulling shoosh-shoosh of a full, mirrory pool; the pool turns the quartz grits at its rim idly and kindly, a lady brooding at jewellery. There might be a hiss of rain on the pane, there might be wind sighing and trying the creaks of the house like keys. I was not deceived by these. The motherly pulse of the sea made a mock of such counterfeits. Like a deep woman, it hid a good deal; it had many faces, many delicate, terrible veils. It spoke of miracles and distances; if it could court, it could also kill. When I was learning to creep, my mother set me down on the beach to see what I thought of it. I crawled straight for the coming wave and was just through the wall of green when she caught my heels.

I often wonder what would have happened if I had managed to pierce that looking-glass. Would my infant gills have taken over, the salt in my blood? For a time I believed not in God nor Santa Claus, but in mermaids. They seemed as logical and possible to me as the brittle twig of a seahorse in the Zoo aquarium or the skates lugged up on the lines of cursing Sunday fishermen – skates the shape of old pillowslips with the full, coy lips of women.

And I recall my mother, a sea-girl herself, reading to me and my brother – who came later – from Matthew Arnold's 'Forsaken Merman':

> Sand-strewn caverns, cool and deep,
> Where the winds are all asleep;
> Where the spent lights quiver and gleam;
> Where the salt weed sways in the stream;
> Where the sea-beasts rang'd all round
> Feed in the ooze of their pasture-ground;
> Where the sea-snakes coil and twine
> Dry their mail and bask in the brine;
> Where great whales come sailing by,
> Sail and sail with unshut eye,
> Round the world for ever and aye.

I saw the gooseflesh on my skin. I did not know what made it. I was not cold. Had a ghost passed over? No, it was the poetry. A spark flew off Arnold and shook me, like a chill. I wanted to cry; I felt very odd. I had fallen into a new way of being happy.

Now and then, when I grow nostalgic about my ocean childhood – the wauling of gulls and the smell of salt, somebody solicitous will bundle me into a car and drive me to the nearest briny horizon. After all, in England, no place is what? more than seventy miles from the sea. 'There,' I'll be told, 'there it is.' As if the sea were a great oyster on a plate that could be served up, tasting just the same, at any restaurant the world over. I get out of the car, I stretch my legs, I sniff. The sea. But that is not it, that is not it at all.

The geography is all wrong in the first place. Where is the grey thumb of the water tower to the left and the sickle-shaped sandbar (really a stone bar) under it, and the Deer Island prison at the tip of the point to the far right? The road I knew curved into the waves with the ocean on one side, the bay on the other; and my grandmother's house, half-way out, faced east, full of red sun and sea lights.

To this day I remember her phone number: OCEAN 1212–W. I would repeat it to the operator, from my home on the quieter bayside, an incantation, a fine rhyme, half expecting the black earpiece to give me back, like a conch, the susurrous murmur of the sea out there as well as my grandmother's Hello.

The breath of the sea, then. And then its lights. Was it some huge, radiant animal? Even with my eyes shut I could feel the glimmers off its bright mirrors spider over my lids. I lay in a watery cradle, and sea gleams found the chinks in the dark green window blind, playing and dancing, or resting and trembling a little. At naptime I clinked my fingernail on the hollow brass bedstead for the music of it and once, in a fit of discovery and surprise, found the join in the new rose paper and with the same curious nail bared a great bald space of wall. I got scolded for this, spanked, too, and then my grandfather extracted me from the domestic furies for a long beachcombing stroll over mountains of rattling and cranking purple stones.

My mother was born and brought up in the same sea-bitten house; she remembered days of wrecks where the townspeople poked among the waves' leavings as at an open market – tea kettles, bolts of soaked cloth, the lone, lugubrious shoe. But never, that she could remember, a drowned sailor. They went straight to Davy Jones. Still, what mightn't the sea bequeath? I kept hoping. Brown and green glass nuggets were common, blue and red ones rare: the lanterns of shattered ships? Or the sea-beaten hearts of beer and whisky bottles. There was no telling.

I think the sea swallowed dozens of tea sets – tossed in abandon off liners, or consigned to the tide by jilted brides. I collected a shiver of china bits, with borders of larkspur and birds or braids of daisies. No two patterns ever matched.

Then one day the textures of the beach burned themselves on the lens of my eye forever. Hot April. I warmed my bottom on the mica-bright stone of my grandmother's steps, staring at the stucco wall, with its magpie design of eggstones, fan shells, colored glass. My mother was in hospital. She had been gone three weeks. I sulked. I would do nothing. Her desertion punched a smouldering hole in my sky. How could she, so loving and faithful, so easily leave me? My grandmother hummed and thumped out her bread dough with suppressed excitement. Viennese, Victorian, she pursed her lips, she would tell me nothing. Finally she melted a little. I would have a surprise when mother came back. It would be something nice. It would be – a baby.

A baby.

I hated babies. I who for two and a half years had been the centre of a tender universe felt the axis wrench and a polar chill immobilize my bones. I would be a bystander, a museum mammoth. Babies!

Even my grandfather, on the glassed-in verandah, couldn't woo me from my huge gloom. I refused to hide his pipe in the rubber plant and make it a pipe tree. He stalked off in his sneakers, wounded too, but whistling. I waited till his shape rounded Water Tower Hill and dwindled in the direction of the sea promenade; its ice-cream and hotdog stalls were boarded up still, in spite of the mild pre-season weather. His lyrical whistle beckoned me to adventure and forgetting. But I didn't want to forget. Hugging my grudge, ugly and prickly, a sad sea urchin, I trudged off on my own, in the opposite direction toward the forbidding prison. As from a star I saw, coldly and soberly, the *separateness* of everything. I felt the wall of my skin: I am I. That stone is a stone. My beautiful fusion with the things of this world was over.

The tide ebbed, sucked back into itself. There I was, a reject, with the dried black seaweed whose hard beads I liked to pop, hollowed orange and grapefruit halves and a garbage of shells. All at once, old and lonely, I eyed these — razor clams, fairy boats, weedy mussels, the oyster's pocked grey lace (there was never a pearl) and tiny white 'ice-cream cones'. You could always tell where the best shells were — at the rim of the last wave, marked by a mascara of tar. I picked up, frigidly, a stiff pink starfish. It lay at the heart of my palm, a joke dummy of my own hand. Sometimes I nursed starfish alive in jam-jars of seawater and watched them grow back lost arms. On this day, this awful birthday of otherness, my rival, somebody else, I flung the starfish against a stone. Let it perish. It had no wit.

I stubbed my toe on the round, blind stones. They paid no notice. They didn't care. I supposed they were happy. The sea waltzed off into nothing, into the sky — the dividing line on this calm day almost invisible. I knew, from school, the sea cupped the bulge of the world like a blue coat, but my knowledge somehow never connected with what I *saw* — water drawn half-way up the air, a flat, glassy blind; the snail trails of steamers along the rim. For all I could tell, they circled that line forever. What lay behind it? 'Spain,' said owl-eyed Harry Bean, my friend. But the parochial map of my mind couldn't take it in. Spain. Mantillas and gold castles and bulls. Mermaids on rocks, chests of jewels, the fantastical. A piece of which the sea, ceaselessly eating and churning, might any minute beach at my feet. As a sign.

A sign of what?

A sign of election and specialness. A sign I was not forever to be cast out. And I *did* see a sign. Out of a pulp of kelp, still shining, with a wet, fresh smell, reached a small, brown hand. What would it be? What did I *want* it to be? A mermaid, a Spanish infanta?

What it was, was a monkey.

Not a real monkey, but a monkey of wood. Heavy with the water it had swallowed and scarred with tar, it crouched on its pedestal, remote and holy, long-muzzled and oddly foreign. I brushed it and dried it and admired its delicately carved hair. It looked like no monkey I had ever seen eating peanuts and moony-foolish. It had the noble pose of a simian Thinker. I realize now that the totem I so lovingly undid from its caul of kelp (and have since, alas, mislaid with the other baggage of childhood) was a Sacred Baboon.

So the sea, perceiving my need, had conferred a blessing. My baby brother took his place in the house that day, but so did my marvellous and (who knew?) even priceless baboon.

Did my childhood seascape, then, lend me my love of change and wildness? Mountains terrify me — they just sit about, they are so *proud*. The stillness of hills stifles me like fat pillows. When I was not walking alongside the sea I was on it, or in it. My young uncle, athletic and handy, rigged us a beach swing. When the tide was right you could kick to the peak of the arc, let go, and drop into the water.

Nobody taught me to swim. It simply happened. I stood in a ring of playmates in the quiet bay, up to my armpits, rocked by ripples. One spoilt little boy had a rubber tyre in which he sat and kicked, although he could not swim. My mother would never let my brother or me borrow water wings or tyres or swimming pillows for fear they would float us over our depth and rubbish us to an early death. 'Learn to swim first,' was her stern motto. The little boy climbed off his tyre, bobbed and clung, and wouldn't share it. 'It's mine,' he reasonably said. Suddenly a cat's paw scuffed the water dark, he let go, and the pink, lifesaver-shaped tyre skimmed out of his grip. Loss widened his eyes; he began to cry. 'I'll get it,' I said, my bravado masking a fiery desire for a ride. I jumped with a sideflap of hands; my feet ceased to touch. I was in that forbidden country − 'over my head'. I should, according to mother, have sunk like a stone, but I didn't. My chin was up, hands and feet milling the cold green. I caught the scudding tyre and swam in. I was swimming. I could swim.

The airport across the bay unloosed a blimp. It went up like a silver bubble, a salute.

That summer my uncle and his petite financée built a boat. My brother and I carried shiny nails. We woke to the tamp-tamp of the hammer. The honey-color of the new wood, the white shavings (turned into finger rings) and the sweet dust of the saw were creating an idol, something beautiful − a real sailboat. From the sea my uncle brought back mackerel. Greeny-blue-black brocades unfaded, they came to table. And we did live off the sea. With a cod's head and tail my grandmother could produce a chowder that set when chilled, in its own triumphal jelly. We made suppers of buttery steamed clams and laid lines of lobster pots. But I never could watch my grandmother drop the dark green lobsters with their waving, wood-jammed claws into the boiling pot from which they would be, in a minute, drawn − red, dead and edible. I felt the awful scald of the water too keenly on my skin.

The sea was our main entertainment. When company came, we set them before it on rugs, with thermoses and sandwiches and colored umbrellas, as if the water − blue, green, grey, navy or silver as it might be, were enough to watch. The grown-ups in those days, still wore the puritanical black bathing suits that make our family snapshot albums so archaic.

My final memory of the sea is of violence − a still, unhealthily yellow day in 1939, the sea molten, steely-slick, heaving at its leash like a broody animal, evil violets in its eye. Anxious telephone calls crossed from my grandmother, on the exposed oceanside, to my mother, on the bay. My brother and I, kneehigh still, imbibed the talk of tidal waves, high ground, boarded windows and floating boats like a miracle elixir. The hurricane was due at nightfall. In those days, hurricanes did not bud in Florida and bloom over Cape Cod each autumn as they now do − bang, bang, bang, frequent as firecrackers on the Fourth and whimsically named after women. This was a monstrous speciality, a leviathan. Our world might be eaten, blown to bits. We wanted to be in on it.

The sulphurous afternoon went black unnaturally early, as if what was to come could not be star-lit, torch-lit, looked at. The rain set in, one huge Noah douche. Then the wind. The world had become a drum. Beaten, it shrieked and shook. Pale and elated in our beds, my brother and I sipped our nightly hot drink. We would, of course, not sleep. We crept to a blind and hefted it a notch. On a mirror of rivery black our faces wavered like moths, trying to pry their way in. Nothing could be seen. The only sound was a howl, jazzed up by the bangs, slams, groans and splinterings of objects tossed like crockery in a giant's quarrel. The house rocked on its root. It rocked and rocked and rocked its two small watchers to sleep.

The wreckage the next day was all one could wish — overthrown trees and telephone poles, shoddy summer cottages bobbing out by the lighthouse and a litter of the ribs of little ships. My grandmother's house had lasted, valiant — though the waves broke right over the road and into the bay. My grandfather's seawall had saved it, neighbors said. Sand buried her furnace in golden whorls; salt stained the upholstered sofa and a dead shark filled what had been the geranium bed, but my grandmother had her broom out, it would soon be right.

And this is how it stiffens, my vision of that seaside childhood. My father died, we moved inland. Whereon those nine first years of my life sealed themselves off like a ship in a bottle — beautiful, inaccessible, obsolete, a fine, white flying myth.

Sylvia Plath
Johnny Panic and the Bible of Dreams (Faber)

(B)   THE PROCESS OF REMEMBERING

REMEMBERING

Remembering is like that. There's what you know happened, and what you think happened. And then there's the business that what you know happened isn't always what you remember. Things are fudged by time: years fuse together. The things that should matter — the stepping-stones that marked the way, the decisions that made one thing happen rather than another — they get forgotten. You are left with islands in a confused and layered landscape, like the random protrusions after a heavy snowfall, the telegraph pole and hump of farm machinery and buried wall. There is time past, and time to come, and time that is continuous, in the head forever.

Penelope Lively
Going Back (Heinemann)

UNCERTAIN MEMORIES

In all these early years I am uncertain what is genuinely remembered. For example I think I can remember a toy motor-car, which now surely – a 1908 vintage toy – might be worthy of a sale at Sotheby's, but since it appears in a photograph of myself and my brother Raymond, this may not be a true memory. My age then was about four, and I wore a pinafore and had fair curls falling around the neck. My elder brother with a proper masculine haircut, an adult of seven, stares fearlessly towards the box-camera, like a future mountaineer of Kamet and Everest, while I still have the ambiguity of undetermined sex.

Of all my first six years I have only such random memories as these and I cannot be sure of the time-sequence. They are significant for me because they remain, the stray symbols of a dream after the story has sunk back into the unconscious, and they cry for rescue like the survivors of a shipwreck.

Graham Greene
A Sort of Life (Penguin)

GRANDMOTHER'S WORDS

'Your mammy has gone to join the angels,' my grandmother said, her old face creased like a shrunk potato.

'When will she be back?' I asked.

I had sensed that I was to be told something of importance. My father had winced off into the shop, where, under no circumstances, was I allowed to follow, and we were sitting in the middle room behind the shop, my grandmother with her back to the window, and I, on my four-legged stool, beside the fire. Somewhere in a blurred, now-forgotten corner of the room was my Auntie Lizzie. It must have been afternoon, for my grandmother had removed the coarse apron she always wore until dinner time. It was fairly early spring, and I have the impression that it was a fine day with the light bright in the back yard. The year was 1919 and I was just turned five.

On my eight-inch stool I was about the right height to stare level into the fire. I have always been a great starer into fires. And this fire was framed like a picture by the old fire-place of black marble, or what I thought was black marble, though I now know it to be of polished and painted slate. Set round it were three long panels – one, upright, on either side, and one, horizontal, above – all of red marble, like red grained wood or red ink running on blotting paper. A few years later I would see the pattern as a map of unendingly explorable archipelagos. The canopy or hood was of iron, embossed with lily stalks, heart-shaped leaves and snakes knotted like bow ties. Similar bows appeared again, red on green ground, on the square tiles my father had set into a kind of entablature on either side of the fire. In the half-light, before the gas was lit, the fire-place turned into a cave, glowing red and green deep down in its gullet, where my fancy could tunnel and hide and lose itself for hours and hours.

But this is surely far too much for a child to remember in his grief! The truth is that I cannot remember any grief. I can remember my grandmother's words, and my answer, but not what I felt about it. As for the fire-place, I do not have to remember that at all.

For, though my grandmother and my aunt are long dead, the fire-place is still there. I stare into it every night. Except that the red and green tiles have been replaced by bronze, it is still just as it was when my grandmother was alive. So, too, are the doors, the window, the shape of the room. Even the little stool still stands in more or less the same place. My childhood is not safely locked off from the present, a world to be revisited or forgotten but never, in either case, to be altered. My childhood is built into the everyday life of today, into the bricks of the house where I live and the walls of the room where I am writing these words. When, a couple of years ago, decorators stripped off the wallpaper in that same middle room, they brought to light the mud-brown, twined-waterweed pattern that must have been there when my grandmother spoke to me – a pattern I had not seen since I was eight years old and had completely forgotten. When at the same time, they burnt off the paint on the stairs, they uncovered, not just the old pash-egg-coloured grain and varnish that I could faintly recall, but also the original green, laid on bare wood, that had been put on when the house was built in 1880. If I pause in my writing and look out of the window, across St George's Terrace, I can see the Post Office that is no longer there, and Seth Slater's tailor's shop that was there before it was a Post Office, and, through long-demolished windows opening on to what is now empty air, I can still watch Mrs Slater and Rosa and John carrying the tea-things from the kitchen to the dining room.

It is not just that the past persists into the present: the present pushes back into the past. I cannot separate what I think I saw from what I know I must have seen. Sometimes the present may even reshape the past. I have memories that seem to be set, quite vividly, in this room, beside that chair, outside that chemist's shop or along the verge of a public footpath – yet second thoughts compel me to admit that, at the time remembered, the chair had not been bought, the chemist's shop was a greengrocer's, and the path had not been laid down across the Park that was then just a field.

And quite apart from such falsifications, the past takes much of its meaning from the present. The whole of my life, in a way, is a follow-through from those first five or ten years, and, whenever I think of them, I see both what they were and what they came to be.

Norman Nicholson
Wednesday Early Closing (Faber)

WRITING AUTOBIOGRAPHY

Autobiography can be the laying to rest of ghosts as well as an ordering of the mind. But for me it is also a celebration of living and an attempt to hoard its sensations.

In common with other writers I have written little that was not for the most part autobiographical. The spur for me is the fear of evaporation – erosion, amnesia, if you like – the fear that a whole decade may drift gently away and leave nothing but a salt-caked mud-flat.

A wasting memory is not only a destroyer; it can deny one's very existence. A day unremembered is like a soul unborn, worse than if it had never been. What indeed was that summer if it is not recalled? That journey? That act of love? To whom did it happen if it has left you with nothing? Certainly not to you. So any bits of warm life preserved by the pen are trophies snatched from the dark, are branches of leaves fished out of the flood, are tiny arrests of mortality.

The urge to write may also be the fear of death – particularly with autobiography – the need to leave messages for those who come after, saying, 'I was here; I saw it too.' Then there are the other uses of autobiography, some less poignant than these assurances – exposure, confession, apologia, revenge, or even staking one's claim to a godhead. In writing my first volume of autobiography, *Cider with Rosie* (1959), I was moved by several of these needs, but the chief one was celebration: to praise the life I'd had and so preserve it, and to live again both the good and the bad.

My book was a recollection of early years set against the village background of my Cotswold upbringing. The end of my childhood also coincided by chance with the end of a rural tradition – a semi-feudal way of life which had endured for nine centuries, until war and the motor-car put an end to it. Technically the book was not so simple. It took two years, and was written three times. In remembering my life, even those first few years of it, I found the territory a maze of paths.

I was less interested, anyway, in giving a portrait of myself, than in recording the details of that small local world – a world whose last days I had seen fresh as a child and which no child may ever see again. It seemed to me that my own story would keep, whereas the story of the village would not, for its words, even as I listened, were being sung for the last time and were passing into perpetual silence.

The village was small, set in a half mile of valley, but the details of its life seemed enormous. The problem of compression was like dressing one tree with leaves chosen from all over the forest. As I sat down to write, in a small room in London, opening my mind to that time-distant place, I saw at first a great landscape darkly fogged by the years and thickly matted by rumour and legend. It was only gradually that memory began to stir, setting off flash-points like summer lightning, which illuminated for a moment some field or landmark, some ancient totem or neighbour's face.

Seizing these flares and flashes became a way of writing, episodic and momentarily revealing, to be used as small beacons to mark the peaks of the story and to accentuate the darkness of what was left out. So I began my tale where this light sparked brightest, close-up, at the age of three, when I was no taller than grass, and was an intimate of insects and knew the details of stones and chair-legs.

This part of the book was of course easiest. I had lived so near to it, with the world no larger than my legs could carry me and no more complex than my understanding. I ruled as king these early chapters. Then the book moved away from me – taking in first my family, then our house and the village, and finally the whole of the valley. I became at this stage less a character than a presence, a listening shadow, a moving finger, recording the flavours of the days, the ghosts of neighbours, the bits of winter, gossip, death.

If a book is to stand, one must first choose its shape – the house that the tale will inhabit. One lays out the rooms for the necessary chapters, then starts wondering about the furniture. The moment before writing is perhaps the most harrowing of all, pacing the empty rooms, knowing that what goes in there can belong nowhere else, yet not at all sure where to find it. There are roofless books in all of us, books without walls and books full of lumber. I realized quite soon, when writing my own, that I had enough furniture to fill a town.

The pains of selection became a daily concern, and progress was marked by what was left out. The flowing chatter of my sisters, for twelve years unstaunched, had to be distilled to a few dozen phrases – phrases, perhaps, which they had never quite uttered, but bearing the accents of all that they had. A chapter about life in my village school also required this type of compression. Here five thousand hours had to be reduced to fifteen minutes – in terms of reading time – and those fifteen minutes, without wearying the reader, must seem like five thousand hours. In another chapter, about our life at home, I describe a day that never happened. Perhaps a thousand days of that life each yielded a moment for the book – a posture, a movement, a tone – all singly true and belonging to each other, though never having been joined before.

Which brings me to the question of truth, of fact, often raised about autobiography. If dates are wrong, can the book still be true? If facts err, can feelings be false? One would prefer to have truth both in fact and feeling (if either could ever be proved). And yet . . . I remember recording some opinions held by my mother which she had announced during a family wedding. 'You got your mother all wrong,' complained an aunt. 'That wasn't at Edie's wedding, it was Ethel's.'

Ours is a period of writing particularly devoted to facts, to a fondness for data rather than divination, as though to possess the exact measurements of the Taj Mahal is somehow to possess its spirit. I read in a magazine recently a profile of Chicago whose every line was a froth of statistics. It gave me a vivid picture, not so much of the city, but of the author cramped in the archives.

In writing autobiography, especially one that looks back at childhood, the only truth is what you remember. No one else who was there can agree with you because he has his own version of what he saw. He also holds to a personal truth of himself, based on an indefatigable self-regard. One neighbour's reaction, after reading my book, sums up this double vision: 'You hit off old Tom to the life,' he said. 'But why d'you tell all those lies about me?'

Seven brothers and sisters shared my early years, and we lived on top of each other. If they all had written of those days, each account would have been different, and each one true. We saw the same events at different heights, at different levels of mood and hunger – one suppressing an incident as too much to bear, another building it large around him, each reflecting one world according to the temper of his day, his age, the chance heat of his blood. Recalling it differently, as we were bound to do, what was it, in fact, we saw? Which one among us has the truth of it now? And which one shall be the judge? The truth is, of course, that there is no pure truth, only the moody accounts of witnesses.

But perhaps the widest pitfall in autobiography is the writer's censorship of self. Unconscious or deliberate, it often releases an image of one who could never have lived. Flat, shadowy, prim and bloodless, it is a leaf pressed dry on the page, the surrogate chosen for public office so that the author might survive in secret.

With a few exceptions, the first person singular is one of the recurrent shams of literature – the faceless 'I', opaque and neuter, fruit of some failure between honesty and nerve. To be fair, one should not confine this failing to literature. One finds it in painting, too, whose centuries of self-portraits, deprecating and tense, are often as alike as brothers. This cipher no doubt is the 'I' of all of us, the only self that our skills can see.

For the writer, after all, it may be a necessary one, the one that works best on the page. An ego that takes up too much of a book can often wither the rest of it. Charles Dickens's narrators were often dry as wafers, but they compèred Gargantuan worlds. The autobiographer's self can be a transmitter of life that is larger than his own – though it is best that he should be shown taking part in that life and involved in its dirt and splendours. The dead stick 'I', like the staff of the maypole, can be the centre of the turning world, or it can be the electric needle that picks up and relays the thronging choirs of life around it.

Laurie Lee
I Didn't Come Too (Penguin)

GOING BACK

It seems smaller, going back: the garden, the house, everything. But the garden, especially. When I was a small child it was infinite: lawns, paths, high hedges, the rose garden, the long reach of the the kitchen garden, the spinney with the silver birches. It was a completed world: beyond lay nothingness. Space. Limbo.

In fact, I now see, a landscape of fields and hills and lanes, tranquil and harmless – but then it was the unpredictable, into which one did not go. We turned back at the gates. The five-barred stable gate, the white gate by the tennis lawn, the drive gates. These defined our world: the safe, controlled world of the garden.

Today, coming out of the other, unpredictable world, it was the garden that was somehow strange – a planned and ordered place amid the random fields and trees.

We stopped the car outside the drive gates.

'I won't be long,' I said.

My husband opened a newspaper. 'No need to hurry.'

I walked down the drive. The leaves were falling, lying in glowing piles at either side. And the conkers. It was a good conker year, I could see. Years ago, years and years ago, when we were five and six, Edward and I, even the drive was a daring extension of our world. We lived then in the hedged bit beyond the kitchen, where the swing was. And then as we got older we made sorties up here, for the conkers and the wild stawberries, and down to the stables, and to the ha-ha at the bottom of the big lawn, and across the field to the spinney and the stream. And then somehow we were over the gates and out there, in that undefined world of light and shape and shadow, and there were no surprises out there any more. No lions: no dragons.

Only the bull in Mr Pitt's field, down at Rodhuish. And daft Ted in the village. And a rabbit's head in the old quarry.

Remembering is like that. There's what you remember, and then there are the things that have never stopped happening, because they are there always, in your head. We are at the orchid place in the quarry, Edward and I, and a rabbit's head lies among the purple-spotted orchids, where the bees unconcernedly feed, a dreadful, shameful thing, and we turn tail and run . . . We sit by the canal in the iris garden, and Edward mangles daisies, his fingers yellow-stained . . . I am standing in a farmyard, and an aeroplane creeps along the sky above a barn . . . There is a noise of rooks, and a grey-haired woman puts her hand on my shoulder in a quiet room where a clock ticks.

Penelope Lively
Going Back (Piccolo)

THE PITFALLS OF AUTOBIOGRAPHY

Before we go any farther, it may be useful to clarify the question: Why am I writing this autobiography? This should have been done in a preface, but prefaces are so boring to read, and to write, that I have postponed the issue until the story got moving.

I believe that people write autobiographies for two main reasons. The first may be called the 'Chronicler's urge'. The second may be called the '*Ecce Homo* motive'. Both impulses spring from the same source, which is the source of all literature: the desire to share one's experiences with others, and by means of this intimate communication to transcend the isolation of the self.

The Chronicler's urge expresses the need for the sharing of experience related to external events. The *Ecce Homo* motive expresses the same need with regard to internal events.

The Chronicler is driven by the fear that the events of which he is a witness and which are part of his life, their colour, shape, and emotional impact, will be irretrievably lost to the future unless he preserves them on tablets of wax or clay, on parchment or paper, by means of a stylus or quill, typewriter or fountain-pen. The Chronicler's urge dominates the autobiographies of persons who themselves have played a part in shaping the history of their times, or felt that they were better equipped than others to record it – as Defoe must have felt when he wrote his *Journal of the Plague Year.*

The *Ecce Homo* motive, on the other hand, urges men to preserve the unique-ness of their inner experiences, and results in the confessional type of autobio-graphy – St Augustine, Rousseau, de Quincey. It prompts dying physicians to record with minute precision their thoughts and sensations during the last hours before the curtain falls.

Obviously the Chronicler's urge and the *Ecce Homo* motive are at opposite poles on the same scale of values, like introversion and extroversion, perception and contemplation. And obviously a good autobiography ought to be a synthesis of the two – which it rarely is. The vanity of men in public life detracts from the autobiographical value of their chronicles; the introvert's obsession with himself makes him neglect the historical background against which he moves. The *Ecce Homo* motive may degenerate into sterile exhibitionism.

Thus the business of writing autobiography is full of pitfalls. On the one hand, we have the starchy chronicle of the stuffed shirt; on the other, the embarrassing nakedness of the exhibitionist – embarrassing because nakedness is only appealing in a healthy body; who but a doctor wants to look at a rash-covered skin? Apart from these two extremes there are various other snares which even competent craftsmen are rarely able to avoid. The most common of these is what one might call the 'Nostalgic Fallacy'.

With an aching, loving, bitter-sweet nostalgia, the author bends over his past like a woman over the cradle of her child; he whispers to it and rocks it in his arms, blind to the fact that the smiles, and howls, and wrigglings of his budding ego lack for his readers that unique fascination which they hold for him. Even experienced authors who know that the reader is a cold fish who has to be tickled behind the gills to make him respond, become victims of this fallacy as soon as they embark on the first chapter with the heading: 'Childhood'. The smell of lavender in mother's linen closet is so intimate; the smile on granny's face so comforting; the water in the brook behind the watercress patch by the garden fence so cool and fresh that it still caresses his fingers holding the pen; and on and on he goes about his linen closets, grannies, ponies, and watercress brooks as if they were a collective memory of all mankind and not, alas, his separate and incommunicable own. Never is the isolation of the self so acutely painful as in the frustrated attempt to share memories of those earliest and most vivid days, when out of the still fluid oneness of the inside and outside world, out of the original mix-up of fact and fantasy, the sharp boundaries of the self were formed. The Nostalgic Fallacy is the result of the craving to melt and undo those boundaries once again.

The sagacious autobiographer will, therefore, with a sigh of regret, put the dry, crumbling, unique sprig of lavender back in the drawer as if it were a packet of common mothballs and restrict himself to relevant facts. But here the trouble starts again, for how is he to know which facts are relevant and which are not? Both the detective and the psycho-analyst affirm that apparently irrelevant facts yield the most important clues. And my experience with sleuths – whether they searched my pockets or my dreams – has convinced me that by and large the affirmation is correct. When one re-reads the entries in one's diary after five years, one is surprised to find that the most significant events are all strangely under-emphasized. Thus the selection of relevant material is a highly problematical affair, and the crux of all autobiography.

Next among the snares is the 'Dull Dog Fallacy'. A great many memoir-writers are so afraid of showing off that they portray themselves as the dullest dogs on earth. The 'Dull Dog Fallacy' requires that the first person singular in an autobiography should always appear as a shy, restrained, reserved, colourless individual; and the reader wonders how he could possibly succeed in making so many friends, in being always in the midst of interesting people, events, and emotional entanglements. But the Dull Dog is, of course, also a paragon of quiet reliability and unobtrusive decency; if he confesses to certain faults, it is merely an added sign of his modesty.

The virtues of understatement and self-restraint make social intercourse civilized and agreeable, but they have a paralysing effect on autobiography. The memoir-writer ought neither to spare himself nor hide his light under a bushel; he must obviously overcome his reluctance to relate painful and humiliating experiences, but he must also have the less obvious courage to include those experiences which show him in a favourable light.

I do not believe that either in life or in literature puritanism is a virtue. Self-castigation, yes. And self-love too – if it is as fierce and humble, exacting and resigned, accepting and rebellious, and as full of awe and wonder as love for other creatures should be. He who does not love himself, does not love well; and he who does not hate himself, does not hate well; and hatred of evil is as necessary as love if the world is not to come to a standstill. Tolerance is an acquired virtue; indifference is a native vice. 'When I have forgiven a fellow everything, I am through with him', said Freud. And even Christ hated the moneylenders.

In 1937, during the war in Spain, when I found myself in prison with the prospect of facing a firing squad, I made a vow: if ever I got out of there alive I would write an autobiography so frank and unsparing of myself that it would make Rousseau's *Confessions* and the *Memoirs* of Cellini appear as sheer cant.

That was fifteen years ago; since then I have tried several times to fulfil that vow. I never got farther than the first few pages. The process of self-immolation is certainly painful, but that isn't the real trouble. The trouble is that it is also morbidly pleasant, like the analyst's couch. It leads to the Nostalgic Fallacy in reverse: the scent of the lavender-bag in the drawer is replaced by the sewer smells so dear to our little id-s. Moreover, it offers that wrong form of catharsis which the artist learns to avoid like the plague. And whatever is bad art is also bad autobiography. I forced myself to go on because I suspected that my loathing for the job, my revulsion against turning an autobiography into a clinical case-history, was due to moral cowardice; and it took me a long time to discover that in this domain the artless truth is obsessional and strident. In short, all art contains a portion of exhibitionism – but exhibitionism is not art.

There is still another aspect to this tricky problem of selecting the relevant material. There is the question: relevant to whom? To the reader, obviously. But what type of reader does the author have in mind? This question, at least, I can answer without ambiguity. The Chronicler's urge is always directed towards the unborn, future reader. This may sound presumptuous, but it is merely the expression of a natural bent. I have no idea whether fifty years from now anybody will want to read a book of mine, but I have a fairly precise idea of what makes me, as a writer, tick. It is the wish to trade a hundred contemporary readers against ten readers in ten years' time and one reader in a hundred years' time. This has always seemed to me what a writer's ambition should be. It is the point where the Chronicler's urge merges with the *Ecce Homo* motive.

Arthur Koestler
Arrow in the Blue (Hutchinson)

WRITING OF THE PAST

In writing of the past, how one transforms and insensibly idealises it, how above all shape and form are imposed upon something which at the time appears a flux of events in themselves sufficiently meaningful. Looking at the scraps of personal correspondence salvaged from those months I find references to people I can no longer remember, acute concern expressed about uncaught trains, confusion over telephone calls, arguments about the merits of social theories put forward in quickly defunct magazines. In re-creating, perhaps even creating, the past we make it inevitably purer and more intelligible than it ever was as seen in the context of a single experience. What we miss out is the vital trivia . . . No picture is complete, of ourselves or certainly of other people. We always put down a personal or imagined truth, even when with the help of memoirs, letters, interviews, tape recordings, we try to evoke a literal one.

Julian Symons
Notes from Another Country
(London Magazine Editions)

AUTOBIOGRAPHY AS AN ATTEMPTED JAIL-BREAK

Memory is not merely recall. Some things we choose to forget. Some, which we cannot forget, we make bearable. Life washes through us like a tide. In its ebb and flow the fragments of the past are ground smooth so that, with time, we can handle them like stones from a rock pool, admiring their colour, shape and texture. We do not know which of them will stir and rattle as the tide ebbs from us for the last time. These are pebbles from my skull.

We get little help from others in living. What we learn from them are mostly the inessentials of life – tricks and skills. But occasionally we exchange obscure signals. They are reassurances that others face or have faced the same difficulties, problems, choices. That they react to the same stimuli, feel the same joy and anguish, make the same sort of shifts to deal with fore-knowledge of mortality. We may record the past for various reasons: because we find it interesting; because by setting it down we can deal with it more easily; because we wish to escape from the prison where we face our individual problems, wrestle with our particular temptations, triumph in solitude and in solitude accept defeat and death. Autobiography is an attempted jail-break. The reader tunnels through the same dark.

Stuart Hood
Pebbles from my Skull
(Hutchinson/Elmfield Press)

WAYS OF WORKING

● Many people find it difficult to get back into their memories. Certain limbering-up activities like asking around within the family, or friends, or focussing on particular incidents may help you. Or being able to have the chance to chat with friends about their experiences can often trigger off related memories. The often-choked process of recollection needs time and a relaxed, supportive context to grow in.

● Look closely at the 'Family photograph' picture and poem. (Brian Jones, *A Family Album* may help here as well.) Bring your own family photograph album in and talk through some of the most intriguing pictures with your friends, telling the stories of the circumstances that are associated with the photographs. Build up your own family album collection of old photographs, poems, stories about autobiographical moments. Perhaps you would like to try out a range of styles as well? Are you going to take a comic view of the past, wry, sincere, ironic, or try to recapture the innocence by trying to write through the eyes of a child?

● Point-of-view exploration: tape or write three different points of view on an early childhood incident that is close to you, e.g. First day at school, Getting lost, Skiving, Getting into trouble. You might choose to look at it (a) through

the eyes of the child at the time the incident took place, (b) through the eyes
of the next-door neighbour, (c) through your own eyes looking back on yourself
when young. To do this effectively you might need to collect more detailed
evidence through interviewing your own family and friends.

● Capturing 'flashpoints' or moments of illumination in your own autobiography.
(Reading Anna Leitrim's stealing toys episode from 'Me and my history', George
Ewart Evans's 'Beetles' memory or Richard Wright's dawning awareness of the
social contrast between his own 'cinder environment' and trim lawns and hedges
of white people's homes, might help you to get started.) Make your own sequence
of 'flashpoints' in free verse or prose poem form. See Seamus Heaney's autobiographical sequence of prose poems called *Stations* (Ulsterman Publications,
70 Eglantine Avenue, Belfast 9) as an example here.

● Make your own public chronicle of a particular period in time, a special area
or district, or the lives, leisure or work of a specific group of people. Possible
starting-points might be people's memories of working and relaxing (see Charles
Forman's material on St Helens in the 1920s and the remembered experiences
of a mortuary technician and a machine worker from the Documentary section;
or a book of photographs like Humphrey Spender's *Worktown people: Photographs
from Northern England 1937–38,* that has sections on Street life, Work, Sport,
Parks, Drinking, Elections, Blackpool and Funerals) or the strength of certain
periods in the popular imagination.

Take, for example, an area of investigation like 'Everyday memories of the
Second World War'. Potential memory-joggers for a good many people are subjects
like evacuation, gas masks, the black market, Saucepans for Spitfires, air-raid
shelters, barrage balloons, dried milk and eggs, utility clothing, ration books, etc.

To catch the flavour of a particular time a chronicle display or collection
might include photocopied newspaper headlines from the local library, taped and
transcribed interviews, photographs, significant objects like a Mickey Mouse gas
mask for children etc. Look at Stephen Humphries' *Hooligans or rebels? – an
oral history of working class childhood and youth 1889–1939* (Basil Blackwell,
Oxford) for many superbly direct examples of oral reminiscence on punishment
in schools, truancy, street gangs, larking about episodes, etc.

● Make a collection of family sayings, catch-phrases, proverbs, jokes and anecdotes
that are connected to memorable events and happenings that you can remember
or have been told about, as in Norman Nicholson's 'Boo to a goose' or Robert
Roberts' piano incident story that passed straight into his family archives.

● In small groups look closely at the editing processes involved in spoken auto-
biography/oral history. For example you might like to contrast the different
transcripts in the passages by Joseph Maddison, Ronald Blythe, and George Ewart
Evans. Which to you seems the most faithful to the way it might have been said?
Or perhaps you would like to share your journal comments on the problems of
transcribing taped memories. Exploration of *The Dillen* by Angela Hewins (OUP),
might prove helpful in this respect.

FURTHER REFERENCES

Autobiography

A Ragged Schooling Robert Roberts, Fontana/Collins
Our Lives Various teenage writers, ILEA English Centre, Sutherland Street, London SW1
An Autobiography Edwin Muir, Hogarth Press/Methuen
A Woman Warrior Maxine Hong Kingston, Picador
Between High Walls Grace Foakes, Pergamon/Shepherd-Walwyn
Black Boy Richard Wright, Longman
Kiddars' Luck Jack Common, Blackie
Tell Freedom Peter Abrahams, Faber
Lark Rise to Candleford Flora Thompson, OUP/Penguin
A Comprehensive Education Roger Mills, Centerprise
In the Castle of My Skin George Lamming, Longman
Destiny Obscure: autobiographies of childhood, education and family from the 1820s to the 1920s John Burnett, Allen Lane
The Life and Writings of a Working Woman Ada Nield Chew, Virago
Pebbles From My Skull Stuart Hood, Elmfield Press
A Boy in Your Situation Charles Hannam, Andre Deutsch
Memoirs Pablo Neruda, Souvenir Press/Penguin
Dobroyed Leslie Wilson, Commonword, Manchester
Places Where I've Done Time William Saroyan, Davis-Poynter
Lifetimes Partington (available from 61 Bloom Street, Manchester)
Aren't You Rather Young to be Writing Your Memoirs? B.S. Johnson, Hutchinson
The Dillen Angela Hewins, OUP
A Model Childhood Christa Wolf, Virago

Spoken personal and public histories

Working Studs Terkel, Penguin
Dutiful Daughters ed. Jean McCrindle and Sheila Rowbotham, Penguin
The Days That We Have Seen George Ewart Evans, Faber
From the Mouths of Men George Ewart Evans, Faber
Working Class Childhood: an oral history Jeremy Seabrook, Gollancz
Fenwomen Mary Chamberlain, Routledge and Kegan Paul
Speak for England ed. Melvyn Bragg, Hodder and Stoughton
Akenfield Ronald Blythe, Penguin
A View in Winter Ronald Blythe, Penguin
London Labour and London Poor Henry Mayhew, Chatto and Windus/Spring Books
Blood of Spain: The Experience of Civil War (1936–39) Ronald Fraser, Penguin
In No Man's Land Tony Parker, Panther
Hooligans or Rebels?: an oral history of working class childhood (1889–1939) Stephen Humphries, Basil Blackwell

Film and television

My Childhood Bill Douglas
Gregory's Girl Bill Forsyth
Blue Remembered Hills Dennis Potter

Photographs

Recall (A slide/tape show in six parts): available from Help the Aged education
   department, 218 Upper Street, London N1
The Child in the City Colin Ward, Architectural Press/Penguin
Down Wapping photographs by Exit, East End Docklands Action Group 1974
   (192 Cable Street, London E1)
Shadow of Light Bill Brandt, Gordon Fraser
Worktown People: photographs from Northern England 1937 — 38 Humphrey
   Spender, Falling Wall Press
The Armley Album Hall Lane Community Centre, 65 Hall Lane, Leeds 12, West
   Yorkshire

2
Travel Writing and the
Sense of Place

INTRODUCTION

Travel writing can seem contrived, a set of '. . trivial circumstances and insignificant happenings . . ', as Lévi-Strauss puts it, self-consciously recorded to satisfy the needs of a publisher; or a cluster of holiday slides paraded after the return in front of polite friends.

Certainly Paul Fussell's examples of tourist dream worlds and pseudo-places seem to confirm our worst suspicions. Without agreeing completely with him that the possibility of travel as genuine exploration is dead, travelling these days can be like moving within a plastic bubble, cosily protected from the raw, unpredictable edge of genuine experience. Just think of all those coaches with orange roofs, airport lounges with endless muzak, the souvenir shops, the sleekly processed tourist routines.

On the other hand, if we are treated to the trained awareness of the more perceptive author—observer, travel writing can open our eyes wider, can often scrape the dull film of local habit and convention from the way we see ourselves and the way we view things. Sleeping rough in the Cévennes in direct contact with the elements prompted Robert Louis Stevenson '. . to come down off this feather-bed of civilisation, and find the globe granite underfoot and strewn with cutting flints.' A jolting escape from routine can serve to stimulate the wondering gaze of a Blaise Cendrars ('Leant over the starboard bulwarks I gaze at the tropical vegetation of an abandoned isle', and in his naked encounter with the dawn at the end of his poem 'Sunsets'), and can help to concentrate our attention more sharply on what we see, as in the diaries of the 'Pennine Way Journey'.

The main reason why travel writing can succeed in rising above the level of 'insignificant happenings', or the purple passage set-piece, is that in the best books it does not only concern itself with physical movement, with the ground shifting under our feet. It can also deal with internal journeys, what John Hillaby has called the workings of the 'skull cinema'. The newness and abrupt dislocation of travelling experiences (being exposed to new places, new relationships, new ways of thinking and feeling) can invite us to stand back from our customary concerns and reflect upon ourselves and the outside world. For many of us the process of travelling can carry with it the need to reconsider and inspect our habitual attitudes. Paul Theroux in *The Great Railway Bazaar* puts it like this: 'Train travel animated my imagination and usually gave me the solitude to order and write my thoughts: I travelled easily in two directions, along the level rails while Asia flashed changes at the window, and at the interior rim of a private world of memory and language. I cannot imagine a luckier combination.' It is this 'private world of memory and language' that adds a further dimension to the experience of travelling. The role of the actual journey becomes rather one of activating a deeper pondering over 'one's past and one's culture from the outside', as W.H. Auden and Louis MacNeice sum it up in their piece on Iceland.

It is the quality of the travel writing that, in the end, persuades the reader to want to participate in the author's journey. The reader allows her or himself to be carried along through the exact observation and authentic detail: the sharp ear for eavesdroppings in Theroux, Auden and Hillaby, the precise, placing detail that makes real to the reader the anticipation of terror in the people and landscapes that Dervla Murphy meets on her cycle journey, and the incisiveness of the satirical comment in Martha Gellhorn's: 'The only aspect of our travels that is guaranteed to hold an audience is disaster. "The camel threw you at the *Great Pyramid* and you broke your leg?" ' — all these qualities help writers to take the reader with them.

The problem of being a traveller is that of seeing things as a series of snatched glances from a passing train window. The empty voyeurism of the tourist (later revealed by Theroux in *The Great Railway Bazaar* when he moves through Vietnam without any real attempt to understand what he sees in an historical or political sense) is sharply exposed through the local, Indian perspective on foreigners in search of Nirvana in the piece by Heather Wood from *Third-Class Ticket*.

The danger for the tourist of contrived cultivation of the picturesque and the exotic and the accompanying standardisation of taste ('exotic spots in a land-scape which may awaken curiosity but do not satisfy a longer interest' — Josef Herman) is shown in Cendrars' 'Sunsets', where:

Everybody talks of sunsets
All the travellers are in agreement in talking about the sunsets in these parts
There are plenty of old books where nothing is described but sunsets. .

This lop-sided attention to the picturesque in scenery tends to isolate landscape from its inhabitants. That is why Auden and MacNeice cram into their *Letters from Iceland* a collage of statistics, letters, a list of proverbs, overheard conversations, recipes, a diary, maps, to indicate something of the cultural reach and variety that they met in their travels across Iceland. As Tom Paulin remarks in an essay on the book (included in *The 1930s: a challenge to orthodoxy* ed. John Lucas, Harvester Press): 'Without human or political content nature means very little . . .'.

As a pointed contrast to this pursuit of the descriptively picturesque we have included pieces that deal with a more rooted sense of place: like Josef Herman's Welsh mining village that in its mood and atmosphere expresses a continuing commitment to a particular kind of working life in the valley.

Landscape does not have to be seen as a hurried glimpse through a window. It can also be viewed as a product of a complicated social and historical process, as in the Raymond Williams piece where 'you must learn to read the whole land as a way of making sense of it'.

TRAVEL WRITING AS BOREDOM

I hate travelling and explorers. Yet here I am proposing to tell the story of my expeditions. But how long it has taken me to make up my mind to do so! It is now fifteen years since I left Brazil for the last time and all during this period I have often planned to undertake the present work, but on each occasion a sort of shame and repugnance prevented me making a start. Why, I asked myself, should I give a detailed account of so many trivial circumstances and insignificant happenings? Adventure has no place in the anthropologist's profession; it is merely one of those unavoidable drawbacks, which detract from his effective work through the incidental loss of weeks or months; there are hours of inaction when the informant is not available; periods of hunger, exhaustion, sickness perhaps; and always the thousand and one dreary tasks which eat away the days to no purpose and reduce dangerous living in the heart of the virgin forest to an imitation of military service . . . The fact that so much effort and expenditure has to be wasted on reaching the object of our studies bestows no value on that aspect of our profession, and should be seen rather as its negative side. The truths which we seek so far afield only become valid when they have been separated from this dross. We may endure six months of travelling, hardships and sickening boredom for the purpose of recording (in a few days, or even a few hours) a hitherto unknown myth, a new marriage rule or a complete list of clan names, but is it worth my while taking up my pen to perpetuate such a useless shred of memory or pitiable recollection as the following: 'At five thirty in the morning, we entered the harbour at Recife amid the shrill cries of the gulls, while a fleet of boats laden with tropical fruits clustered round the hull'?

Nevertheless, this kind of narrative enjoys a vogue which I, for my part, find incomprehensible. Amazonia, Tibet and Africa fill the bookshops in the form of travelogues, accounts of expeditions and collections of photographs, in all of which the desire to impress is so dominant as to make it impossible for the reader to assess the value of the evidence put before him. Instead of having his critical faculties stimulated, he asks for more such pabulum and swallows prodigious quantities of it. Nowadays, being an explorer is a trade, which consists not, as one might think, in discovering hitherto unknown facts after years of study, but in covering a great many miles and assembling lantern-slides or motion pictures, preferably in colour, so as to fill a hall with an audience for several days in succession. For this audience, platitudes and commonplaces seem to have been miraculously transmuted into revelations by the sole fact that their author, instead of doing his plagiarizing at home, has supposedly sanctified it by covering some twenty thousand miles.

Claude Lévi-Strauss
Tristes Tropiques (Penguin)

TOURIST FANTASIES

For tourist fantasies to bloom satisfactorily, certain conditions must be established. First, the tourist's mind must be entirely emptied so that a sort of hypnotism can occur. Unremitting Musak is a help here, and it is carefully provided in hotels, restaurants, elevators, tour buses, cable-cars, planes, and excursion boats. The tourist is assumed to know nothing, a tradition upheld by the American magazine *Travel* (note the bogus title), which is careful to specify that London is in England and Venice in Italy. If the tourist is granted a little awareness, it is always of the most retrograde kind, like the 30s belief, which he is assumed to hold, that 'transportation,' its varieties and promise, is itself an appropriate subject of high regard. (Think of the 1939 New York World's Fair, with its assumption that variety, celerity, and novelty in means of transport are inherently interesting: 'Getting There Is Half the Fun.') A current day-tour out of Tokyo honors this convention. The ostensible object is to convey a group of tourists to a spot where they can wonder at the grandeurs of natural scenery. In pursuit of this end, they are first placed in a 'streamlined' train whose speed of 130 miles per hour is frequently called to their attention. They are then transferred to an air-conditioned 'coach' which whisks them to a boat, whence, after a ten-minute ride, they are ushered into a funicular to ascend a spooky gorge, after which, back to the bus, etc. The whole day's exercise is presented as a marvel of contrivance in which the sheer variety of the conveyances supplies a large part of the attraction. Hydrofoils are popular for similar reasons, certainly not for their efficiency. Of the four I've been on in the past few years, two have broken down spectacularly, one in Manila Bay almost sinking after encountering a submerged log at sophomoric high speed.

Tourist fantasies fructify best when tourists are set down not in places but in pseudo-places, passing through subordinate pseudo-places, like airports, on the way. Places are odd and call for interpretation. They are the venue of the traveler. Pseudo-places entice by their familiarity and call for instant recognition: 'We have arrived.' Kermanshah, in Iran, is a place; the Costa del Sol is a pseudo-place, or Tourist Bubble, as anthropologists call it. The Algarve, in southern Portugal, is a prime pseudo-place, created largely by Temple Fielding, the American author of *Fielding's Travel Guide to Europe*. That book, first published in 1948, was to tourism what Baedeker was to travel. It did not, says John McPhee, 'tell people what to see. It told them . . . what to spend, and where.' Bougainville is a place; the Polynesian Cultural Center, on Oahu, is a pseudo-place. Touristically considered, Switzerland has always been a pseudo-place, but now Zermatt has been promoted to the status of its pre-eminent pseudo-place. Because it's a city that has been constructed for the purpose of being recognized as a familiar image, Washington is a classic pseudo-place, resembling Disneyland in that as in other respects. One striking post-Second War phenomenon has been the transformation of numerous former small countries into pseudo-places or tourist commonwealths, whose function is simply to entice tourists and sell them things. This has happened remarkably fast. As recently as 1930 Alec Waugh could report that Martinique had no tourists because there was no accommodation for them. Now, Martinique would seem to be about nothing but tourists, like Haiti, the Dominican Republic, Barbados, Bermuda, Hong Kong, Fiji, and the Greek Islands.

Paul Fussell
Abroad (OUP)

TRAVEL AS DISASTER

We can't all be Marco Polo or Freya Stark but millions of us are travellers never-theless. The great travellers, living and dead, are in a class by themselves, unequalled professionals. We are amateurs and though we too have our moments of glory we also tire, our spirits sag, we have our moments of rancour. Who has not heard, felt, thought or said, in the course of a journey, words like: 'They've lost the luggage again, for God's sake?' 'You mean we came all this way just to see this?' 'Why do they have to make so damn much noise?' 'Call that a room with a view?' 'I'd rather kick his teeth in than give him a tip.'

But we persevere and do our best to see the world and we get around; we go everywhere. Upon our return, no one willingly listens to our travellers' tales. 'How was the trip?' they say. 'Marvellous,' we say. 'In Tbilisi, I saw . . .' Eyes glaze. As soon as politeness permits or before, conversation is switched back to local news such as gossip, the current political outrage, who's read what, last night's telly; people will talk about the weather rather than hear our glowing reports on Copenhagen, the Grand Canyon, Katmandu.

The only aspect of our travels that is guaranteed to hold an audience is disaster. 'The camel threw you at the *Great Pyramid* and you broke your leg?' 'Chased the pickpocket through the Galeria and across Naples and lost *all* your travellers' cheques and your passport?' 'Locked and forgotten in a *sauna* in Viipuri?' 'Ptomaine from eating *sheep's eyes* at a Druze feast?' That's what they like. They can hardly wait for us to finish before they launch into stories of their own suffering in foreign lands. The fact is, we cherish our disasters and here we are one up on the great travellers who have every impressive qualification for the job but lack jokes.

Martha Gellhorn
Travels with Myself and Another (Penguin)

A CAMP IN THE DARK

The author has tried unsuccessfully to find lodgings for the night in the small village of Fouzilhac in the Cévennes, France. Modestine is his donkey.

The lanterns had somewhat dazzled me, and I ploughed distressfully among stones and rubbish-heaps. All the other houses in the village were both dark and silent; and though I knocked at here and there a door, my knocking was unanswered. It was a bad business; I gave up Fouzilhac with my curses. The rain had stopped, and the wind, which still kept rising, began to dry my coat and trousers. 'Very well,' thought I, 'water or no water, I must camp.' But the first thing was to return to Modestine. I am pretty sure I was twenty minutes groping for my lady in the dark; and if it had not been for the unkindly services of the bog, into which I once more stumbled, I might have still been groping for her at the dawn. My next business was to gain the shelter of a wood, for the wind was cold as well as boisterous. How, in this well-wooded district, I should have been so long in finding one, is another of the insoluble mysteries of this day's adventures; but I will take my oath that I put near an hour to the discovery.

At last black trees began to show upon my left, and, suddenly crossing the road, made a cave of unmitigated blackness right in front. I call it a cave without exaggeration; to pass below that arch of leaves was like entering a dungeon. I felt about until my hand encountered a stout branch, and to this I tied Modestine, a haggard, drenched, desponding donkey. Then I lowered my pack, laid it along the wall on the margin of the road, and unbuckled the straps. I knew well enough where the lantern was; but where were the candles? I groped and groped among the tumbled articles, and, while I was thus groping suddenly I touched the spirit-lamp. Salvation! This would serve my turn as well. The wind roared unwearyingly among the trees; I could hear the boughs tossing and the leaves churning through half a mile of forest; yet the scene of my encampment was not only as black as the pit, but admirably sheltered. At the second match the wick caught flame. The light was both livid and shifting; but it cut me off from the universe, and doubled the darkness of the surrounding night.

I tied Modestine more conveniently for herself, and broke up half the black bread for her supper, reserving the other half against the morning. Then I gathered what I should want within reach, took off my wet boots and gaiters, which I wrapped in my waterproof, arranged my knapsack for a pillow under the flap of my sleeping-bag, insinuated my limbs into the interior, and buckled myself in like a *bambino*. I opened a tin of Bologna sausage and broke a cake of chocolate, and that was all I had to eat. It may sound offensive, but I ate them together, bite by bite, by way of bread and meat. All I had to wash down this revolting mixture was neat brandy: a revolting beverage in itself. But I was rare and hungry; ate well, and smoked one of the best cigarettes in my experience. Then I put a stone in my straw hat, pulled the flap of my fur cap over my neck and eyes, put my revolver ready to my hand, and snuggled well down among the sheepskins.

I questioned at first if I were sleepy, for I felt my heart beating faster than usual, as if with an agreeable excitement to which my mind remained a stranger. But as soon as my eyelids touched, that subtle glue leaped between them, and they would no more come separate.

The wind among the trees was my lullaby. Sometimes it sounded for minutes together with a steady even rush, not rising nor abating; and again it would swell and burst like a great crashing breaker, and the trees would patter me all over with big drops from the rain of the afternoon. Night after night, in my own bedroom in the country, I have given ear to this perturbing concert of the wind among the woods; but whether it was a difference in the trees, or the lie of the ground, or because I was myself outside and in the midst of it, the fact remains that the wind sang to a different tune among these woods of Gévaudan. I hearkened and hearkened; and meanwhile sleep took gradual possession of my body and subdued my thoughts and senses; but still my last waking effort was to listen and distinguish, and my last conscious state was one of wonder at the foreign clamour in my ears.

Twice in the course of the dark hours — once when a stone galled me underneath the sack, and again when the poor patient Modestine, growing angry, pawed and stamped upon the road — I was recalled for a brief while to consciousness, and saw a star or two overhead, and the lace-like edge of the foliage against the sky. When I awoke for the third time (Wednesday, September 25th), the world was flooded with a blue light, the mother of the dawn. I saw the leaves labouring in the wind and the ribbon of the road; and, on turning my head, there was Modestine tied to a beech, and standing half across the path in an attitude of inimitable patience. I closed my eyes again, and set to thinking over the experience of the night. I was surprised to find how easy and pleasant it had been, even in this tempestuous weather. The stone which annoyed me would not have been there, had I not been forced to camp blindfold in the opaque night; and I had felt no other inconvenience, except when my feet encountered the lantern or the second volume of Peyrat's *Pastors of the Desert* among the mixed contents of my sleeping-bag; nay, more, I had felt not a touch of cold, and awakened with unusually lightsome and clear sensations.

With that, I shook myself, got once more into my boots and gaiters, and, breaking up the rest of the bread for Modestine, strolled about to see in what part of the world I had awakened.

For my part, I travel not to go anywhere, but to go. I travel for travel's sake. The great affair is to move; to feel the needs and hitches of our life more nearly; to come down off this feather-bed of civilisation, and find the globe granite underfoot and strewn with cutting flints. Alas, as we get up in life, and are more preoccupied with our affairs, even a holiday is a thing that must be worked for. To hold a pack upon a pack-saddle against a gale out of the freezing north is no high industry, but it is one that serves to occupy and compose the mind. And when the present is so exacting, who can annoy himself about the future?

Robert Louis Stevenson
Travels with a Donkey (Heinemann)

67

PENNINE WAY JOURNEY

May 16

Going far?
All the way.
Over Kinder?
Seems best.
It'll be mucky.
Could be.

Later that day

Up there you blink. Mounds of bare peat rise in all directions, like waves. On the top there are no signposts, no markers, only the choice of channels between the chocolate-coloured peat.

The channel I followed swung off in the wrong direction. I tried another with the same result. *And* another until, fed-up with the sight of peat, I took off my shoes and socks and climbed onto a crest of the soggy stuff. I didn't sink in far, but the prospect from the top was appalling. The peat extended for miles. It rose, gradually in the direction of a mound of rocks. And it seemed, like manure. The top of Kinder Scout looks as if it's entirely covered in the droppings of dinosaurs.

May 17

Over-plump grouse scutter ahead like mechanical toys, alarmed, clucking until they bounce into the air, turn in the wind, and glide down the fell slopes on improbably small, bow-shaped wings. At your approach sheep panic, barging into each other until at a safe distance, with foreleg raised, they slew around and stare at you with mad, watery-blue eyes.

May 19

Two pied wagtails turned up for breakfast. I tossed them bits of bacon sandwich, packed my gear, folded the tent, strapped it down on top of the rucksack, and set off. In six hours I saw but one soul, a farmer who whistled commands to his sheep-dog from the driving seat of a tractor. He waved, I waved, I went on.

May 23

The little road shrinks to a path, the path to a track and as the last visible farm house shrinks far behind, the sense of space is tremendous and is forever. I went up to Fountains Fell, to where Great Whernside, Littondale, and Langstroth appeared as dark clefts in the undulations of the hills. The men who put names to those places knew what they were about. There is Green Hackeber, and Gauber, Gatekirk, Eller Beck, Blackshiver, Quaking Pot, and some deep holes called Boggart Roaring.

May 31

'It's difficult, you know, here in the winter,' said the woman in the shop. An understatement, since the snow has been known to cover the local station so deep that the station-master couldn't find the train he was supposed to flag out. Glad I walked the Way in spring.

John Hillaby
Journey Through Britain
(Paladin)

Mist on Kinder Scout

I stood still, straining my eyes.
The mist was closing in,
It was thickening
To dense-grey like sheep-wool.
What if I ran or stumbled
This way, that way?
A gully could gulp me,
Swampy rain-slime swallow me;
And what if I plunged
Off the lip of the plateau,
Like a medieval seaman
Fearing the edge of the world?

I heard nothing but rasping
Voices of invisible rams.
I was lost, and afraid to move —
Till a stranger gloomily

Appeared, and guided me
Over rubbery peat-hags,
Spongy moss and spiked grass,
To the head of Grinds Brook.

And when I thanked him,
He'd gone. There was nothing
But mist, like peat-smoke,
And water trickling to Edale.

Harold Massingham

CROSSING THE BORDER INTO NORTHERN IRELAND:
A Cyclist's Journal

9 June

Today I left Cavan town soon after eight o'clock — a sunny morning with a strong cool wind and swift white clouds. In Belturbet post office advice about cross-border routes was offered by a friendly clerk and a tall old farmer with a leathery face. They thought a cyclist might be able to get across, if the water was low, where the bridge used to be. 'It was blown up twice,' explained the clerk, 'so now they'll leave it that way.' When I asked who had blown it up, and why, they obviously thought I was 'leading them on' and changed the subject. But I genuinely wanted to know. I have a very limited understanding of these matters.

Beyond Belturbet the hilly third-class road passed a few poor little farms and presented two crossroads without signposts. Uncertain of the way, I approached a depressed-looking farm dwelling. As I crossed the untidy yard I called out 'Anybody at home?' — not realizing (stupidly) the effect an unknown voice would have quarter of a mile from the border. As I stood at the open door the whole family faced me silently like figures in a tableau, eyes full of fear, everybody motionless. A thin bent grandad stood in the centre of the kitchen floor leaning on an ash-plant, his hat pushed back off his forehead. A woman of about my own age, with unkempt foxy hair and a torn pink jersey, had been making bread and stood with floury hands held over a basin. A young woman with impetigo, a ragged skirt and sandals not matching was just inside the door holding an empty pail. A skinny, freckled little boy had been pulling a cardboard carton full of turf sods across the floor and he it was who broke the silence by beginning to cry. It is many years since I last saw that degree of slovenly poverty in my own part of rural Ireland. (Yet the inevitable television set stood in one corner.) But it was the fear, not the poverty, that shook me; that instant of pure terror before my harmlessness was recognized. Then everybody relaxed – except the child – and the women came out to the road to give me precise instructions. They didn't think the stepping-stones would be above water today – and they were right.

Round the next corner a concrete roadblock supported a NO ROAD sign. Then I saw a river lined with willows and alders. Its fast brown water was swirling and glinting in the sun below the trees' fresh green, and it seemed incongruous – yet obscurely reassuring – to find such a troublesome border taking such a lovely form. Standing on the remains of the old narrow bridge (it must have been very attractive) I looked at a newish county council cottage twenty yards away – deserted, all its windows blown in, yet a framed photograph of a County Cavan football team still hanging on an inside wall. Across the border was a thatched cottage half-hidden by trees: probably it was empty, too. I could see not a sign of life anywhere and suddenly I remembered the Turkish–Soviet border at Ani. Though there are no watch-towers here one gets the same feeling of animation artifically suspended by politics. I looked down at the rusty carcass of a bus filled with boulders; the locals' attempt – plus these submerged stepping stones – to replace the bridge. How much more efficiently the Baltis or Nepalese would have coped, with so many boulders and trees available!

Back on the road I was nearly run down by two Irish Army Land-Rovers going towards the non-bridge at top speed. As I turned off on to another by-road they raced back towards Belturbet. Pedalling slowly along a deserted hilly road parallel with the border, I looked north when the high hedges permitted. Fermanagh was a long ridge of wooded or cultivated land with little houses that even from a distance were perceptibly neater than most Co. Cavan homesteads. Within only a few miles I passed several abandoned farmhouses, cottages and hovels; it must be easy to go to ground hereabouts. Most gates had been improvised from old bedsteads, tar-barrels and/or bundles of thorn. I surmounted one bedstead to attend to my morning duty, leaving Roz [the bike] in the ditch and paying no attention to an approaching vehicle. But it stopped beside Roz with a squeal of brakes and three young soldiers clutching rifles came over the 'gate' so quickly that it collapsed. As my activities were at a crucial stage I could do nothing but squat on, causing the Irish Army to retreat in such confusion that one youth tripped over his rifle.

Dervla Murphy
A Place Apart (Penguin)

ICELAND JOURNEY

1   Every exciting letter has enclosures,
        And so shall this – a bunch of photographs,
      Some out of focus, some with wrong exposures,

Press cuttings, gossip, maps, statistics, graphs;
I don't intend to do the thing by halves.
I'm going to be very up to date indeed.
It is a collage that you're going to read.

I want a form that's large enough to swim in,
And talk on any subject that I choose,
From natural scenery to men and women,
Myself, the arts, the European news:
And since she's on a holiday, my Muse
Is out to please, find everything delightful
And only now and then be mildly spiteful.

2   Dear Christopher,
        Thank you for your letter. . . Now, as to your questions:

1 'I can't quite picture your arrival. What was your impression of Reykjavik harbour? Is there any attempt to make the visitor feel that he is arriving at a capital city?'

Not much. There is nothing by the pier but warehouses and piles of agricultural implements under tarpaulin. Most of the town is built of corrugated iron. When we arrived, it was only half-past seven and we had to wait outside the harbour, because the Icelandic dockhands won't get up early. The town was hidden in low-lying mist, with the tops of the mountains showing above it. My first impression of the town was Lutheran, drab and remote. The quay was crowded with loungers, passively interested, in caps. They seemed to have been there a long time. There were no screaming hawkers or touts. Even the children didn't speak.

2 'What does R. look like?'

There is no good building stone. The new suburban houses are built of concrete in sombre colours. The three chief buildings are the Roman Catholic church, the (unfinished) theatre and the students' hostel, which looks like waiting-rooms of an airport. There is a sports ground, with a running-track and tennis courts, where the young men play most of the night. In the middle of the town there is a shallow artificial lake full of terns and wild duck. The town peters out into flat rusty-brown lava-fields, scattered shacks surrounded by wire-fencing, stockfish drying on washing-lines and a few white hens. Further down the coast, the lava is dotted with what look like huge laundry-baskets; these are really compact heaps of drying fish covered with tarpaulin. The weather changes with extraordinary rapidity: one moment the rain blots out everything, the next, the sun is shining behind clouds, filling the air with an intense luminous light in which you can see for miles, so that every detail of the cone-shaped mountains stands out needle-sharp against an orange sky. There is one peak which is always bright pink.

3   *Soups:* Many of these are sweet and very unfortunate. I remember three
with particular horror, one of sweet milk and hard macaroni, one tasting
of hot marzipan, and one of scented hair oil. (But there is a good sweet soup,
raspberry coloured, made of bilberry, L.M.)

Fish: Dried fish is a staple food in Iceland. This should be shredded with
the fingers and eaten with butter. It varies in toughness. The tougher kind
tastes like toe-nails, and the softer kind like the skin of the soles of one's
feet.

In districts where salmon are caught, or round the coast, you get excellent
fish, the grilled salmon particularly.

Meat: This is practically confined to mutton in various forms. The Danes
have influenced Icelandic cooking, and to no advantage. Meat is liable to be
served up in glutinous and half-cold lumps, covered with tasteless gravy.
At the poorer farms you will only get Hangikyrl, i.e. smoked mutton. This
is comparatively harmless when cold as it only tastes like soot, but it would
take a very hungry man indeed to eat it hot.

Vegetables: Apart from potatoes, these, in the earlier part of the summer,
are conspicuous by their absence. Later, however, there are radishes, turnips,
carrots, and lettuce in sweet milk. Newish potatoes begin to appear about
the end of August. Boiled potatoes are eaten with melted butter, but beware
of the browned potatoes, as they are coated in sugar, another Danish
barbarism.

Fruit: None, except rhubarb and in the late summer excellent bilberries.

Cold Food: Following the Scandinavian custom, in the hotels, following
the hot dish there are a number of dishes of cold meats and fishes eaten with
bread and butter. Most of these are good, particularly the pickled herring.
Smoked salmon in my opinion is an overrated dish, but it is common for
those who appreciate it.

Sweets: The standard sweet is skyr, a cross between Devonshire cream
and a cream cheese, which is eaten with sugar and cream. It is very filling
but most people like it very much. It is not advisable, however, to take coffee
and skyr together just before riding, as it gives you diarrhoea.

4   *Sandakrökur*

We caught the Icelandic Train Bleu all right. Two coaches crammed to
capacity. How embarrassing it is to get into an already crowded bus when
the passengers have got to know each other. We felt like the Germans invading
Belgium. But the atmosphere soon thawed; I got my travelling rug well over
my knees, found that my cigarettes had come out of their packet into my
pocket, and settled down as an accepted citizen of a temporary regime.

The hills are all covered in mist. Road menders peered out of wayside
tents, bridge sides suddenly shaved the bus. Loud cries of excitement told
that someone had hit his head very hard on the roof at a bump. Thomas
Hardy offered me some snuff and the bus roared when I sneezed. Now we
were passing through a district of terminal moraines which looked too like
the illustrations in a geography text book to be real. Here the last public

execution took place in the early nineteenth century. Sweets were passed round. Sick streamed past the windows.

At four o'clock we reached Blonduos, a one-horse sort of place, where we were to have lunch. Everyone clattered off to their respective lavatories and then down to the dining-room, where I was lucky to arrive early enough to get a real chair instead of a bench. The first course was rice and raisins and ginger. I could have wept, I was so hungry. And the rest was scarcely better, enormous hunks of meat that might have been carved with a chopper, smeared with half-cold gravy. No one can accuse the Icelander of being dainty. I watched a large man opposite leisurely stuffing down large pieces of tepid fat like the hero of a Sunday-school story.

On again, grinding over a watershed, up test gradients. The view from the top is said to be one of the best in the island, but it wasn't today. We came down to Vidamyri, where stands the oldest church in Iceland. Unfortunately we didn't stop, and I only caught a glimpse of it, squat and turf covered, like a shaggy old sheep with a bell round its neck. Shortly afterwards we reached the crossroads where we were to change horses. There was a hurricane blowing and the temperature outside wasn't far off freezing. As I paid the driver, a ten krónur note blew away and I had to chase it for a hundred yards. The bus from Akureyri had also arrived, and Ragnar was talking to one of his old schoolmasters. I got into the primitive local bus and tried to get warm. Luckily it was only forty minutes or so to Sandakrökur, and we got there at eight.

5   R.   And so we came to Iceland —
         C.   Our latest joyride.
         G.   And what have you found in Iceland?
         C.   What have we found? More copy, more surface,
                Vignettes as they call them, dead flowers in an album —
                The harmoniums in the farms, the fine-bread and pancakes
                The pot of ivy trained across the window,
                Children in gumboots, girls in black berets.
         R.   And dead craters and angled crags.

6   I went to eat and then ran into some drunk Norwegian sailors. An Icelandic acquaintance of theirs passed and greeted one by slapping him on the bottom, which started a furious argument conducted entirely in English, something like this.
    — Why did you do that?
    — Why shouldn't I?
    — Don't you know it's an insult to slap a man on his arse?
    — No, it isn't.
    — Yes, it is.
    — No it isn't. It's an Icelandic custom.
    — Oh no, it isn't.
    — How do you know?

— How do I know. Everybody knows.
— No, they don't.
— I tell you it's an insult to slap a chap's arse.
— How can you tell me when you don't know about Iceland?
— If you don't know that, you're goddam uneducated.
— How should I know that when I know it isn't.
(Two officers stroll up and stand by. The crowd begins to disperse.)
— Well, be more careful, next time, Mister, see.
— Same to you.

7   In the bus today I had a bright idea about this travel book. I brought a Byron
with me to Iceland, and I suddenly thought I might write him a chatty letter
in light verse about anything I could think of, Europe, literature, myself.
He's the right person I think, because he was a townee, a European, and
disliked Wordsworth and that kind of approach to nature, and I find that
very sympathetic. This letter in itself will have very little to do with Iceland,
but will be rather a description of an effect of travelling in distant places
which is to make one reflect on one's past and one's culture from the outside.
But it will form a central thread on which I shall hang other letters to different
people more directly about Iceland. Who the people will be I haven't the
slightest idea yet, but I must choose them, so that each letter deals with
its subject in a different and significant way. The trouble about travel books
as a rule, even the most exciting ones, is that the actual events are all extremely
like each other—meals—sleeping accommodation—fleas—dangers, etc, and the
repetition becomes boring. The usual alternative, which is essays on life
prompted by something seen, the kind of thing Lawrence and Aldous Huxley
do, I am neither clever enough nor sensitive enough to manage.

8   The day was now getting misty and the ride dreary. I held in my beast and
trailed along humbly with the jingling pack-horses, losing the sense of time.
I thought the ride would never come to an end. But it did. Suddenly we
came over a rise and there was a long and shallow valley, desolate enough
for anyone and smoking away like the dumping-ground of a great city. I
thought the whole valley was on fire but coming closer I saw that the smoke
was trails of steam, dozens of ribbons of steam blowing from left to right.
This was our destination — the hot springs of Hveravellir. It would now be
about teatime, the others had already left their horses by the hut and were
walking back to look at the springs. 'You *must* see the hut,' Maisie shouted
to me, 'it is just like a henhouse.' And it *was*, my dear, but only the sort of
henhouse you would find in a depressed area. The walls are of rough stone
banked outside with turf, the corrugated iron roof is also covered with turf;
the stone walls inside are unlined and the whole place is incredibly damp.
There is a nasty platform to sleep on three foot up from the floor and
another platform higher up under the roof which you reach by a ladder.
After surveying these apartments I went to have a look at the springs. A
real witches' laundry with the horizontal trailers of steam blowing through

the mist, some from little pop-holes in the ground and others from quite large pools, most of them circular. Some of these latter were lovely, might have been invented by Arthur Rackham – stone basins of highly coloured water varying from Reckitt's blue to green, and round the edge yellowish growths of sulphur. The crust of stone around them seems only about four inches thick and you expect any moment to go down like Dathan and Abiram. The water is practically boiling and the whole valley smells of bad eggs.

9   Our progress today was again stony once we had left the short stretch of grassland. We got in between Langjökull on the left and a mountain with the charming name of Ok on the right and once we had done that all we could think of was getting somewhere else. But we didn't. We went on and on and the landscape remained the same. It was like walking the wrong way on a moving staircase. We were close in under the Langjökull but it was covered with mist. Maisie was in a frightful temper. This valley is called Kaldidalur which means Cold Dale – apt but inadequate. The Icelanders are rather proud of it as a show-piece of scenery and no doubt on a clear day it may be quite beautiful if one drives through it quickly in a car. But all we could see was a thirty-foot radius of stones. The stones were too much for my horse and it took to stumbling. We came across the ancient wreck of a very primitive touring car – more desolate than the bones of a camel in a film about the Foreign Legion.

W.H. Auden and Louis MacNeice
Letters from Iceland (Faber)

KEEPING A TRAVEL LOG

A   Overheard conversations

'Reggie's got awfully small,' said the first man.
'Do you think so?' said the second.
'I'm afraid I do. Awfully small. His clothes don't fit him.'
'He was never a big man.'
'I know that. But have you seen him?'
'No. Godfrey said he'd been sick.'
'I'd say *very* sick.'
'Getting old, poor chap.'
'And awfully small.'

B   Visual snapshots

It was after eleven, and most of the apartment blocks were in darkness. But in one bright window there was a dinner party ending, like a painting of a city interior, hung and illuminated in the shadowy gallery of rooftops and balconies. The train passed and printed the window on my eye: two men and two women around a table on which there were three wine bottles, the remains of a large meal, coffee cups, a raided bowl of fruit. All the props, and the men in shirt sleeves, spoke of amiable intimacy, the sad comedy of a reunion of friends. Jean and Marie had been away. Jean was smiling, preparing to clown, and had pulled one of those confounded French faces. He waved his hand back and forth and said, 'She got up on the table like a madwoman and began shaking it at me like this. Incredible! I said to Marie, "The Picards will never believe this!" This is the truth. And then she —'

Looking out a train window in Asia is like watching an unedited travelogue without the obnoxious soundtrack: I had to guess at the purpose of activities — people patting pie-shaped turds and slapping them onto the side of a mud hut to dry; men with bullocks and submerged ploughs, preparing a rice field for planting; and at Badami Bagh, just outside Lahore, a town of grass huts, cardboard shelters, pup tents, and hovels of paper, twigs, and cloth, everyone was in motion — sorting fruit, folding clothes, fanning the fire, shooing a dog away, mending a roof.

C Characters

I returned to my compartment to find a young man sitting on my berth. He greeted me in an accent I could not quite place, partly because he lisped and also because his appearance was somewhat bizarre. His hair, parted in the middle, reached below his shoulders; his thin arms were sheathed in tight sleeves and he wore three rings with large orange stones on each hand, bracelets of various kinds and a necklace of white shells. His face frightened me: it was that corpselike face of lunacy or a fatal illness, with sunken eyes and cheeks, deeply lined, bloodless, narrow, and white. He had a cowering stare, and as he watched me — I was still dripping from my shower — he played with a small leather purse. He said his name was Hermann; he was going to Delhi.

D Dramatic incident

There was a drama outside Niš. At a road near the track a crowd of people fought to look at a horse, still in its traces and hitched to an overloaded wagon, lying dead on its side in a mud puddle in which the wagon was obviously stuck. I imagined its heart had burst when it tried to free the wagon. And it had just happened: children were calling to their friends, a man was dropping his bike and running back for a look, and farther along a man pissing against a fence was straining to see the horse. The scene was composed like a Flemish painting in which the pissing man was a vivid detail. The train, the window frame holding the scene for moments, made it a picture. The man at the fence flicks the last droplets from his penis and, tucking it in his baggy pants, begins to sprint; the picture is complete.

E Places

Venice, like a drawing room in a gas station, is approached through a vast apron of infertile industrial flatlands, criss-crossed with black sewer troughs and stinking of oil, the gigantic sinks and stoves of refineries and factories, all intimidating the delicate dwarfed city beyond. The graffiti along the way are professionally executed as the names of the firms: MOTTA GELATI, LOTTA COMMUNISTA, AGIP, NOI SIAMO TUTTI ASSASSINI, RENAULT, UNITA. The lagoon with its luminous patches of oil slick, as if hopelessly retouched by Canaletto, has a yard-wide tidewrack of rubble, plastic bottles, broken toilet seats, raw sewage, and that bone white factory froth the wind beats into drifts of foam. The edges of the city have succumbed to industry's erosion, and what shows are the cracked back windows and derelict posterns of water-logged villas, a few brittle Venetian steeples, and farther in, but low and almost visibly sinking, walls of spaghetti-coloured stucco and red roofs over which flocks of soaring swallows are teaching pigeons to fly.

F Anecdotes

It was my inability to understand these occupations that led these Indian railway conversations into ancedotes of the oddest sort. The engineer, seeing that my grasp of hydraulics was slender, told me a story about a yogi who neither ate nor drank a thing in his life. 'What did he live on?' I asked. It seemed a fair question. 'Air only,' he said, 'because he did not want to contaminate the body with food and drink.' The yogi lived to a ripe old age — over seventy. Mr Gopal, the liaison man, had been stumped by my ignorance of liaising. His story concerned a monkey and a tiger who always travelled together. No one could understand why the tiger didn't gobble up the monkey, but a man watched them closely (from behind a tree, unseen) and realized that the tiger was blind: the monkey guided the tiger from place to place. I had heard a story about a man in Bombay who walked on water, and another about a man who taught himself to fly using wings from palm leaves; the canvasser for seamless tubes told me about a bridge of monkeys from Ceylon to Dhanushkodi, across the Palk Strait. I saw these tall stories as a flight from the concrete, the Indian imagination requiring something more than the prosy details of the ledger.

G Reflection

Train travel animated my imagination and usually gave me the solitude to order and write my thoughts: I travelled easily in two directions, along the level rails while Asia flashed changes at the window, and at the interior rim of a private world of memory and language. I cannot imagine a luckier combination.

Paul Theroux
The Great Railway Bazaar (Penguin)

TRAVELLING POEMS

Passengers

They are all there sitting in deck chairs
Or playing cards
Or taking tea
Or being bored
All the same there's a little group of sportsmen playing shuffle-board
Or deck tennis
And another little group who are going to swim in the pool
At night when everyone is asleep the rows of empty chairs along the deck are like
    a collection of skeletons in a museum
Old dried up women
Chameleons dandruff nails

Rio de Janeiro

Everyone is up on deck
We are in the middle of the mountains
A lighthouse goes out
You look everywhere for the Sugar-Loaf and ten people discover it at once in a
    hundred different directions these mountains look so alike in their pear-shaped
    forms
M. Lopart shows me a mountain whose profile on the sky is like a stretched out
    corpse and whose silhouette looks very much like that of Napoleon on his death-
    bed
I find that it looks more like Wagner a Richard Wagner puffed up with pride or
    flooded with grease
Rio is close by now and you can make out the houses on the beach
The officers compare this panorama with the Golden Horn
Others tell the story of the revolt of the fort
Others unanimously regret the construction of a huge modern hotel high and
    square which disfigures the bay (it's very beautiful)
Others again protest vehemently at the abrasion of a mountain
Leant over the starboard bulwarks I gaze at
The tropical vegetation of an abandoned isle
The big sun which ploughs the big vegetation
A little boat manned by three fishermen
These men with slow methodical movements
Who work
Who fish
Who haul in their catch
Who don't even look at us
Totally at their work

Sunsets

Everybody talks of sunsets
All the travellers are in agreement in talking about the sunsets in these parts
There are plenty of old books where nothing is described but sunsets
Tropical sunsets
Yes it's true they're splendid
But I prefer the sunrise by far
The dawn

I never miss one
I am always on the bridge
Naked
And I am always alone in my admiration
But I am not going to describe the dawn
I am going to keep it for myself

Blaise Cendrars
Selected Poems (Penguin)

FOREIGNERS

A group of poor Indian villagers are being taken on a journey through India, paid for by money left by a rich benefactress.

Slowly the old ones ascended the steps, turned for a farewell look at the river and then disappeared among the other pilgrims. Not long thereafter they reached the station and the carriage to find Ashin worrying, breakfast ready, and the clothes washed and dripping. They explained the nature of their absence and Ashin shyly smiled his respect for the worshippers. Soon they were off, weaving here and there through the crowd, noticing a more colourful shop, a funeral procession, a garland maker, as they walked. Through the labyrinth of alleys they found a way to the Durga temple and were shocked when a family of monkeys appeared on the wall to greet them. This was an old temple, rather dingy to the villagers' eyes. Amiya, who had stopped to watch a mother monkey feeding her baby, suddenly looked up and realized that once again a crowd of foreigners was watching the worship from a neighbouring house. She fumed, she shouted, she raged at Ashin, and all that happened was that one of the foreigners raised a camera and appeared to take a picture of Amiya pointing at him. The shock of this effrontery made her recoil, she ran away from the sight of the window. Deepaka came and tried to distract her by pointing out a seller of coloured powders who had made his wares into a line of beautiful little mountains, gracing the edge of the temple wall. Amiya would not respond, nor would she talk. Ashin led the rest of his charges from the temple. Over and again Amiya asked Ashin:

'But do they pay to watch worship in their own countries?'

Over and again she received the same reply:

'I do not know, Amiya. They come to learn and do not know what they do is an insult.'

Amiya's distress was contagious and it was a confused and somewhat sullen group which made its way down a wide avenue to a wooded park. They left the main road and followed Ashin up a flight of steps. Everywhere there were priests and holy men. And everywhere there were groups of foreigners taking pictures of the priests.

'This is the Hannumanji temple,' announced Ashin.

The villagers started forward eagerly along the cobbled walk. They loved the monkey helper of Rama, and to pay him homage in his own temple caused them great excitement and delight. Amiya walked a little more slowly than the others, Deepaka beside her trying to remind her of the wonderful nonsense of Hannuman. A cluster of women who always tried to imitate Amiya stayed close to the friends. They were walking behind a pair of foreigners, a boy and a girl. Amiya was stiffening with anger, and Deepaka was trying to hurry her past them when a voice addressed the foreigners:

'Good day to you. Do you like our temple?'

Amiya watched the couple pause and then saw their confusion as they looked at the wizened little holy man smiling to them from under his umbrella. The two bowed and waited. Amiya and the others paused to watch.

'You spoke to us in English,' the girl said hesitantly.

'Yes, once very long ago I was a student in England. Where do you come from?'

The boy replied, 'I am from the States and my friend is from London.'

'Why have you come to India?' asked the little man.

'We want to reach . . .' but Amiya and the others did not know what he said. Harischandra could not translate. The little man bent forward to the boy.

'I beg your pardon. I did not understand. Please say it again.'

The boy blushed and said, 'You know, enlightenment, release,' and then again the strange word.

'Ah, you mean you wish a revelation of God, or as we say, to be absorbed in unity.' The old seer sat back, pleased to have understood, but the boy and girl were distressed.

'No, no, enlightenment, nirvana, release into nothing, like in the old books, you know.'

'But enlightenment is recognition of unity, or in your tradition, knowledge of God.' The old man stated this flatly.

'No, we learned all about it, the big self and and the little self, and finding nothingness.'

'But my young friend, the great self is the Universe, or God, and absorption into that unity is what we are all seeking.'

'We spent time in Rishikesh with a guru,' the girl tried to explain. 'He said we had to meditate to make ourselves empty.'

'Yes, as vessels for the god, or unity, within and without.'

'No, to be not attached to life, so we can be released. You know, initiated.'

'But you are young, you have not yet begun to live, this is not the time to be released. You must wait until you are old like me, and all your duties done, then you can go out to seek release.' The old man changed his attack. His audience was growing and they murmured approval at this remark.

'We have no duties, we just want to get released.'

'Of course you have duties: to learn, to work, to marry and have children, to raise them as best you can. Then when they have children you can choose to take this path.'

'But we don't want all that. We don't have to do it. We want to get released now.'

'My friend, I do not understand this phrase "get released". Here we view enlightenment as an achievement of study, discipline and devotion. One earns release, or revelation, one cannot be made aware by any other agent than one's mind, or the tools of one's spirit. First you must master the languages of revelation, either in our tradition or in your own, and then you must practise hard until you are able to reach that one moment of joy. Nothing can obtain it for you except work and constant awareness.' The small man was revelling in the phrases of the foreign language. Harischandra struggled to translate.

'But does not a guru do that? He releases you and you get enlightened. It is not hard, they said so in Rishikesh. We have been looking for a guru who will take us together.' The boy put his arm around the girl. Amiya looked away. The old teacher smiled and then his face grew sad. Slowly he withdrew into himself and the Indians knew that the interview was over. The couple looked confused as people started to walk on and as the old man began to murmur, oblivious of them all.

'Why did he stop talking like that? Why did he look so sad?'
The couple turned to the remaining watchers. A studious-looking man looked at the holy man and at the boy's honest bewilderment. Finally he spoke:

'I think he fears that you have only disappointments ahead, and he does not wish you to go from our country with this disappointment. There is no easy way to truth.'

'But we won't go until we've got enlightenment. You Indians know about spiritual things and the easy ways to get release. That is why we came here.'

'Then I must wish you a happy time. But please, remember that the holy man here in Benares had studied too, and that he recommended work. Perhaps he was once an engineer.' The clerk moved away and Amiya and Deepaka with the other villagers followed him up the path.

'They were not like the watchers at the temple,' said Deepaka.

'No, they were dirty.' Amiya did not like to be puzzled as she now was.

'They said they had come to learn from Indians.'

'And they said they had no duties.' Amiya spat. Someone else muttered. 'Where are their families and how do they feel about these children wandering about in dirty clothes, to get released?'

Deepaka paused and looked back. The couple was walking hand in hand along the path. They looked like small children returning home from a party; sad, tired, depleted.

'No wonder the old man wished to weep,' sighed Deepaka. She caught Amiya and the others as they were about to enter the temple and for the next hour she forgot about the couple. When she came out of the enclosure a monkey plucked at her sari and she squealed in fright, to be teased at once by the others. The villagers were gathered under a tree eating some fruit. Amiya related the tale of the couple with bitterness and scorn, and was shocked when Harischandra, Ashin, Reena and Deepaka expressed pity for the young couple:

'They come to learn, Amiya, they do not come to offend.'

'They were dirty. The girl was wearing blue trousers like the man. Why do not they learn from books in their own lands?'

'Perhaps they tried.'

'No, they come to be lazy and not wash. There is much work to do here and in their own countries.' Amiya grew more stern as she saw her supporters nodding.

'They must be rich, or they could not come here and not work. How much does it cost to come across the seas?'

'Thousands of rupees.'

'You see, they are just mocking us like the people at the temple who took pictures of our prayers. They are rich but they pretend to be poor. They say they have no duties and come to find an easy way to be released into nothingness. Foolishness. Would they not offend fewer if they just cast themselves into a river in their own lands? That is the easy way to nothingness!' There was uncomfortable laughter for a moment and the villagers were relieved when Ashin urged them to move on to the bus.

Heather Wood
Third-Class Ticket
(Routledge & Kegan Paul)

PEOPLE IN A LANDSCAPE
A Welsh Mining Village

This mining village differs from others I know first of all in its colour.

The collieries are on the outskirts of the village, and the air is therefore clear. A friend of mine who knows the French landscapes by heart, compares the place, when bright-lighted, with Brittany.

Violet roofs at the foot of green hills. Pyramids of black tips surrounded by cloud-like trees the colour of dark bottles.

When the sun appears and gilds the air, the streets, otherwise uniform grey, become copper brown. This happens usually in the evenings, for the days are mostly behind a screen of slow rains, cold and blue like steel dust; the kind of rains which never promise to stop, and awaken in you a feeling as hopeless as that arising when you are faced with many roads on a lost track. To be truthful, I must add that only at the beginning did they awaken in me a feeling of impatient anger. Afterwards I discovered, to my own surprise, that the rains here are more than part of the general atmosphere. It is the rain that weaves the strange tapestry of mood in which life here finds its order.

While the air becomes oily, the roofs and roads glossy, the river fuller and noisier, men bite their pipes, and finding cover in the entrances of the shops, enjoy, as always, a talk for talk's sake. Only dogs disappear from the streets, for the heavy doors of street philosophy are closed to them.

On the square of the village, blue and red buses appear and disappear. A colourful little cart with the standing figure of the milkman inside; in the twittering noise of the rain the tapping steps of the tiny brown pony.

A woman walking over the bridge at the end of the street, the wind blowing

against her, the white shawl rising from her shoulders and spreading like two huge wings.

A brown bus with miners returning from work.

Singly or in groups of two or three, short silhouettes with logs of wood under their arms fill up the square. The black statue of the policeman gleams like silk.

'Shwmai, Wyn!' 'Shwmai, Sid!' 'Shwmai, shwmai!'

Some turn left, others turn right.

Some remain and talk awhile under the awning with red and gold letters – 'Fish and Chips Restaurant'; others walk forward to the bridge.

But even the glossy rainy hours are numbered. A sunlit evening glazes the village.

The River Tawe which always has two colours more than the sky – black of coal and yellow of clay – is now red.

White stones in the river.

Gilded cows walk over the stones.

Children in pink shirts hang on the trees near the bridge.

The hills are bright blue. Over them lie brassy yellow clouds.

'There you are,' said a man with the soft voice of secrecy to me, 'such is life here; mostly grey, but there is also a drop of gold in it.'

For weeks I wandered here on the hills, in the little streets, looking at the landscape, looking at walls and at men, at pits from far and near, sketching and talking to miners on the surface and underground, at work and at rest, studying their movements and their appearance.

This was a way of exercising my faculties of concentration, of clearing my mind; a way of piercing the thick cloud of insignificant incident which enshrouds every new reality.

84

There is a tradition among artists, particularly among writers, when they come to a small place, to look for the so-called 'characters', and to represent them and their acts as the colour of the village. Yet a less easily satisified observer will soon find out that the so-called 'characters' are lamentably alike everywhere. They rather remind one of exotic spots in a landscape which may awaken curiosity but do not satisfy a longer interest. There is no real depth in them; and therefore they surely do not typify and place. They only have connected anecdotes, which do not possess a big enough form to embrace a full-blooded living man, nourished by tradition, formed by labour and moved by aspiration.

The miner is the man of Ystradgynlais.

In his appearance, although at first sight like other workers, the miner is more impressive and singular.

Sometimes I thought of old Egyptian carvings walking between sky and earth, or of dark rocks fashioned into glorious human shapes, or of heavy logs in which a primitive hand had tried to synthesize the pride of human labour and the calm force which promises to guard its dignity.

It would be true to say that the miner is the walking monument to labour.

By this singularity of appearance, amid the clean figures of the shop-keepers, the tall and thin figures of the town councillors, the robust figures of the insurance agents, the respectable figures of the ministers, and the fatigued figures of the schoolmasters, the miners form, like trees among vegetables, a solid group. But what makes the group so singular outside is but the strong similarity within the group.

Like the houses with doors smaller than men, like the two china dogs on the mantelpieces, like the taste of the blackberry tart, they are similar in each house.

The kind of mauve scarf and the way they wear it: the manner of nodding their heads sideways in greeting, the feelings of relief and comfort they express as they stride down the middle of the road, their way of sitting near a wall and supporting their bodies with the heel of the foot.

Also similar are their troubles and joys.

What happens today to one happens tomorrow to another. Therefore there is a sincere concern for each other's lives, and duties become habits.

Men must give each other a hand.

Familiarity breaks the ice of strangeness.

'You're no stranger here,' I was told the very day I arrived. A day later I was addressed as Joe, and soon I was nick-named Joe-bach.

If someone more individualistically-tempered does not like the familiarity, people here will easily find out, and even the dogs won't bark after him.

Men need each other if only to talk to — or just to make the heart easier. Thus men listen with heavy concentration, and share feelings, laughter, tears.

Birth and death are faced as matters of fact, the first without too much fuss, the other without too much gloom. But the unexpected is encountered with gravity.

One afternoon a little street was empty but for a few dogs walking here and there. The two rows of houses and the black road between them were bathed in a peaceful light.

An old man, bent like a walking-stick, with his head hanging down on his chest, was knocking at every door, one after another, all the way down the street. At every door he spent just a moment.

A woman or a man or the two together would come to the open door and listen to the old man; some would take their apron to their eyes, others just nod sadly.

When he came nearer to me, I thought that evening that Welsh must be the only language of music of sorrow.

He had lost his son in the Far East.

Then, on the Teddy Bear Bridge, I met three pregnant women. Their shapes were enormous and of earthy beauty. Next to them all Venuses would look but pale girls. Looking at them, Walt Whitman would have repeated his psalm-sounding phrase: 'And I say there is nothing greater than mother of man.'

The three mothers of man talked of death.

The whole village talked of death.

As in most small places, time and energy do not find their expression in movement, but rather in density. In passionate calm, rather, that brings out not so much the vivid as the heroic, not so much the ornamental as the dignifying simplicity.

This fashions primarily the form of speech. Emotion replaces sentimentality, the quality of voice replaces the choice of smart words. Not all music is expressed in the songs and instrumental compositions of a people. Music lives first of all in the everyday modelling of the language, in the way of pressing our feelings into sounds for which words are but natural tails.

Here tradition gives its lead. The most admired is the man able to speak in the tradition of the Welsh preacher.

How does an old Welsh preacher speak? His voice knows only two colours: the bright yellow of a peaceful sun, and the threatening red of hell. Only two sounds: the whisper of a branch moved by the wind, and the thundering of an empty barrel falling downstairs. His hands know only two movements: the gentle movement of reaching for a flower, and the whirling of mill-sails in a storm. Only two expressions on his face – eyebrows, eyes, nostrils and mouth working simultaneously; first, that of comfort from looking into a garden; second, that of surprise from facing the dark mysteries of a forest.

As his voice goes higher, his body rises up in the air.

As his voice sinks, his body falls across the pulpit rail, and to make sure that now he is in earnest, that he is now on the earth, he hammers a closed fist on the open palm of his hand.

Even underground I saw men falling naturally into oratory.

Even fireside conversations are seldom 'clever' or dispassionate, although there are quite a few who have learnt the art of working out a case and swiftly proving a point; but the will to carry us closer to the object at the end of their vision keeps passion alive. It is this passion that brings even to the loud unordered life of the local pubs a nostalgic atmosphere half dreamy and half joyful. It is this passion which lights up their aspirations, and makes some of them read through heavy volumes of economics, sociology and philosophy, and prepare themselves for the task of leadership. It is this passion which makes others sing, or write. It is this traditional passion, this monumental appearance, that broadens the local and incidental, and makes the individual become typical and symbolic.

But there are others who have no more passion left.

They are waiting for death.

Victims of silica dust.

You can pick them out with your finger.

They will say with a sad smile: 'A bit short of breath.'

This is Ystradgynlais, a Welsh mining village.

Josef Herman
Related Twilights (Robson Books)

BLACK MOUNTAINS

1

See this layered sandstone among the short mountain grass. Place your right hand on it, palm downward. See where the sun rises and where it stands at noon. Direct your middle finger midway between them. Spread your fingers, not widely. You now hold this place in your hand.

The six rivers rise in the plateau of the back of your hand. The first river, now called Mynwy or Monnow, flows at the outside edge of your thumb. The second river, now called Olchon, flows between your thumb and the first finger, to join the Mynwy at the top of your thumb. The third river, now called Honddu, flows between your first and second fingers and then curves to join the Mynwy, away from your hand. The fourth river, now called Grwyne Fawr, flows between your second and third fingers, and then curves the other way, joining the fifth river, now called Grwyne Fechan, that has been flowing between your third and your little finger. The sixth river, now called Rhiangoll, flows at the outside edge of your little finger. Beyond your hand are the two rivers to the sea. Mynwy carrying Olchon and Honddu flows into the circling Wye. Grwyne and Rhiangoll flow into the Usk. Wye and Usk, divided by the Forest of Gwent, flow to the Severn Sea.

It was by Wye and Usk, from the Severn Sea and beyond it, that men first came to this place.

The ridges of your five fingers, and the plateau of the back of your hand, are now called the Black Mountains. Your thumb is Crib y Gath or Cat's Back. Your first finger is Haterall. Your second finger is Ffawyddog, with Bal Mawr at the knuckle. Your third finger is Gader, with Gader Fawr at the knuckle. Your little finger is Allt Mawr, and its nail is Crug Hywel, giving its name to Crickhowell below it. On the back of your hand are Twyn y Llech and Twmpa and Rhos Dirion and Waun Fach. Mynwy and Olchon flow from Twyn y Llech. Honddu flows from Twyn y Llech and Twmpa. Grwyne Fawr flows from Rhos Dirion. Grwyne Fechan and Rhiangoll flow from Waun Fach.

You hold the shapes and the names in your hand.

2

It was by Wye and Usk, from the Severn Sea and beyond it, that men first came to this place.

> We have no ready way to explain ourselves to you. Our language has gone utterly, except for the placename which you now say as Ewyas. The names by which we knew ourselves are entirely unknown to you. We left many marks on the land but the only marks that you can easily recognize are the long stone graves of our dead. If you wish to know us you must learn to read the whole land.

3

The long barrows of the first Black Mountain shepherds are clustered on flat grasslands between the steep northern scarp, at your wrist, and on one side the wide valley of the Wye, on the other the valley of the Usk and the basin of Llyn Syvadon, now called Llangorse Lake.

When the first shepherds came there was thick oak forest from the rivers to the level of these grasslands. Then the forest thinned, and there was good pasture among the scattered trees. On the ridges above them, in the climate of that time, there were great winter bogs in the peat above the deep sandstone, but there was some summer grazing on the slopes. They lived at that chosen level, at first only in the summers, going back to the rivers in the winters, but later yearthrough.

These are still flat grasslands, grazed by thousands of sheep and hundreds of ponies. Below them and above them the land has changed and been changed.

4

We can count in generations. Say two hundred and twenty generations from the first shepherds to us. Then a new people came. Say one hundred and sixty generations from them to us. They came when the climate was changing. Winters were much colder and summers hotter and drier. While elsewhere in the island men were moving down from chalk uplands, because the springs were failing, here the sandstone ridges and the plateau were drying, and there was new summer grazing. Surviving tracks show the change. To every ridge, now, there are long transverse, sometimes zigzag, tracks from the middle heights to the crests. They are often sunken, making a characteristic notch where they break the ridge. The local name for such a track is *rhiw*. Along these tracks, sheep and cattle were driven for the summer grazing. Meanwhile, below the old grasslands, the forest was changing. The damp oak forest fell back, and new clearings were made among the more diverse woods. And this people felled along the slopes of the ridges. There was then more grass but also the heather began to spread. They lived and worked in these ways for sixty generations.

5

New peoples came. Say a hundred generations from them to us. And again the climate was changing. Winters were milder, summers cooler and wetter. They settled a little higher than the first shepherds, and in new ways. They built folds and camps at the ends of ridges: at Pentwyn, Y Gaer, Crug Hywel, Castell Dinas. There were summer pastures behind them, along the lower ridges, for their sheep and cattle and horses. And still they cleared towards the valleys, in small square fields. There were peaceful generations, but increasingly, now, more peoples were coming from the east. The folds and steadings became armed camps. The names of history begin with the Silures. But then a different arrival: an imperial people: Romans. These said of the Silures: 'non atrocitate, non clementia mutabatur': changed neither by cruelty nor by mercy. Literate history, imperial history, after more than a hundred generations of history.

6

In literate history the Black Mountains are marginal. They are still classified today as marginal or as waste land. After the Silures no new people settled them. The tides of conquest or lordship lapped to their edges and their foothills, leaving castles facing them – Ewyas Harold, Ewyas Lacy, Grosmont, Skenfrith, White Castle, Abergavenny, Crickhowell, Bronllys, Hay, Clifford – to command their peoples. Romans drove military roads at their edges. Normans pushed closer, but had no use for land above seven hundred feet. In the mountains and their valleys the people were still there, with their animals. They were the children of the first shepherds and of the upland people and of the camp-builders. Roman governors wanted them to come down and live in new towns. Some went, some stayed. When the Romans left the island, some came back to the mountains. By at latest the sixth century, in modern reckoning, the Black Mountains were a kingdom, which lasted, precariously, until the twelfth century. Twenty generations of Roman rule and its aftermath. Twenty-five generations of a small native kingdom. They called the kingdom by a very old name: Ewyas.

7

Where then are the Black Mountains? The physical answer is direct. The literate and administrative answer is more difficult.

At a certain point on the narrow and winding road which we drive in summer for shopping – past Pentwyn and Parc y Meirch, below the source of the Mynwy and over the brooks of Dulas and Esgyrn – at a certain point on this secluded road between high banks and hedges of hazel and holly and thorn, at this indistinguishable point there is a ridged bump in the roadway, where the roadmen of Brecon (now Powys) and the roadmen of Hereford (now Hereford and Worcester) have failed to see eye to eye. It is a trivial unevenness, deep within this specific region. It is the modern border between England and Wales.

And this is how it has gone, in literate and administrative history. The small kingdom of Ewyas – not small if you try to walk it, but politically small – was often, while it still had identity, redrawn or annexed or married into the neighbouring kingdoms of Brycheiniog or Gwent or Erging (Archenfield). Its modern political history is differently arbitrary. A dispute between the London court and a local landowning family, at the time of the Act of Union between England and Wales, led to a border which follows no natural feature or, rather, several in an incomprehensible series. In the twentieth century, three counties had lines drawn across and through the Black Mountains: lines on maps and in a few overgrown and lichened stones. Brecon pushed one way, Monmouthshire another, Hereford a third. The first was part of Wales, the third part of England; Monmouthshire, until it became Gwent, anomalous between them. A national park boundary followed these amazing administrative lines. The Brecon was incorporated into the new Powys. Monmouthshire in name became the old Gwent. Hereford and Worcester, unwillingly joined, considered and rejected the name of West Mercia. It was almost, even in name, a very old situation: this marginal, this waste land, taken in at the very edges of other, more powerful, units.

Within the Black Mountains, these lines on the map mean nothing. You have only to stand there to see an unusually distinct and specific region. Or go on that midsummer Sunday – Shepherds' Sunday – when they drive the tups from above the Usk to above the Monnow and track down unmarked sheep. An old internal organization, in the region's old activity, still visibly holds. Later, of course, the externally drawn lines and their consequences arrive, administratively, in the post. They are usually bills.

8

How to see it, physically? At first it is so strange. You need your hand on the stone to discern its extraordinary structure. Within the steep valleys, or from any of the ridges, this basic shape of the hand is not visible. And of course at every point there are minor features: cross valleys, glaciated cwms, rockfalls (*darens*), steeply gouged watercourses. It is so specific a country, yet its details take years to learn.

Black mountains? From a distance, like others, they are blue. From very close they are many colours: olive-green under sunlight; darker green with the patches of summer bracken; green with a reddish tinge when there are young leaves on the whinberries; dark with the heather out of flower, purple briefly in late summer; russet in the late autumn bracken; a pale gold, often, in the dead winter bracken, against the white of snow. Black? Entirely so, under heavy storm clouds. Very dark and suddenly solid under any thick cloud. The long whaleback ridges can be suddenly awesome.

But then their valleys are so different. Now Mynwy and Olchon and Honddu and Rhiangoll are farmed; Grwyne Fawr is forested and dammed; Grwyne Fechan is farm, a little forest and then upland pasture. The oldest modern farms are halfway up each slope from the valley beds, where the springs mostly rise. The old valley roads are at this level. But there are now roads and farms right down by the rivers, where there can be some flat fields. Then from these and the others the cleared fields climb the slopes, to uneven heights. Ash and thorn and rowan and cherry are still felled, bracken ploughed, to enclose a new field from the mountain. Others, once cleared, have gone back to scrub and bracken. At the farthest points, often surprisingly close, are old ruined stone farms, thick now with the nettles marking human occupation. In the Napoleonic wars there was this high and intensive settlement. It fell back with the decline of the Welsh woollen industry. The fields have been taken in to other farms. The rest of the story is what is called depopulation.

But the valleys are bright green, under the different colours of the mountains. Trees flourish in them. From some ridges the valleys still look like woodland, with the farms in clearings. But there is always a sharp contrast between the bleak open tops, with their heather and whinberry and cotton sedge and peat pools, their tracks which dissolve into innumerable sheep tracks, their sudden danger, in bad weather, in low cloud and mist with few landmarks, and the green settled valleys, with the fine trimmed farm hedges, the layered sandstone houses – colours from grey and brown towards pink or green, the patchwork of fields. At mid-summer the valleys are remarkable, for on the trimmed hedges of thorn and holly and hazel and ash and field maple there is an amazing efflorescence of stands of honeysuckle and pink or white wild roses, and on the banks under them innumer-able foxgloves. It is so close to look up from these flowers to the steep ridges. By one of the ruined farms there was once a whole field of foxgloves. It is now back to bracken and thistle. But in the next field they are felling and clearing again, and the ploughed earth above the sandstone goes through a range of colours from wet dark red to dried pink among the bright grass.

So this extraordinarily settled and that extraordinarily open wild country are very close to each other and intricately involved. Either, with some strictness, can be called pastoral, but then with very different implications. As the eye follows them, in this unusually defining land, the generations are distinct but all suddenly present.

9

It is a place where you can stand and look out. From Haterall there is the vast patchwork of fields of the Herefordshire plain, across to the Malverns and the Clees. From Twmpa there is distance after distance of upland Wales, from Radnor and Eppynt to Plynlimmon and Cader Idris and the neighbouring Beacons. From Allt Mawr there is the limestone scarp, on the other side of the Usk, where the iron industry came, and in the valleys behind it, Rhymney and Taff and Rhondda, the mining for coal.

Land, labour, and history. It can be cold standing there. The winds sweep those ridges. You go back down, into the settled valleys, with their medley of map names.

Different views, different lives. But occasionally, laying your right hand, palm downward, on the deep layered sandstone, you know a whole, intricate, distinct place. The Black Mountains. Ewyas.

Raymond Williams
Places ed. Ronald Blythe (OUP)

TRAVEL BOOKS

After encountering a number of these books, it's time to inquire what they are. Perhaps it is when we cannot satisfactorily designate a kind of work with a single word (*epic, novel, romance, story, novella, memoir, sonnet, sermon, essay*) but must invoke two (*war memoir, Black autobiography, first novel, picture book, travel book*) that we sense we're entering complicated territory, where description, let alone definition, is hazardous, an act closer to exploration than to travel. Criticism has never quite known what to call books like these. Some commentators, perhaps recalling the illustrated travel lectures of their youth or the travel films that used to be shown as 'short subjects', call them *travelogues*. Others, more literary, render that term *travel logs*, apparently thinking of literal, responsible daily diaries, like ships' logs. This latter usage is the one preferred by David Lodge, who says of 30s writing that 'it tended to model itself on historical kinds of discourse – the autobiography, the eye-witness account, the travel log: *Journey to a War, Letters from Iceland, The Road to Wigan Pier, Journey without Maps, Autumn Journal,* "Berlin Diary", are some characteristic titles.' Even Forster is uncertain what to call these things. In 1941 he calls them *travelogues*, in 1949 *travel books*.

Let's call them travel books, and distinguish them initially from guide books, which are not autobiographical and are not sustained by a narrative exploiting the devices of fiction. A guide book is addressed to those who plan to follow the traveler, doing what he has done, but more selectively. A travel book, at its purest, is addressed to those who do not plan to follow the traveler at all, but who require the exotic or comic anomalies, wonders, and scandals of the literary form *romance* which their own place or time cannot entirely supply. Travel books are a sub-species of memoir in which the autobiographical narrative arises from the speaker's encounter with distant or unfamiliar data, and in which the narrative – unlike that in a novel or a romance – claims literal validity by constant reference to actuality. The speaker in any travel book exhibits himself as physically more free than the reader, and thus every such book, even when it depicts its speaker trapped in Boa Vista, is an implicit celebration of freedom. It resembles a poetic ode, an Ode to Freedom. The illusion of freedom is a precious thing in the 20s and 30s, when the shades of the modern prison-house are closing in, when the passports and queues and guided tours and social security numbers and customs regulations and currency controls are beginning gradually to constrict life. What makes travel books seem so necessary between the wars is what Fleming pointed to in *One's Company,* 'that lamb-like subservience to red tape which is perhaps the most striking characteristic of modern man.' Intellectual and moral pusillanimity is another characteristic of modern man. Hence Douglas's emphasis on the exemplary function of the travel writer's internal freedom and philosophic courage:

It seems to me that the reader of a good travel-book is entitled not only to an exterior voyage, to descriptions of scenery and so forth, but to an interior, a sentimental or temperamental voyage, which takes place side by side with the outer one.

Thus 'the ideal book of this kind' invites the reader to undertake three tours simultaneously: 'abroad, into the author's brain, and into his own.' It follows that 'the writer should . . . possess a brain worth exploring; some philosophy of life – not necessarily, though by preference, of his own forging – and the courage to proclaim it and put it to the test; he must be naif and profound, both child and sage.' And if the enterprise succeeds, the reader's 'brain' will instinctively adjust itself to accord in some degree with the pattern established by the author's travel, both external and internal: that is, it will experience an access of moral freedom. It is thus possible to consider the between-the-wars travel books as a subtle instrument of ethics, replacing such former vehicles as sermons and essays.

Paul Fussell
Abroad (OUP)

WAYS OF WORKING

● Try to capture the spirit of some of the tourist dream worlds or 'pseudo-places' (see 'Tourist Fantasies', Paul Fussell) taken from your own experience in a series of short prose snapshots, or free verse poems; then make them up into a wall display, connecting your writing to some of the most lurid colour supplement/ travel brochure dream-holiday pictures.

● Keep a travel log or journal recording your everyday journeys, or experiences of a school camp or visit abroad, throughout a half-term of your course. Before you start, talk through (in small groups) Paul Theroux's precise examples of what you might like to look out for in your daily observations, e.g. overheard conversations, visual snapshots, characters, dramatic incidents, places, anecdotes and more general reflections and commentaries on the process of travelling. At the end of the project select some of the most striking moments from your logs to share with the rest of your group. You might like to include illustrations, cartoons, sketches to accompany the written entries.

● Modern travellers' tales: make a taped collection of the most weird, mysterious, bizarre travelling encounters from people (friends *and* strangers) in the local community and share them with the group.

● Travel as disaster: working in small groups, build up a wall display of single or strip cartoons that illustrate disastrous travelling moments, like the examples given by Martha Gellhorn: 'They've lost the baggage again, for God's sake?', 'You mean we came all this way just to see this?', 'Why do they have to make so damn much noise?', 'Call that a room with a view?' Collect the anecdotes from other members of the school/college.

● A collage sequence: when you next have an outing to a new city or part of the country, or a memorable holiday experience, try to record in detail what you see and hear. Carefully arrange your observations in the form of a travel journey, like 'The Pennine Way journey', including drawings or photocopies of maps, descriptions, poems, photographs, sketches, tickets, objects found, extracts from Guide books, etc.

● Find out as much as you can about women travel writers like Freya Stark, Angela Carter, Mary Kingsley, Dervla Murphy, etc. from your college/school library and local libraries. Select two or three extracts from the work of one of the writers that you find most intriguing and present your general findings and extracts to the rest of the group. Try to express a direct, personal response to the writer rather than giving a dutiful, potted biography.

● How do different types of travelling affect the writer's perception of the journey? Explore in your own way the possible contrasts between the experiences of cycle rider (Dervla Murphy), train rider (Paul Theroux), donkey rider (Robert Louis Stevenson), long-distance walker (John Hillaby).

● External journeys and internal journeys: write a short story about an actual, physical journey that you've lived through yourself that also involved you in a journey of personal discovery through having to reflect upon your life. You could show the difference between the two journeys by putting the internal journey inside brackets.

● Look closely at the 'Travelling poems' by Blaise Cendrars. Pick out one poem that puzzles you and makes you want to ponder over it. Then decide how you would read it aloud to the rest of your group. First go for the whole feel of the poem rather than concentrating on single words and phrases. Detailed, written jottings on rough paper on how to read it might help you to make sense of it. Then try it out on your friends in small groups before you share it with the whole group.

● Some of these writers (Herman, Williams) think that a place or landscape cannot be understood unless you are prepared 'to read the whole land' and see the layers upon layers of history and previous forms of cultivation and living that make up that place. Re-explore your own local district and try to trace the pattern of its physical and social development. Try the local library for earlier records, photographs, old maps, newspaper articles. Ask residents about their impressions and memories of the place. Take photographs (or make sketches) from unusual viewpoints. Finally produce a descriptive article on the area, drawing on all your sources, and presented for readers who are strangers to the place.

FURTHER REFERENCES

Travels with a Donkey in the Cévennes Robert Louis Stevenson, Heinemann
Travels through West Africa Mary Kingsley, Virago
The Aran Islands J.M. Synge, OUP

Twilight in Italy and *Sea and Sardinia* D.H. Lawrence, Penguin
Journey Without Maps Graham Greene, Penguin
Letters from Iceland W.H. Auden and Louis MacNeice, Faber
Tristes Tropiques Claude Lévi-Strauss, Jonathan Cape and Penguin
The Great Railway Bazaar Paul Theroux, Penguin
Third-Class Ticket Heather Wood, Routledge & Kegan Paul
Journey through Britain John Hillaby, Paladin
A Place Apart Dervla Murphy, Penguin
A Short Walk in the Hindu Kush Eric Newby, Paladin
In Patagonia Bruce Chatwin, Picador
Millstone Grit Glyn Hughes, Sphere
Arabia Through the Looking Glass Jonathan Raban, Fontana
Selected Poems Blaise Cendrars, Penguin
The Road to Oxiana Robert Byron, Picador
Sea to the West Norman Nicholson, Faber
No Particular Place to Go Hugo Williams, Picador
Abroad Paul Fussell, OUP
'Oriental Romances—Japan' from *Nothing Sacred* Angela Carter, Virago

3
Documentary

INTRODUCTION

Although many people associate documentary with TV and the cinema, it is a genre which has a long tradition in print (e.g. Daniel Defoe's *A Journal of the Plague Year*) and which is thriving in the 1980s and still developing new forms (e.g. John Berger's *Pig Earth*). John Grierson's classic definition, 'the creative treatment of actuality', makes it clear that documentary has its roots in the real world but, in practice, it is a mixed form, having links with oral history, sociology, reporting and realistic fiction. All of these methodologies have their sources in 'actuality' but each has its own way of working. Documentary, as an art form, seems to have adapted various features from them in its many different ways of depicting the world of reality.

Some of its raw material, like oral history, may be drawn from people's anecdotes and memories of the past, but documentary often tries to advance a wider, more public perspective (e.g. John Berger's *A Seventh Man*). However, unlike sociology, it makes no formal attempt to construct theories or models nor to apply a statistical approach, for a documentary-maker works in the closest possible contact with what he or she finds in the field (e.g. Jeremy Seabrook's *A City Close-up*). Press reporters are engaged with deadlines and the news value of their material as well as with the particular editorial stance of their paper, whereas the authors of documentaries make time to undertake an in-depth study of their subject, and are generally their own master. Realistic fiction, like many documentaries, presents graphic descriptions of people and places which often mirror particular reality, but novelists have the freedom to invent and create their own imaginative world. Although a documentary writer may share some of those insights we regard as a novelist's, as Paul Rotha stated, 'he is dedicated to *not* inventing'. However, as Rotha continues, 'he cannot escape his subjectivity' and 'presents *his* version of the world'.

More often than not the writer or investigator has a strong social or political purpose and wishes to expose, educate or reform. It was a growing social consciousness in a group of artists that led to the rise of the Documentary movement in the cinema in the 1930s, and often writers choose minority or oppressed communities to study (e.g. Jeremy Seabrook's *Unemployment*). Whether an author's intentions are explicit or implicit in the tone and presentation, as readers we shall be looking for writers whose integrity we can trust, who show respect for the evidence they have collected and whose text can survive attentive reading. In documentary, then, the relationship between the author as observer and his subject is no more important than that between the author as presenter and his audience. If we consider those two main strands of documentary separately, the process of looking and listening, and the way of recording what has been seen or heard, some of the key problems become clearer.

Who is doing the observing and what are their credentials? What is their background and previous experience in that field? Why are they concerned with that specific area of life? Are they observing as a stranger like William Cobbett in *Rural Rides,* or from the inside, like George Orwell in *Down and Out in Paris and London?* Reality can be distorted by the very presence of an observer, as well as by their kind of interpretation of what occurs. What are their motives and purposes? Even if an author is only seeking his own clarification, that will influence what he concentrates on and what he ignores. But of all these questions, those about intentions are the most important.

If a writer's intentions are clearly prior to his study they will powerfully affect his editorial decisions and mode of presentation. When unexpected information is uncovered or an author's perspective is shifted during his investigations these will still be major influences on how he sifts his material. We can learn much of a writer's intentions by comparing his notebooks or early drafts to the completed text. In our other volume, *The Process of Writing,* we include extracts from Orwell's *Road to Wigan Pier* diary (in effect not first jottings but a later draft) and the published text. What is highlighted or rejected in the latter offers vital clues to the author's tacit purpose; the selected portraits and incidents illuminate his political purpose.

As a genre, documentary continues to evolve, with artists like John Berger trying out new approaches to the form. Popular modes of presentation include simple narratives or chronological accounts, transcripts of recorded speech introduced by portraits of the people concerned (as in Ronald Blythe's *Akenfield*) or more structured interviews and information. John Berger and the photographer, Jean Mohr, interweave narrative and photographs in *A Fortunate Man* and *A Seventh Man,* and in *Pig Earth* Berger recreates stories told him by peasants and includes short, symbolic poems.

It is unlikely that a student reader will appreciate the importance of editorial decisions in a documentary until he has had the opportunity to make his own. The final text will be a culmination of a series of decisions, choices and rejections (see 'Ways of Working' below).

One final point: a writer's use of images and metaphors in a documentary deserve close attention because they may show us how he is seeking the consensus of a sympathetic audience.

Comments on the extracts

We have tried to illustrate some of the range of approaches. In the passage from *Working Lives,* George Wood, a mortuary technician, begins by admitting his uncertainty about how to talk about his work — 'I do not want to upset anybody'. Starting from taped interviews, he expanded the original transcription into a coherent written account, and had full control of the way he presented his own experience.

In contrast, Jeremy Seabrook in *Unemployment* describes Sunderland as an informed visitor might see it, but with a kind of camera eye hovering over the town that places the individual stories in a wider, more public context.

A different approach was taken by Tony Wilkinson who, like George Orwell in the 1930s, temporarily became a down-and-out and tried to view that world from the inside, but with the skills and insights of a professional reporter. He does not disguise his concern over his own physical and mental health, but in his elaborate role-play he was dependent on how people treated him and had to accept the self-imposed limitations. For example, he was never able to interview any of the down-and-outs he met.

Grierson's account of the filming of *Drifters* in 1929 shows how the shaping of such documentaries is largely determined by the purpose and aesthetic concern of the director. Grierson was determined to show on screen what he saw as the heroic nature of the daily work of fishermen.

A very different view of life at sea is narrated in Tony Wailey's account of the 1966 seamen's strike. Not only do we have the insider's slant on the conditions of work but a perspective on the situation quite unlike some of the public ones in the press, on radio and on TV. A fuller documentary on that strike would include more voices, more points of view, but this unofficial seamen's history is one the public rarely gets in such detail.

In James Agee's study of tenant farmers in the USA in 1936, there is the same meticulous detail found in Orwell and Wilkinson, but the narrative is dramatised and the reader is invited into what the writer experienced: 'Leave this room and go quietly down into the hall . . .'

Similar rhetorical devices are used in other parts of his book, which instead of involving the reader may tend to alienate him.

Daniel Defoe was only five years old at the time of the Plague so his *Journal of the Plague Year,* published in 1722, is a reconstruction of events, using many of the devices of current drama-documentaries seen on TV. There are graphic eye-witness reports and what look like transcripts of real conversations, and yet in places Defoe disarms the reader by admitting that he does not relate many of the stories as facts within his own knowledge. When we view historical reconstructions on TV we may not always be sure about the authenticity of the dialogue or the way the characters are interpreted. The border line in such cases between fact and fiction becomes increasingly blurred.

Finally we include Berger's account of how he compiled *A Seventh Man.* His comments on how he and Mohr tried to relate key statements and photographs to each other contain insights into the process of selecting and editing which determines the finished work.

WORKING LIVES

George Wood – Mortuary Technician

George Thomas Wood was born in 1914. He spent most of his working life in and out of hospital jobs. He first joined Hackney hospital in 1961 as a mortuary attendant but left after a few years and went to the Whipps Cross Hospital as a telephonist. He rejoined Hackney Hospital after about two years and resumed his old job in the mortuary.

From about the end of 1975 his health began to deteriorate but he carried on working. Then in July 1976 his wife fell ill and died towards the end of the month. Six weeks after this George was admitted into Hackney Hospital where he died in August 1976.

I am not sure how to talk about my work, because it concerns the dead. I do not want to upset anybody. I'll start by describing my day.

I start at 8.00 in the morning. I get to the main gate of the hospital and collect the keys and the book. Then I come down to the mortuary and check the bodies that have come in overnight, since I left at 5.00 the previous day. I enter them in the book and measure them up for the undertakers – for coffins, of course. I put the name of the deceased and the measurements on to a form and take it down to Medical Records when they open at 9.00. They hand it to the relatives, who hand it to the undertaker. Eventually it comes back to me. It's a kind of cycle. Then I release the body to the undertakers. There are exceptions, like Coroner's cases, when the body is taken from the mortuary to the Coroner's Court. There is a form to say the Coroner's man can take it. It says they have the Coroner's permission to remove the body. He takes it whether you say Yea or Nay. The Coroner is quite powerful.

After I've been to put these forms in Records, anybody from the wards may phone or my bleep may go. I answer and they say they want a body removed from so-and-so ward. So I go and collect the body, bring it down from the ward to the mortuary, enter it in the book, measure it up, put it in the fridge, write out another form, take it to Medical Records, and so it goes on. After dealing with a body I go for a cup of tea or something and then maybe get a notice from Records that they want a PM done on so-and-so. A PM is a Post Mortem, or, I should say, an autopsy. I prepare the bodies for the pathologist to examine. I don't want to go into the grisly details, so I will tell you what happens when I go to a ward for a body. I take a trolley with me. Sister will screen all the patients off, naturally, before I get there. We go to the bedside, and put the body in this trolley, which is known as a consumer trolley. It opens up on a hinge and you put the body inside. It is essential that the living patients don't see the body. It spoils the image of the hospital if they see a corpse. They lay the body out on the ward before I get there; wash it, cut the fingernails and toenails and make it look nice. I won't talk about plugging, but this has to be done too. Then they tie the legs together, comb the hair and put a shroud on. On the shroud they put all the details: name, how long they've been there, any property they've got on them — anything like that. There is supposed to be an Hour of Reverence, too — when they die there's supposed to be an hour before they make a start on them; but the wards are a bit pushed and in fact they get on with the job immediately because they need the bed for another patient. It's understandable. The exceptions to this procedure are the Jewish people. They are not put in a shroud; they're just wrapped in a sheet. The shroud is indicative of something Christian, I think. Anyway, it's something the Jews don't approve of. And when the undertaker comes to collect Jewish bodies after I've taken them to the mortuary and put them in the. fridge, they are washed again because they've been handled by Christians, or something like that. They're washed by Jewish people. The men wash the men and the women wash the women. Then they put clothes on them — trousers, jacket and prayer shawl. They put the prayer shawl in the coffin first and put the body in afterwards. It's entirely different to the Christian way of doing things.

I will have to say a bit more about PM's, because they are a big part of my job. When we hear that they want to do a PM on Mr or Mrs So-and-so, we get the body out of the fridge, take the shroud off and put it on the PM table, which is in a room next door to the fridges. Then we prepare the body for the PM. It's done by the attendant or the technician. It's difficult to talk about without upsetting or offending somebody. You open up the chest and take out the sternum; if you want to get to the brain, you cut across the scalp and fleck back the scalp both ways, which leaves the skull exposed. Then you get the electric saw, and saw the top of the skull off, which leaves the brain exposed. The doctors come down and do the PM itself until they ascertain the cause of death. When they're finished, we reconstitute the body, which means sew it up. When the doctors have finished dissecting the organs, we place everything back and sew the body up again. We do the donkey work. You learn how to do it by experience, mostly. I have got a certificate to show I can do it — I took it in 1965. But you learn more by experience than anything else. When you first come to the job you've got to be shown how to do it — you can't just walk into it. So you're shown the job and you pick it up as you go along. First you're a mortuary porter, then a mortuary attendant.

It's a long story how I came into the job. I came out of the army from Burma in 1946. I was demobbed. I went to the Labour Exchange. The chap said,

'What do you want to do?'

I said, 'It makes no difference to me.'

'Hospital work?'

'Sure.' I said.

I went to the Connaught Hospital in Walthamstow.

The Head Porter said, 'Have you ever done a PM?'

I said, 'No', laughing.

'Would you like me to show you?'

'Sure.'

So he did. After that I used to do it when he was sick or away. In 1951 I went to Whipps Cross Hospital and I got into the mortuary there. I left there in 1961 and came here to Hackney. I've been here ever since.

The work has never upset me. It may have upset my wife, but not me, not really, not seriously. I have never had nightmares about it or anything, I have come to accept the fact that when people are dead, that's it. A body is just an inanimate object. Where the soul or the spirit goes to I wouldn't know. I have never had experience of spirits — at least, only in the bottle! No, seriously, that side of the work has never bothered me at all. The job has to be done. I do it. It has never worried me, opening up people. You open up a side of beef. What's the difference? They're both dead, aren't they? I am religious to a certain degree, but I don't think that has anything to do with my work. Once people are dead, their spirits go somewhere else.

I do an average of 300 PMs every year. I do about one a day, but sometimes three or four. I might do none for a few days, then have three or four in one day. PMs are done on about 25 per cent of bodies, so that the doctors concerned can try and settle any query about why someone died. But a PM is only done if the relatives agree. If they say no, that's the end of it, unless it's a Coroner's case. I have already mentioned the Coroner's powers. He takes up a case if there is any mystery about a death. If a body comes in from outside, for example, the doctors here might ring up the GP concerned and he might say,

'I haven't seen So-and-so for perhaps a year, 18 months or even two years. That's odd. Why did he die suddenly?'

So the case is referred to the Coroner. The Coroner decides whether to do a PM or not. Most times he wants one done, to see if there's been any foul play — a bash on the head or poisoning; maybe 99 times out of 100 there's nothing; it's natural causes, but they have the PM just in case.

About 1100 bodies pass through here per year. That's an average of three or four a day. It includes those from the wards, people who die a natural death and BIDs as we call them (Brought in Dead). BIDs are the Coroner's cases. There are two mortuaries in Hackney — this one and the one in St John's Churchyard. That's a public mortuary. This one is for the hospital. It's closed to the public, although I do let relatives in to see a body if they want to. I bring them into the waiting room while I get the body out of the fridge, make it look nice with a little red on the lips, and a cross on it, put it on a trolley and wheel it into the Chapel. Then I show the visitors in. This is if they are Christians. Its the same for all denominations. It's only different if they're Jewish, as I've said. The Jewish bodies have somebody to stay with them all night. The relatives bring in what they call a body watcher to look after the body until it's removed by the undertaker next day. Incidentally, they like their burials to be as near sunset on the day after death as possible, although it can't always be done: if it's a Coroner's case and there's an inquest to follow, it can't be done; nor if the person died on a Friday afternoon — in that case nothing can be done until Sunday at the earliest, because Saturday is their Sabbath, of course.

While I am describing my work, I would like to clear up a few queries and mistaken ideas about dead bodies. First, Rigor Mortis. How soon it sets in depends on the temperature. You hear of old people dying in a warm room, with an electric fire on, and wrapped in a blanket. It might be a couple of days before they start getting stiff — a day, at least. But here, normally, it's a few hours.

Funnily enough, it starts to disappear after three or four hours. They come out of it. The body starts to relax again. So these stories about bodies sitting up with Rigor Mortis are nonsense. I have never seen a body sit up in thirty years. If one has, then all I can say is, I've missed it. If you move a body, though, you do get wind expelled. It makes an awful noise, but it happens. Next I would like to dispose of all this rubbish about there being no blood at PMs. Of course there is blood. There is pints of it. Also, the pathologist tells me that the hair and nails keep growing for a while. That is why they cut the nails when they are laying out the body in the ward.

Many people wonder what happens to rings and other jewellery on bodies. They are removed in the ward, if possible. They go to the property office. All property is taken down there, if it's open. If the death is in the middle of the night or early in the morning, it goes down first thing, at 9.00, when they open. If they can't get a ring off on the ward, it's entered on the shroud and noted down in the book when I come on in the morning. I check to see if there is anything there. If there is, I remove it. All property is returned to the relatives. If they don't collect anything left on the body, it's signed out by the undertakers when they collect it. We try to get everything off, but sometimes rings are stuck on. Sometimes, when old people die, you can't get their wedding ring off. They might have had it on for 60 years – and your knuckles tend to swell up in old age. The joints swell. To get a ring over a joint is jolly difficult at times. There are tricks: you can put soap round it and use a piece of thin twine or thread. The soap makes the ring slide more easily. You twirl the twine round the ring and pull it towards you. It usually comes off. They don't use these tricks on the wards, but we can.

Another common query is about stillbirths. We do deal with them. The maternity block is opposite the mortuary here. I go and collect them or the porters do. They're brought down plus the part called the placenta, which is the afterbirth. They are entered in the book as stillbirths. They never lived. But if the pregnancy was more than 28 weeks they must be registered at the Town Hall in the register of births, marriages and deaths. If it's less than 28 weeks, they can be done away with, incinerated or something, without being registered. Funeral arrangements for those over 28 weeks are done mostly by the contract under-takers for the hospital, the same as for adults who die with nobody to bury them – no money or no relatives. The contract undertakers bury them for the hospital.

I have got to know the local undertakers pretty well over the years. You do get one from out of town occasionally and you don't know him: they come from Scotland, up north or Wales. They'll phone and say, 'Can I pick up a body at such-and-such a time?' and I'll say, 'Yeah, of course,' and maybe stay open late for them. Or they'll come overnight and say, 'Can we pick it up in the morning? We're coming from Wales, Scotland, or whatever.' But normally, 99 times out of 100, they're people I know, from round the area.

I have only had one misunderstanding with an undertaker. People ask whether bodies ever get mixed up. Well, it can happen. It shouldn't, but where the human element comes in, it can happen. It happened to me once. An undertaker came and took the wrong body. We were busy in the PM room at the time. It was my fault for not checking and it was his fault for not checking. I just said, 'That's the one'; he took it and it was the wrong body. After a while we found out. There was quite a kerfuffle. We phoned the undertaker and he said,

'Oh, it's in my Chapel,' which was fortunate. If it had been a cremation, it would have been taken straight to the cemetary and we wouldn't have got it back. There would have been an awful stink then, of course. As it was, it was a burial. These things do happen. They shouldn't, but they do. It's happened to me now, once. That's the only case I can remember. I do check that the undertaker takes the right body if possible, but if you're busy in the PM room and an undertaker knocks on the door, you go, 'Help yourself, like.' You shouldn't, but you do.

On the front of the fridge you've got brown cards which show the name of the body, which ward, how long it's been dead, and all the necessary details. So there's no reason for mix-ups. The fridge takes 21 bodies and stores the amputations from the hospital until they can be taken away and incinerated. We can usually cope, but if we have to use more space, we use the PM table, the waiting room and anywhere that's available in the winter time, when it's bad.

I can manage on my own. They wanted to give me an assistant, but I don't know that the work here warrants two. It's quite busy, but I can cope. I'm on a 38 hour week now, being a technician. When I was a porter, I was on 40. I'm not ancillary staff now; I'm technical. I work a lot of overtime, which they pay me for. I work from 8 till 5 – that's five days a week – and I come in on Saturday mornings to measure up bodies and enter them in the book to keep up the records, which they like. I'm not obliged to do that, but I do. I belong to the ASTMS, which is the Association of Scientific, Technical and Managerial Staff. Our big chief is Clive Jenkins.

I've been at it thirty years. It suits me, this job. There are no guv'nors breathing down my neck. Certain things have to be done, so I do them; but nobody tells me to. I used to come under the Head Porter, but now I'm under the Path. Lab.

After work I forget about it. I might think 'I'll go in a bit earlier tomorrow' if I've got a PM first thing, but I don't take the work home with me (metaphorically speaking, of course!). Once I've finished, I've finished. Most people who do this work tend to live with it all the time. They're married to it; it's their whole life. But not me, to me it's just a means to an end. I get money on a Friday, which is all I'm interested in.

Working Lives Vol. 2 (Centerprise)

Sunderland. The river opens the town, a deep wound in its granite base, and the cliffs glitter like silver beneath the grass that partly covers them. In the old docks area, some reminders of the old seaport: the orphanage for the children of men drowned at sea; an abandoned warehouse that used to hold stores of the woods from tropical Africa, teak and sapele; some gutted pubs with the weathered figure-head of the bows of a ship; the shops that incorporate the remains of a chandler's business; a compass manufacturer. But the streets where the dockers and ship-workers lived have gone, even though there are still red-brick chasms of warehouses, rusting hoists still hanging from third-floor windows. Some of the area was cleared in the thirties, and there are monumental blocks of flats — themselves a little like the shell of a great sea-going vessel — called Wear Garth and Covent Garden. But most of the buildings are from the fifties; hastily assembled flats and houses which display all the flaws of the beginning of an age of instant consumption. The future has already caught up with them — stained concrete and rusty metal, broken glass, leaky pipes and graffiti.

The houses of the shipowners and the tradespeople who provisioned them stand in elegant late-Georgian terraces, many of them now occupied by solicitors and estate agents and small workshops, their red brick ingrained with the soot from chimneys long demolished, but their pillars painted cream and white, and the street names etched on ornamental plaster scrolls on the street corner. In this part of the town, there is that sense of exhaustion which pervades those places where human beings have worked for generations, have expended their life energy in making and creating things, which for the most part they never enjoyed the use of. It isn't really the place that seems exhausted so much as some of the people, those who have continued to pay for the privation and harshness of those years when they or their parents stood begging at the shipyard gates.

Not far from the river were the pits. Sky and sea seem to offer false freedoms to the dark single-storey cottages that still cluster round some of the pitheads. In the same way, the red shells of churches and Victorian pubs offered possibly more real freedoms. In Southwick, the terraces are still full of smoke blown through them like a funnel by the cold wind off the North Sea. The lights from the shipyard in midwinter are brighter than the sun that lingers on the green hilltops to the north of the town; the harsh beauty of a place where epic struggles have occurred. The Miners' Hall, now a car showroom, with its bas-relief of lions, rams and boars, its foliate fresco and the Italianate tower with constellations of iron stars in the metalwork, was once a place where children whose fathers were not miners used to plead with their friends to take them inside for the warmth and the company. The Primitive Methodist chapel is now the Majestic furniture store, offering another kind of comfort to the recently poor, while on the opposite side of the ring road Genevieve's Discotheque lights the night sky above the great iron bridge over the Wear, with its spikes to prevent people climbing it, and 'Nil Desperandum Auspice Deo' worked into the metal panel in the centre. In a brick-and-glass old people's rest centre — a sort of bus shelter with doors – the old men with white stubble and coal-grained skin play dominoes and remember the magnificence and harshness of their childhood, when they walked to school barefoot in the snow, feet so calloused they could slide like hooves over the frozen surfaces.

In a big Victorian pub on the corner of a main road, a man of about fifty-five sits with a single pint of beer which he makes last the whole evening. He smokes Players No. 6, smokes them until his fingers are burned by the heat, and still he manages to draw some smoke from what is left before crushing the end between his thumb and forefinger and placing the few shreds of tobacco that remain into a leather pouch. He says 'That's how to make twenty cigarettes into twenty-two.' He wears a sports jacket, flannel trousers, black shoes elasticated at the side, an open-neck shirt with a frayed collar; clothes that had been his best until he lost his job two years ago. He had been a cabinet maker, and he had been in his last place for sixteen years.

There is a snooker table and a dartboard. The younger men come in, put 20p in the slot to release the balls for a game of snooker. They scarcely speak to each other, and they acknowledge each other only by a nod or a brief touch on the arm as they leave. There is no conversation. The music of Boney M singing 'Ra-Ra-Rasputin' recurs frequently, filling the space between the high pillars with their Corinthian capitals and the space between the men who do not speak. An old man comes in. A gust of wind accompanies him, and some dust and waste-paper from the street. He sits at one of the round glass-topped tables. The girl behind the bar brings him a pint; he acknowledges a man at the dartboard who has bought it for him. If people do not say much, it is because little has happened since they last saw each other that is worthy of the telling.

The man who has been a cabinet maker says: 'The same things happen every day. Bugger-all.' He has thinning hair, straight and brown, through which the skull shines pink. His eyes are deep and bright blue, although the face is lined and heavy, with two parallel furrows like scars at the side of the mouth. 'The firm just closed down. We didn't hear about it till the day we finished. He went bust. That was it. I'd got eight hundred pounds in my last wage packet. You can't believe it you know. We were raised on work up here. I find myself even now thinking it's time to get up, and I put my feet out of bed, grab my trousers before I remember I don't have to go. Then you get back into bed, and you're glad you're not late; till it dawns on you you'll never have to get up early ever again. I miss the early mornings. In winter I used to love it. I used to walk to work from where we lived. I saw the sun rise over the cranes and the shipyards; the snow made everything look different; and in summer the sky was open and clear, you never minded going to work. You don't realize what it means to you. I worked with three good blokes over ten years. You get to know them, you respect them, you know all about their families. You talk about the football or the horses or the telly; you know exactly where they stand, what they think. But if I see them now, there's none of them working, we haven't anything to say to each other.

'When I lost my job, the family was grown up, the boy married, the girl courting; she's married now. It was all right for a few weeks, you think "Well, I deserve a holiday." I used to go shopping with the wife; it was all right. We went to the Lake District for a fortnight, that was an ambition we'd always had. That was beautiful. But then you start to look for work. There's nothing doing, and you start to resent it. The wife is still doing what she has to do, what she's always done over the years. But she's got it all worked out, she doesn't even want you to help her. That's the first thing. I irritated her. I'd got nothing to tell her. I used to go to the betting shop, I never won much. But then I felt I had to stay out all day, otherwise she might think I wasn't really looking for work. She did think that. She didn't know it's not very clever trying to find work at fifty-four.

'After a year, things between me and her started getting really bad. We rowed. I felt I didn't want to be with her. We stopped having much of a sex life – oh, years ago. It didn't bother me, not really. I've always made things. I'd got a shed where I'd make models out of wood, metal; I like modelling things, planes, boats. I'd like to have been a sculptor; I chip away at stones, anything; I feel I can get a shape out of almost anything; I can see something waiting to get out.

'I felt restless. I used to walk; I'd wander round the town. I couldn't stay in, but there was nowhere I wanted to go. I found myself looking at women, girls. And I even used to sit on a bench where I could see the girls coming out of school. I don't know why. It was on my way home in the afternoon. And it came to me that I was deliberately getting there at about four o'clock, so I could watch them. Girls, not more than thirteen or fourteen some of them. I found I was getting all sexed up watching them, you know what I mean?

'Of course I was upset. I told myself I must never go back there again; but I did. I kept on going back. I thought somebody'll report me for hanging around. I never did anything. I never spoke to any of them. I felt I wanted something. I wanted something I couldn't have. Oh, I thought about it, the ignorance we grew up in, I'd never had a woman when I met my wife . . .

'I got scared. It was sitting and having all that time to think about yourself. All the years you'd never really bothered; you'd done what you had to do. I think I never knew what was going on in my own mind till I started to have time on my hands.

'Then I thought I'd better stop going out. I felt I was somebody else, I wasn't myself any more. I felt like Jekyll and Hyde; there was this other man inside me. I saw a film on telly where this man changed into a monster at night; it was a horror film. I thought, Christ that's me. I felt so ashamed. I went to see the minister at the church, but I couldn't tell him.

'I mean, with the blokes at work, you joke, you talk about sex. But it's open; pictures in the paper, you look at it, but you don't think of it for yourself. Nothing like this. I thought I was ill. I went to my doctor in the end. He was a very good bloke. I talked to him. He gave me some tablets for depression. I said, "But I'm not depressed, I'm frightened." I even found myself looking at my own daughter, God forgive me. I used to leave the bathroom door open and hope she'd come in to see me with nothing on. I used to pick her dirty bits of washing out, it fascinated me. When she left to live with her bloke I was glad. The missis said it was wrong not getting married straight away, but I was pleased when she went.

'I've never done anything, don't get me wrong. I can control myself. I wouldn't.

It was like a great gap in your life, and all the things you've never thought about – they get through the gap and come into your conscious mind. Idleness. My mother always said the devil finds work for idle hands. It's true of idle minds, I can tell you.

'It's funny. I've always been broadminded. At work, when they used to go on about queers or prostitutes, I've always defended them. I've always stuck up for those who people have a down on, I never knew why.

'But I do know of people's lives that's been smashed apart by having nowt to do. Time. It can be a funny thing. There's times of the day that definitely go slower than others, did you know that? There is definitely times when the hands move slower on the clock. I hate the middle of the day. And the long summer evenings. I go for walks sometimes, to Hebburn, along the beach, in the wind. It helps block things out. You walk twelve to fifteen miles on an afternoon, come back tired out. That reminds me of coming home from work, when I felt tired but knowing you'd given a good day's work. That was satisfying; something I haven't known since. You feel now you've got nothing to give, nothing to offer. You feel ashamed of yourself.'

Jeremy Seabrook
Unemployment (Paladin)

DOWN AND OUT

I walked to Waterloo, a distance of some three or four miles, hoping to eat in the same Spanish café I had found at the weekend. It meant hanging about the station for a few hours, but I was getting used to that. Waterloo Station was much more crowded than I'd remembered it, thousands of people milling in the concourse, jostling for position as they scuttled to and from the platforms. I sat on a bench seat near the bookstall. It had been moved since my previous visit six days before to make way for workmen installing screens and barriers. One man was drilling into the newly laid concrete, another was ferrying loads of paving slabs with a fork-lift truck.

Beside me was a one-legged old man in clothes even shabbier than my own. His crutches lay by his side, together with three or four plastic carrier-bags which seemed to be filled with old clothes. Another dosser joined us, a stocky man with wild curly hair and a skin so blackened he might have spent the night in a coal cellar. Even his bald patch was dark, like cow-hide.

We had been sitting for about a quarter of an hour, watching the men at work, when a policeman approached us.

'Right,' he said, looking at us each in turn, 'on your way.'

The blackened man started to gather his belongings. I looked at the policeman quizzically.

'Are you travelling anywhere?' he asked.

'Yes,' I said. 'I'm just waiting for a friend to come, then we'll be on our way.'

It was true. I had an appointment with the film crew, who had arranged to meet me there.

'I mean,' said the policeman with infinite patience, 'are you travelling on a train?'

'No,' I said.

'Well, in that case, you're not entitled to sit there. That seat is reserved for the travelling public.'

'But I've arranged to meet my friend here,' I said.

'Look, I don't want any talk,' said the policeman becoming agitated. 'Either you move or I nick you, all right?'

The two other dossers had already packed their bags and were beginning to move away. They had said nothing during this exchange, and looked vaguely embarrassed by my apparent stupidity. I stood up, and walked over to the book-stall, where I began to look at some magazines. The policeman watched me, satisfying himself that I had no immediate intention of resuming my seat, and then he walked away into the crowd.

The one-legged man limped after him on crutches. My other companion had quietly sat down on another bench, out of view. I waited a few minutes in the bookstall, then I resumed my seat. Next to me was an old man who told me he was staying at the Salvation Army hostel in Blackfriars Road near by. I began to wonder if any of the seats were occupied by travellers at all.

He said the Salvation Army was quite strict – if you even smelt of drink, they threw you out. But, he said, they did not shove religion down his throat, a fact for which he was grateful.

'A man tried to sell me his meal ticket the other day,' he said. 'He wanted to buy a bottle of cider. I told him I wasn't having anything of that, because his ticket had his name and his bed number on it, and I'd have been out on my ear if they'd found out.'

His accent sounded like those I had heard in Suffolk, and I asked him if he was from those parts.

'No, I'm not from Suffolk, you've got the wrong bloke,' he shouted, as if I had accused him of a crime. 'I'm from St Albans, Hurts, you understand? St Albans, Hurts.' His voice was getting louder, and he pronounced the name of the county as it was spelt. 'ST ALBANS HURTS,' he continued, 'ST A–L–B–A–N–S H–E–R–T–S. ST ALBANS HURTS!' He was at screaming pitch, and his voice echoed round the girders above our heads. Scores of people looked round to see what was happening. They glared at me as if I had tried to rob the old man.

I tried to calm him down, but it was several minutes before he regained his composure. He told me he was sixty-two, and he gave me the exact address of his birthplace in St Albans as though he were filling in yet another government form.

'I go back to St Albans every Thursday on the train,' he said. 'But there's nowhere to stay in St Albans. There's no Salvation Army hostel like here.'

I decided to get weighed. It had been ten days since I took to the streets, and my diet had changed dramatically. I wanted to find out if the high fat content of my meals had altered my weight, or if all the walking I was doing had counter-balanced the higher carbohydrate intake. I went down into the Gents in the basement, where I found a large red weighing machine with a huge circular dial, like the ones I had stepped on at the seaside when I was small.

I took off my heavy overcoat, and laid it on a shoe-shining machine, then I placed my bag and my radio on the floor. The machine took a 5 pence piece. The needle registered 10 stones, 7 pounds, exactly the same weight as when I had set out. I stepped off the machine, smiling, pleased that I had at least managed to keep my weight up in spite of my reduced circumstances. I bent to pick up my coat from the shoe-shine machine, when I became aware of a young man approaching me rapidly from behind. He was smartly dressed, in his early twenties, and as he drew level with me he thrust out an arm as if he were about to seize my coat. I jumped back in surprise, and I saw his hand dart towards a folder which was propped up on the shoe-shining machine against the wall. I had not noticed it before, and it struck me that he must have thought that I had been trying to steal it. He stared at me aggressively, and I thought he was going to speak, but he tucked the folder under his arm and hurried away, bounding up the stairs two at a time.

I left Waterloo Station and walked to the Victoria Embankment where I joined the lunchtime strollers in the park. A Scotsman in a kilt, his hair tied up in a pony tail, was walking a tiny dog, striding out, oblivious to the wry smiles he left in his wake. A decrepit old gardener was sweeping leaves from under a tree one at a time, more a caress than a business-like attempt to clear the debris. I wondered if he would manage to uncover the lawn before the tree shed its next leaves. On a park bench two skinheads were eating fish and chips, feeding tit-bits to the pigeons. One of them was clearly frightened of the birds, and from time to time he leaped on to the bench itself to avoid them as they crowded round his friend's feet. He continued to feed them, however, making sure he was at a safe height.

I walked into Soho to see if the traders in Berwick Street Market would give me any of the fruit they considered unfit for sale. As I walked through the streets, the pictures of naked women in the shop windows surprised me. How many times, I wondered, had I walked through these streets and considered them merely colourful, amusing. Now they seemed almost threatening. Berwick Street was busy, working wives laden with their lunchtime shopping, buying pounds of this, half pounds of that. Could I, I thought, afford to buy fruit on my budget? I looked hard at the prices. One apple would cost me around 8 pence, a large orange nearer 12 pence. The doctor had advised me against salads, because, he said, I stood a greater risk of catching typhoid or a similar disease from foods which might have been in contact with flies. But, in the cold weather, that possibility seemed greatly lessened. He had told me to look for foods with high carbohydrate and high fat, for energy. Still, a free apple or orange would not hurt, I thought, as a supplement to all the junk food. I found a crate on a barrow which contained abandoned fruit from one of the near-by stalls. There were three oranges with the beginnings of mould on one side, several mouldy bunches of grapes, each with good fruit among the bad, and a bag of reject figs. I took an orange and popped it in my bag.

Tony Wilkinson
Down and Out (Quartet Books)

ON MAKING 'DRIFTERS'

Drifters is about the sea and about fishermen, and there is not a Piccadilly actor in the piece. The men do their own acting, and the sea does its — and if the result does not bear out the 107th Psalm, it is my fault. Men at their labour are the salt of the earth; the sea is a bigger actor than Jannings or Nitikin or any of them; and if you can tell me a story more plainly dramatic than the gathering of the ships for the herring season, the going out, the shooting at evening, the long drift in the night, the hauling of nets by infinite agony of shoulder muscle in the teeth of a storm, the drive home against a head sea, and (for finale) the frenzy of a market in which said agonies are sold at ten shillings a thousand, and iced, salted and barrelled for an unwitting world — if you can tell me a story with a better crescendo in energies, images, atmospherics and all that make up the sum and substance of cinema, I promise you I shall make my next film of it forthwith.

But, of course, making a film is not just the simple matter of feeling the size of the material. If that were so every fool who fusses over a nondescript sunset, or bares his solar plexus to the salt sea waves on his summer holiday, would be an artist. I do not claim the brave word, though I would like to, but I think I know what it mostly means. It has very little to do with nondescript enthusiasm, and a great deal to do with a job of work.

In art, as in everything else, the gods are with the big battalions. You march on your subject with a whole regiment of energies: you surround it, you break in here, break in there, and let loose all the shell and shrapnel you can (by infinite pushing of your inadequate noddle) lay hands on. Out of the labour something comes. All you have to do then is to seize what you want. If you have really and truly got inside, you will have plenty — of whatever it is — to choose from.

So in this rather solid adventure of the herring fishery I did what I could to get inside the subject. I had spent a year or two of my life wandering about on the deep sea fishing-boats, and that was an initial advantage. I knew what they felt like. Among other things they had developed in me a certain superior horsemanship which was proof against all bronco-buckings, side-steppings and rollings whatsoever. I mention this because the limiting factor in all sea films is the stomach of the director and his cameramen. It is a super fact, beyond all art and non-art. Of my cameramen one also was an ex-seaman. The other, for all his bravery, was mostly unconscious.

In this matter I was altogether to blame. What I know of cinema I have learned partly from the Russians, partly from the American westerns, and partly from Flaherty, of *Nanook*. The westerns give you some notion of the energies. The Russians give you the energies and the intimacies both. And Flaherty is a poet.

The net effect of this cinematic upbringing was to make me want a storm: a real storm, an intimate storm, and if possible a rather noble storm. I waited in Lowestoft for weeks till the gale signal went up, and I got it. So did the cameramen. The wild Arabian breeze of the drifter's bilges did not help matters.

Taking the film as a whole I got the essentials of what I wanted. I got the most beautiful fishing-village in the world – I found it in the Shetlands – for a starting point. I staged my march to the sea, the preparations, the procession out. I ran in detail of furnace and engine-room for image of force, and seas over a headland for image of the open. I took the ships out and cast the nets in detail: as to the rope over the cradle, the boy below, the men on deck against the sea; as to the rhythm of the heaving, the run on the rollers, the knotted haul of each float and net; as to the day and approaching night; as to the monotony of long labour. Two miles of nets to a ship: I threw them in a flood of repetition against a darkening sky.

The life of Natural cinema is in this massing of detail, in this massing of all the rhythmic energies that contribute to the blazing fact of the matter. Men and the energies of men, things and the functions of things, horizons and the poetics of horizons: these are the essential materials. And one must never grow so drunk with the energies and the functions as to forget the poetics.

I had prepared against that as best I knew how. Image for this, image for that. For the settling of darkness, not darkness itself, but flocks of birds silhouetted against the sky flying hard into the camera: repeated and repeated. For the long drift in the night, not the ship, not the sea itself, but the dark mystery of the underwater. I made the night scene a sequence of rushing shoals and contorting congers. For the dawn, not a bleary fuss against the sky (which in cinema is nothing), but a winding slow-rolling movement into the light. Then a bell-buoy.

Then a Dutch lugger rolling heavily into the light. Three images in a row.

You can never have your images too great, and I think there are none of us poets enough to make cinema properly. It is in the end a question of suggesting things, and all the example of Shakespearian metaphor is there to tell you how short we stand of the profundities.

The most solid scene, I would say, was the spectacle of the hauling. Camera and cameraman were lashed on top of the wheelhouse, and the nets came up through the heavy sea in great drifts of silver. We got at it from every angle we could and shot it inside-out with the hand camera; and, put together, it made a brave enough show. But even then the fact of the matter, however detailed, however orchestrated, was not enough. The sea might lash over the men and the ship plunge, and the haul of the nets tauten and tear at the wrists of the men: it was still not enough. This business of horizons had to be faced over again. By fortune a whale came alongside to clean the nets, and I used it for more than a whale. I used it for a ponderous symbol of all that tumbled and laboured on that wild morning. It adds something, but it is possible that something else, had I but felt it properly, would have carried the scene still further to that horizon I speak of. Images, images — details and aspects of things that lift a world of fact to beauty and bravery — no doubt half a hundred passed under my nose, and I did not see them.

So through the procession into harbour, and the scenes in the market-place at Yarmouth — fact joined to fact and detail to detail. But here, of course, because of the size and variety of the scene, rather greater possibilities in the matter of orchestration. The gathering procession of buyers and sellers on the quayside, the procession of ships through the harbour mouth: the two processions interwoven. The selling itself, the unloading, the carrying: mouth work and shoulder work interwoven, made complementary to each other, opposed to each other as your fancy takes you. Rivers of fish, being slid into a ship's hold, cartfuls of baskets, girls gutting, barrels being rolled: all the complex detail of porterage and export dissolved into each other, run one on top of the other, to set them marching. It is the procession of results. Cranes and ships and railway trains — or their impressionistic equivalents — complete it.

The problem of images does not arise so plainly here, for cinematic processions, if you bring them off, are solid affairs that carry their own banners. Two, however, I did try. As the labour of the sea turned to the labour of the land, I carried forward a wave theme. It is played heavily for accompaniment as the ships ride in; but as life on the quayside takes charge of the picture, it is diminished in strength till it vanishes altogether. Through breaking waves the buyers and sellers go to their business. Count that, if you will, for an image of opposition. It is a far cry from the simple and solid labour of the sea to the nepman haggling of the market-place.

The last was of similar type. As the catch was being boxed and barrelled I thought I would like to say that what was really being boxed and barrelled was the labour of men. So as the herring were shovelled in, and the ice laid on, and the hammer raised to complete the job, I slid back for a flash or two to the storm and the hauling. The hammer is raised on mere fish: it comes down on dripping oilskins and a tumbling sea. This notion I kept repeating in flashes through the procession of barrels and the final procession of railway trucks. The barrels of the dead pass for a second into the living swirl of a herring shoal, in and out again; the smoke in a tunnel dissolves for a moment into the tautened wrist of a fisherman at the net-rope.

I cannot tell you what the result of it all is. Notions are notions and pictures are pictures, and no knowledge of cinematic anatomy can guarantee that extra something which is the breath of life to a picture. If I raise this matter of images it is rather to give you some idea of how the movie mind works. It has to feel its way through the appearances of things, choosing, discarding and choosing again, seeking always those more significant appearances which are like yeast to the plain dough of the context. Sometimes they are there for the taking; as often as not you have to make a journey into a far country to find them. That, however, is no more difficult for cinema than for poetry. The camera is by instinct, if not by training, a wanderer.

John Grierson
Grierson on Documentary, ed. F. Hardy (Faber)

Then the nets rose and fell
in the swell. Then the dark water
went fiery suddenly, then black.
Then with a haul it was all
fire, all silver fire
fighting down the black. Then the fire
rose in the air slowly,
struggling over the side of the boat.
Then it was deck and hold.
Then it was the dance of death
in silver with grey gulls.
Then it was low clouds, bars of light,
high water slapping, choppy wake
and oilskin tea then.

Edwin Morgan
The New Divan (Carcanet)

THE SEAMEN'S STRIKE, LIVERPOOL 1966

So you've come to stand on the stones of the dock road, the warehouses shimmering in the sunlight and throwing shadows across the water where the rubble of the Wirral rises out beyond the locks and you hold up the placard in your hand as an odd lorry goes by and kicks up the dust. And you look over at the ships all laid up in their berths and think of how dead they look, no more than iron hulks without the men. And the coppers watch you from their hut as you stroll up and down and try to remember how it all started and it's funny that you can't, can't remember anything except walking up and down on the picket line each Friday as though you'd been doing it all your bloody life. Then you remember the song, the only bloody song he ever knew and you picture him that night with his hair blowing and his fists up and him saying don't let them fool you and the song of the 'Saints' going rolling around the deck and getting lost on the wind. And now it's a quiet afternoon in late May and no one goes down to the ships any more and the strike is two weeks old and still the song keeps dancing in your head.

And you mind that time the year gone by, homeward bound and two weeks from Liverpool and the football on the wireless and the mess room below deck where the lads had gathered with their mugs of tea and tins of baccy and the smoke drifting up surrounding the bulwarks and being cut by the plum voice of the world news that tell you all seamen are to get a big rise within a few weeks.

And Joe Conlan smiled that funny way he had of crinkling up his big face and turned to his donkeyman mate and you hear him say they'll want something back for that. And Wally Jolly nodded the way he did when he'd finished telling you anything important, like the way donkey men got their name from having to lug their own mattresses down to the ships in the old days, and nodded again. You look out beyond the deck and see the sun flitting across the crests as the after end dips and rises in the late afternoon and the masthead a moving shadow along the water and inside the swirl of voices and shouts as Liverpool go one up and you thought about the extra few bob and what Conlan meant about them wanting something back.

You soon found out. You had to work seven days a week now before overtime. Then the union bloke took some papers out of his briefcase and showed you what the agreement had been and a couple of lads told him that ever since they'd gone to bloody sea the story had been to fight for less hours not more and didn't they have us enough by the balls already? The union bloke shrugged and you got the feeling he wasn't so happy either but he didn't say anything. Mates and Masters could now turn you out any time they wanted to, weekends away were to be just the same as any other day, the big rise had taken care of that.

Tony Wailey
History Workshop

THREAT OF SEAMEN'S STRIKE GROWS

The nation last night seemed to slip a little nearer towards the seamen's strike, which is due to start on Monday. The executive of the National Union of Seamen is to discuss this morning an appeal by Mr Gunter, Minister of Labour, that they should give serious consideration to the damage the strike would inflict on the economy, but it seems extremely unlikely that they will call off the strike.

Mr Gunter spent about an hour with the executive indicating the serious effects the strike will have, and listening to the union's point of view. But the meeting appears to have been totally fruitless in the sense that the Minister had no concession to offer, and the union did not reveal any change of attitude.

Mr William Hogarth, general secretary of the union, said he did not want to prejudge the issue, but he thought there was no chance of the executive having a change of mind when it considered Mr Gunter's appeal. They were 'definitely no nearer a settlement'.

He said: 'None of us wants to see the economy of the country disrupted, but we have a feeling that our membership is saying once and for all that the seamen want a decent life.'

The Times, 12 May 1966

DISCOVERING THE WAY OF LIFE OF A TENANT FARMER –
SOUTHERN STATES OF USA, 1936

Where they live

There are on this hill three such families I would tell you of: the Gudgers, who are sleeping in the next room; and the Woods, whose daughters are Emma and Annie Mae; and besides these, the Ricketts, who live on a little way beyond the Woods; and we reach them thus:

Leave this room and go very quietly down the open hall that divides the house, past the bedroom door, and the dog that sleeps outside it, and move on out into the open, the back yard, going up hill: between the tool shed and the hen house (the garden is on your left), and turn left at the long low shed that passes for a barn. Don't take the path to the left then: that only leads to the spring; but cut straight up the slope; and down the length of the cotton that is planted at the crest of it, and through a space of pine, hickory, dead logs and blackberry brambles (damp spider webs will bind on your face in the dark; but the path is easily enough followed); and out beyond this, across a great entanglement of clay ravines, which finally solidify into a cornfield. Follow this cornfield straight down a row, go through a barn, and turn left. There is a whole cluster of houses here; they are all negroes, the shutters are drawn tight. You may or may not waken some dogs: if you do, you will hardly help but be frightened, for in a couple of minutes the whole country will be bellowing in the darkness, and it is over your movements at large at so late and still an hour of the night, and the sound, with the knowledge of wakened people, their heads lifted a little on the darkness from the crackling hard straw pillows of their iron beds, overcasts your very existence, in your own mind, with a complexion of guilt, stealth, and danger:

But they will quiet.

They will quiet, the lonely heads are relaxed into sleep; after a while the whip-poorwills resume, their tireless whipping of the pastoral night, and the strong frogs; and you are on the road, and again up hill, that was met at those clustered houses; pines on your left, one wall of bristling cloud, and the lifted hill; the slow field raised, in the soft stare of the cotton, several acres, on the right; and on the left the woods yield off, a hundred yards; more cotton; and set back there, at the brim of the hill, the plain small house you see is Woods' house, that looks shrunken against its centers under the starlight, the tin roof scarcely taking sheen, the floated cotton staring:

The house a quarter-mile beyond, just on the right of the road, standing with shade trees, that is the Ricketts'. The bare dirt is more damp in the tempering shade; and damp, tender with rottenness, the ragged wood of the porch, that is so heavily littered with lard buckets, scraps of iron, bent wire, torn rope, old odors, those no longer useful things which on a farm are never thrown away. The trees: draft on their stalks their clouds of heavy season; the barn: shines on the perfect air; in the bare yard a twelve-foot flowering bush: in shroud of blown bloom slumbers, and within: naked, naked side by side those brothers and sisters, those most beautiful children; and the crazy, clownish, foxy father; and the mother; and the two old daughters; crammed on their stinking beds, are resting the night:

Fred, Sadie, Margaret, Paralee, Garvrin, Richard, Flora Merry Lee, Katy, Clair Bell; and the dogs, and the cats, and the hens, and the mules, and the hogs, and the cow, and the bull calf:

Woods, and his young wife, and her mother, and the young wife's daughter, and her son by Woods, and their baby daughter, and that heavy-browed beast which enlarges in her belly; Bud, and Ivy, and Miss-Molly, and Pearl, and Thomas, and Ellen, and the nameless plant of unknown sex; and the cat, and the dog, and the mule, and the hog, and the cow, and the hens, and the huddled chickens:

And George, and his wife, and her sister, and their children, and their animals; and the hung wasps, lancing mosquitoes, numbed flies, and browsing rats:

All, spreaded in high quietude on the hill.

What they earn

Woods and Ricketts work for Michael and T. Hudson Margraves, two brothers, in partnership, who live in Cookstown. Gudger worked for the Margraves for three years; he now (1936) works for Chester Boles, who lives two miles south of Cookstown.

Gudger has no home, no land, no mule; none of the more important farming implements. He must get all these of his landlord. Boles, for his share of the corn and cotton, also advances him rations money during four months of the year, March through June, and his fertilizer.

Gudger pays him back with his labor and with the labor of his family.

At the end of the season he pays him back further: with half his corn; with half his cotton; with half his cottonseed. Out of his own half of these crops he also pays him back the rations money, plus interest, and his share of the fertilizer, plus interest, and such other debts, plus interest, as he may have incurred.

What is left, once doctors' bills and other debts have been deducted, is his year's earnings.

Gudger is a straight half-cropper, or sharecropper.

Woods and Ricketts own no home and no land, but Woods owns one mule and Ricketts owns two, and they own their farming implements. Since they do not have to rent these tools and animals, they work under a slightly different arrangement. They give over to the landlord only a third of their cotton and a fourth of their corn. Out of their own parts of the crop, however, they owe him the price of two thirds of their cotton fertilizer and three fourths of their corn fertilizer, plus interest; and, plus interest, the same debts or rations money.

Woods and Rickets are tenants: they work on third and fourth.

A very few tenants pay cash rent: but these two types of arrangement, with local variants (company stores; food instead of rations money; slightly different divisions of the crops) are basic to cotton tenantry all over the South.

From March through June, while the cotton is being cultivated, they live on the rations money.

116

From July through to late August, while the cotton is making, they live however they can.

From late August through October or into November, during the picking and ginning season, they live on the money from their share of the cottonseed.

From then on until March, they live on whatever they have earned in the year; or however they can.

During six to seven months of each year, then – that is, during exactly such time as their labor with the cotton is of absolute necessity to the landlord – they can be sure of whatever living is possible in rations advances and in cottonseed money.

During five to six months of the year, of which three are the hardest months of any year, with the worst of weather, the least adequacy of shelter, the worst and least of food, the worst of health, quite normal and inevitable, they can count on nothing except that they may hope least of all for any help from their landlords.

Gudger – a family of six – lives on ten dollars a month rations money during four months of the year. He has lived on eight, and on six. Woods – a family of six – until this year was unable to get better than eight a month during the same period; this year he managed to get it up to ten. Ricketts – a family of nine – lives on ten dollars a month during this spring and early summer period.

This debt is paid back in the fall at eight per cent interest. Eight per cent is charged also on the fertilizer and on all other debts which tenants incur in this vicinity.

At the normal price, a half-sharing tenant gets about six dollars a bale from his share of the cottonseed. A one-mule, half-sharing tenant makes on the average three bales. This half-cropper, then, Gudger, can count on eighteen dollars, more or less, to live on during the picking and ginning: though he gets nothing until his first bale is ginned.

Working on third and fourth, a tenant gets the money from two thirds of the cottonseed of each bale: nine dollars to the bale. Woods, with a mule, makes three bales, and gets twenty-seven dollars. Ricketts, with two mules, makes and gets twice that, to live on during the late summer and fall.

What is earned at the end of a given year is never to be depended on and, even late in a season, is never predictable. It can be enough to tide through the dead months of the winter, sometimes even better: it can be enough, spread very thin, to take through two months, and a sickness, or six weeks, or a month: it can be little enough to be completely meaningless: it can be nothing: it can be enough less than nothing to insure a tenant only of an equally hopeless lack of money at the end of his next year's work: and whatever one year may bring in the way of good luck, there is never any reason to hope that that luck will be repeated in the next year or the year after that.

What their houses are like inside

Four rooms make a larger tenant house than is ordinary: many are three; many are two; more are one than four: and three of these rooms are quite spacious, twelve feet square. For various reasons, though, all of which could easily enough have been avoided in the building of the house, only two of these rooms, the kitchen and the rear bedroom, are really habitable. There is no ceiling to either of the front rooms, and the shingles were laid so unskillfully, and are now so multitudinously leaky, that it would be a matter not of repairing but of complete re-laying to make a solid roof. Between the beams at the eaves, along the whole front of the house, and the top of the wall on which the beams rest, there are open gaps. In the front room on the right, several courses of weatherboarding have been omitted between the level of the eaves and the peak of the roof: a hole big enough for a cow to get through. The walls, and shutters, and floors, are not by any means solid: indeed, and beyond and aside from any amount of laborious caulking, they let in light in many dozens of places. There are screens for no windows but one, in the rear bedroom. Because in half the year the fever mosquitoes are thick and there are strong rainstorms, and in the other half it is cold and wet for weeks on end with violent slanted winds and sometimes snow, the right front room is not used to live in at all and the left front room is used only dubiously and irregularly, though the sewing machine is there and it is fully furnished both as a bedroom and as a parlor. The children use it sometimes, and it is given to guests (as it was to us), but storm, mosquitoes and habit force them back into the other room where the whole family sleeps together.

The Gudgers' house, being young, only eight years old, smells a little dryer and cleaner, and more distinctly of its wood, than an average white tenant house, and it has also a certain odor I have never found in other such houses: aside from these sharp yet slight subtleties, it has the odor or odors which are classical in every thoroughly poor white southern country house, and by which such a house could be identified blindfold in any part of the world, among no matter what other odors. It is compacted of many odors and made into one, which is very thin and light on the air, and more subtle than it can seem in analysis, yet very sharply and constantly noticeable. These are its ingredients. The odor of pine lumber, wide thin cards of it, heated in the sun, in no way doubled or insulated, in closed and darkened air. The odor of woodsmoke, the fuel being again mainly pine, but in part also, hickory, oak, and cedar. The odors of cooking. Among these, most strongly, the odors of fried salt pork and of fried and boiled pork lard, and second, the odor of cooked corn. The odors of sweat in many stages of age and freshness, this sweat being a distillation of pork, lard, corn, wood-smoke, pine, and ammonia. The odors of sleep, of bedding and of breathing, for the ventilation is poor. The odors of all the dirt that in the course of time can accumulate in a quilt and mattress. Odors of staleness from clothes hung or stored away, not washed. I should further describe the odor of corn: in sweat, or on the teeth, and breath, when it is eaten as much as they eat it, it is of a particular sweet stuffy fetor, to which the nearest parallel is the odor of the yellow excrement of a baby. All these odors as I have said are so combined into one that they are all and always present in balance, not at all heavy, yet so searching that all fabrics of bedding and clothes are saturated with them, and so clinging that they stand softly out of the fibers of newly laundered clothes. Some of their components are extremely 'pleasant,' some are 'unpleasant'; their sum total has great nostalgic power. When they are in an old house, darkened, and moist, and sucked into all the wood, and stacked down on top of years of a moldering and old basis of themselves, as at the Ricketts', they are hard to get used to or even hard to bear. At the Woods', they are blowsy and somewhat moist and dirty. At the Gudgers', as I have mentioned, they are younger, lighter, and cleaner-smelling. There too, there is another and special odor, very dry and edged: it is somewhat between the odor of very old newsprint and of a victorian bedroom in which, after long illness, and many medicines, someone has died and the room has been fumigated, yet the odor of dark brown medicines, dry-bodied sickness, and staring death, still is strong in the stained wallpaper and in the mattress.

Their belongings

On the mantel above this fireplace:

A small round cardboard box:

(on its front:)

Cashmere Bouquet Face Powder

Light Rachel

(on its back:)

The Aristocrat of Face Powders.

Same quality as 50¢ size.

Inside the box, a small puff. The bottom of the box and the bottom face of the puff carry a light dust of fragrant softly tinted powder.

A jar of menthol salve, smallest size, two thirds gone.

A small spool of number 50 white cotton thread, about half gone and half unwound.

A cracked roseflowered china shaving mug, broken along the edge. A much worn, inchwide varnish brush stands in it. Also in the mug are eleven rusty nails, one blue composition button, one pearl headed pin (imitation), three dirty kitchen matches, a lump of toilet soap.

A pink crescent celluloid comb: twenty-seven teeth, of which three are missing; sixteen imitation diamonds.

A nailfile.

A small bright mirror in a wire stand.

Hung from a nail at the side of the fireplace: a poker bent out of an auto part.

Hung from another nail, by one corner: a square pin-cushion. Stuck into it, several common pins, two large safety-pins, three or four pins with heads of white or colored glass; a small brooch of green glass in gilded tin; a needle trailing eighteen inches of coarse white thread.

Above the mantel, right of center, a calendar: a picture in redbrown shadows, and in red and yellow lights from a comfortable fireplace. A young darkhaired mother in a big chair by the fire: a little girl in a long white nightgown kneels between her knees with her palms together: the mother's look is blended of doting and teaching. The title is Just a Prayer at Twilight.

James Agee
Let Us Now Praise Famous Men (Peter Owen)

Being observations or memorials of the most remarkable occurrences, as well publick as private, which happened in London during the last great visitation in 1665. Written by a citizen who continued all the while in London; never made publick before.

It was about the Beginning of September 1664, that I, among the Rest of my Neighbours, heard in ordinary Discourse, that the Plague was return'd again in Holland; . . .

We had no such thing as printed News Papers in those Days, to spread Rumours and Reports of Things; and to improve them by the Invention of Men, as I have liv'd to see practis'd since. But such things as these were gather'd from the Letters of Merchants, and others, who corresponded abroad, and from them was handed about by Word of Mouth only; so that things did not spread instantly over the whole Nation, as they do now. But it seems that the Government had a true Account of it, and several Counsels were held about Ways to prevent its coming over; but all was kept very private. Hence it was, that this Rumour died off again, and People began to forget it, as a thing we were very little concern'd in, and that we hoped was not true; till the latter End of November, or the Beginning of December 1664, when two Men, said to be French men, died of the Plague in Long Acre, or rather at the upper End of Drury Lane.

. . . for now the Weather set in hot, and from the first Week in June, the Infection spread in a dreadful Manner, and the Bills rise high, the Articles of the Feaver, Spotted-Feaver, and Teeth, began to swell: For all that could conceal their Distempers, did it to prevent their Neighbours shunning and refusing to converse with them; and also to prevent Authority shutting up their Houses, which though it was not yet practised, yet was threatened, and People were extremely terrify'd at the Thoughts of it.

The Second Week in June, the Parish of St Giles's, where still the Weight of the Infection lay, buried 120; whereof though the Bills said but 68 of the Plague, every Body said there had been 100 at least, calculating it from the usual Number of Funerals in that Parish as above.

Till this Week the City continued free, there having never any died except that one Frenchman, who I mention'd before, within the whole 97 parishes. Now there died four within the City, one in Wood street, one in Fenchurch street, and two in Crooked-lane: Southward was entirely free, having not one yet died on that Side of the Water.

I liv'd without Aldgate about mid-way between Aldgate Church and White-Chappel-Bars, on the left Hand or North-side of the Street; and as the Distemper had not reach'd to that Side of the City, our Neighbourhood continued very easy: But at the other End of the Town, their Consternation was very great; and the richer sort of people, especially the Nobility and Gentry, from the West-part of the City throng'd out of Town, with their Families and Servants in an unusual Manner; and this was more particularly seen in White-Chapel; that is to say, the

Broad-street where I liv'd: Indeed nothing was to be seen but Waggons and Carts, with Goods, Women, Servants, Children, &c., Coaches fill'd with People of the better Sort, and Horsemen attending them, and all hurrying away; then empty Waggons, and Carts appear'd and Spare-horses with Servants, who it was apparent were returning or sent from the Countries to fetch more People: Besides innumerable Numbers of Men on Horseback, some alone, others with Servants, and generally speaking, all loaded with Baggage and fitted out for travelling, as any one might perceive by their Appearance.

This was a very terrible and melancholy Thing to see, and as it was a Sight which I cou'd not but look on from Morning to Night; for indeed there was nothing else of Moment to be seen, it filled me with very serious Thoughts of the Misery that was coming upon the City, and the unhappy Condition of those that would be left in it.

A Watchman, it seems, had been employed to keep his Post at the Door of a House, which was infected, or said to be infected, and was shut up; he had been there all Night for two Nights together, as he told his Story, and the Day Watchman had been there one Day, and was now come to relieve him: All this while no Noise had been heard in the House, no Light had been seen; they call'd for nothing, sent him of no Errands, which us'd to be the chief Business of the Watchman; neither had they given him any Disturbance, as he said, from the Monday afternoon, when he heard great crying and screaming in the House, which, as he supposed, was occasioned by some of the Family dying just at that Time: it seems the Night before, the Dead-Cart, as it was called, had been stopt there, and a Servant-Maid had been brought down to the Door dead, and the Buriers or Bearers, as they were call'd, put her into the Cart, wrapt only in a green Rug, and carried her away.

The Watchman had knock'd at the Door, it seems, when he heard that Noise and Crying, as above, and no Body answered, a great while; but at last one look'd out and said with an angry quick Tone, and yet a Kind of crying Voice, or a Voice of one that was crying, What d'ye want, that ye make such a knocking? He answer'd, I am the Watchman! how do you do? What is the Matter? The Person answered, What it that to you? Stop the Dead-Cart. This, it seems, was about one a-Clock; soon after, as the Fellow said, he stopped the Dead-Cart, and then knock'd again, but no Body answered: He continued knocking, and the Bellman call'd out several Times, Bring out your Dead; but no Body answered, till the Man that drove the Cart being call'd to other Houses, would stay no longer, and drove away.

The Watchman knew not what to make of all this, so he let them alone, till the Morning-Man, or Day Watchman, as they call'd him, came to relieve him, giving him an Account of the Particulars, they knock'd at the Door a great while, but no body answered; and they observed, that the Window, or Casement, at which the Person had look'd out, who had answered before, continued open, being up two Pair of Stairs.

Upon this, the two Men to satisfy their Curiosity, got a long Ladder, and one of them went up to the Window, and look'd into the Room, where he saw a Woman lying dead upon the Floor, in a dismal Manner, having no Cloaths on her but her Shift: But tho' he call'd aloud, and putting in his long Staff, knock'd hard on the Floor, yet no Body stirr'd or answered; neither could he hear any Noise in the House.

He came down again, upon this, and acquainted his Fellow, who went up also, and finding it just so, they resolv'd to acquaint either the Lord Mayor, or some other Magistrate of it, but did not offer to go in at the Window: The Magistate it seems, upon the Information of the two Men, ordered the House to be broken open, a Constable, and other Persons being appointed to be present, that nothing might be plundred; and accordingly it was so done, when no Body was found in the House, but that young Woman, who having been infected, and past Recovery, the rest had left her to die by her self, and were every one gone, having found some Way to delude the Watchman, and get open the Door, or get out at some Back Door, or over the Tops of the Houses, so that he knew nothing of it; and as to those Crys and Shrieks, which he heard, it was suppos'd, they were the passionate Cries of the Family, at the bitter parting, which, to be sure, it was to them all; this being the Sister to the Mistress of the Family. The Man of the House, his Wife, several Children, and Servants, being all gone and fled, whether sick or sound, that I could never learn; nor, indeed, did I make much Enquiry after it.

I went all the first Part of the Time freely about the Streets, tho' not so freely as to run my self into apparent Danger, except when they dug the great Pit in the Church-Yard of our Parish of Algate; a terrible Pit it was, and I could not resist my Curiosity to go and see it; as near as I may judge, it was about 40 Foot in Length, and about 15 or 16 Foot broad; and at the Time I first looked at it, about nine Foot deep; but it was said, they dug it near 20 Foot deep afterwards, in one Part of it, till they could go no deeper for the Water: for they had, it seems, dug several large Pits before this, for tho' the Plague was long a-coming to our Parish, yet when it did come, there was no Parish in or about London, where it raged with such Violence as in the two Parishes of Algate and White-Chapel.

I say they had dug several Pits in another Ground, when the Distemper began to spread in our Parish, and especially when the Dead-Carts began to go about, which was not in our Parish, till the beginning of August. Into these Pits they had put perhaps 50 or 60 Bodies each, then they made larger Holes, wherein they buried all that the Cart brought in a Week, which by the middle, to the End of August, came to, from 200 to 400 a Week; and they could not well dig them larger, because of the Order of the Magistrates, confining them to leave no Bodies within six Foot of the Surface; and the Water coming on, at about 17 or 18 Foot, they could not well, I say, put more in one Pit; but now at the Beginning of September, the Plague raging in a dreadful Manner, and the Number of Burials in our Parish increasing to more than was ever buried in any Parish about London, of no larger Extent, they ordered this dreadful Gulph to be dug, for such it was rather than a Pit.

Much about the same Time I walk'd out into the Fields towards Bow; for I had a great mind to see how things were managed in the River, and among the Ships; and as I had some Concern in Shipping, I had a Notion that it had been one of the best Ways of securing ones self from the Infection to have retir'd into a Ship, and musing how to satisfy my Curiosity, in that Point, I turned away over the Fields, from Bow to Bromley, and down to Blackwall, to the Stairs, which are there for landing, or taking Water.

Here I saw a poor Man walking on the Bank, or Sea-wall, as they call it, by himself; I walked a while also about, seeing the Houses all shut up; at last I fell into some Talk, at a Distance, with this poor Man; first I asked him, how People did thereabouts? Alas, Sir! says he, almost all desolate; all dead or sick: Here are very few Families in this Part, or in that Village, pointing at Poplar, where half of them are not dead already, and the rest sick. Then he pointed to one House, There they are all dead, said he, and the House stands open; no Body dares go into it. A poor Thief, says he, ventured in to steal something, but he paid dear for this Theft; for he was carried to the Church-Yard too, last Night. Then he pointed to several other Houses. There, says he, they are all dead; the Man and his Wife, and five Children. There, says he, they are shut up, you see a Watchman at the Door; and so of other Houses. Why, says I, What do you here all alone? Why, says he, I am a poor desolate Man; it has pleased God I am not yet visited, tho' my Family is, and one of my Children dead. How do you mean then, said I, that you are not visited. Why, says he, that's my House, pointing to a very little low boarded House, and there my poor Wife and two Children live, said he, if they may be said to live; for my Wife and one of the Children are visited, but I do not come at them. And with that Word I saw the Tears run very plentifully down his Face; and so they did down mine too, I assure you.

But said I, Why do you not come at them? How can you abandon your own Flesh, and Blood? Oh, Sir! says he, the Lord forbid; I do not abandon them; I work for them as much as I am able; and blessed be the Lord, I keep them from Want; and with that I observ'd, he lifted up his Eyes to Heaven, with a Countenance that presently told me, I had happened on a Man that was no Hypocrite, but a serious, religious good Man, and his Ejaculation was an Expression of Thankfulness, that in such a Condition as he was in, he should be able to say his Family did not want. Well, says I, honest Man, that is a great Mercy as things go now with the Poor: But how do you live then, and how are you kept from the dreadful Calamity that is now upon us all? Why, Sir, says he, I am a Waterman, and there's my Boat, says he, and the Boat serves me for a House; I work in it in the Day, and I sleep in it in the Night; and what I get, I lay down upon that Stone, says he, shewing me a broad Stone on the other Side of the Street, a good way from his House, and then, says he, I alloo, and call to them till I make them hear; and they come and fetch it.

Well, Friend, says I, but how can you get any Money as a Waterman? does any Body go by Water these Times? Yes, Sir, says he, in the Way I am employ'd there does. Do you see there, says he, five Ships lie at Anchor, pointing down the River, a good way below the Town, and do you see, says he, eight or ten Ships lie at the Chain, there, and at Anchor yonder, pointing above the Town. All those Ships have Families on board, of their Merchants and Owners, and such like, who have lock'd themselves up, and live on board, close shut in for fear of the Infection; and I tend on them to fetch Things for them, carry Letters, and do what is absolutely necessary, that they may not be obliged to come on Shore; and every Night I fasten my Boat on board one of the Ship's Boats, and there I sleep by my self, and blessed be God, I am preserv'd hitherto.

I heard of one infected Creature, who running out of his Bed in his Shirt, in the anguish and agony of his Swellings, of which he had three upon him, got his Shoes on and went to put on his Coat, but the Nurse resisting and snatching the Coat from him, he threw her down, run over her, run down Stairs and into the Street directly to the Thames in his Shirt, the Nurse running after him, and calling to the Watch to stop him; but the Watchmen frighted at the Man, and afraid to touch him, let him go on; upon which he ran down to the Stillyard Stairs, threw away his Shirt, and plung'd into the Thames, and being a good swimmer, swam quite over the River; and the Tide being coming in, as they call it, that is running West-ward, he reached the Land not till he came about the Falcon Stairs, where landing, and finding no People there, it being in the Night, he ran about the Streets there, Naked as he was, for a good while, when it being by that time High-water, he takes the River again, and swam back to the Stillyard, landed, ran up the Streets again to his own House, knocking at the Door, went up the Stairs, and into his Bed again; and that this terrible Experiment cur'd him of the Plague, that is to say, that the violent Motion of his Arms and Legs stretched the Parts where the Swellings he had upon him were, that is to say, under his Arms and his Groin, and caused them to ripen and break; and that the cold of the Water abated the Fever in his Blood.

I have only to add, that I do not relate this any more than some of the other, as a Fact within my own Knowledge, so as that I can vouch the Truth of them, and especially that of the Man being cur'd by the extravagant Adventure, which I confess I do not think very possible, but it may serve to confirm the many desperate Things which the distress'd People falling into, Diliriums, and what we call Lightheadedness, were frequently run upon at that time, and how infinitely more such there wou'd ha' been, if such People had not been confin'd by the shutting up of Houses; and this I take to be the best, if not the only good thing which was performed by that severe Method.

Daniel Defoe
Journal of the Plague Year (Penguin)

THE PROCESS OF MAKING A DOCUMENTARY

Why has photography lent itself so easily to usages which are relatively independent of the photographers' intentions? I think the reason is fairly simple. The photograph offers a set of appearances prised away from their context and therefore from their meaning, because meaning is always a question of process – meaning lies in narrative, meaning is born out of development and process. If you stop that process, and take a set of images out of their context, they are prised away from their meaning. Something of the violence of that prising away of appearances from the continuum in which they once existed is suggested by the following thought. Imagine that the life of a photograph is only ten years, and most photographs last longer, the ratio between that life and the instant it represents will be something like 200,000 million to one. This perhaps gives one some idea of the violence of the fission that occurs when a set of appearances is prised away from its context. The violence destroys meaning. And the set of appearances is then available to *any* meaning being put upon it.

How in practice can we use photographs, so that, even though we are using them publicly, they are replaced in a context which is comparable to that of private photographs? This is what Jean Mohr, Sven Blomberg and myself have tried to do in our books. What we have achieved is only a tentative beginning, others later will make us look like primitives.

The problem is to construct a context for a photograph, to construct it with words, to construct it with other photographs, to construct it by its place in an ongoing text of photographs and images.

If we want to put a photograph back into the context of experience, social experience, social memory, we have to respect the laws of memory. We have to situate the printed photograph so that it acquires something of the surprising conclusiveness of that which *was* and *is*.

John Berger
Camerawork No. 4

'A Seventh Man' – theory in practice

In *A Seventh Man* there is a photograph, which is in a wooden barracks where Portuguese and Yugoslavs live. They work in a tunnel, they live in a wooden barracks, they have bunks two above the other. Around the bunks, on the roof of the bunk above, all the way round are pictures, sexy pictures, which they did not of course bring with them. They bought them in Germany or Switzerland or somewhere. The room is absolutely plastered with these. We wanted to use that picture because it was important, first of all because it was like that, secondly because it is, in a sense, an indirect index of the sexual deprivation suffered by these men. How to do it? Because you put that picture on a page and what does it say? How is that image going to work?

It firstly, maybe, approves of the virulent sexism of the images stuck up. It's going to confirm the superstition that these men are all sex maniacs and it's probably also going to give a vicarious thrill to some. You see, it's not going to work and it was a problem which we actually worked on for about a week. How could we use this in order to escape this automatic and false meaning? We tried juxtaposing that picture with pictures of the men's faces, it doesn't work because it doesn't really mean anything – it really only adds the personalities of these people. We tried putting in a photograph of something in the street, some sex shop in the street where the bourgeois of the city go. But again that says it is o.k. the petty bourgeois go to the sex shop the same as the migrant workers. It doesn't help. I'm not saying that the solution we found is the ideal one, but finally we found a photograph of an old peasant woman in her village who could have been the mother of any of those workers – in fact she wasn't – but she could have been. It was a picture of a mother, quite influenced in some respects by Catholic iconography with the Madonna and so on. The kind of picture that one of those workers might have carried around with him. It had a kind of icon value, it was sacred. We then put next to it not a photograph at all but a reproduction of a Madonna, a painting by Perugino. There begins to be a juxtaposition between idealised maternity and real maternity – that's to say a woman of 45 looking like 65 and probably with eight children. Then we turned the page and in that context we put the picture of the barracks with the sexy pictures all round. Beginning to relate, to talk about a life story, beginning to talk about women in more than one dimension, beginning to talk about the experience of those men. And then finally we chose to put opposite that barracks picture an extraordinary photograph that Jean took of a young Polish peasant girl – at that time totally uninfluenced and untouched by sexist consumerist glamour, who at the same time has a very beautiful face, young and questioning, the exact opposite in fact of the women in the barracks picture but corresponding very likely to one of the girls in the village. Now with those four pictures we perhaps began to put back the first one – that is to say the barracks one – in a context.

John Berger
Camerawork No. 4

The medical

From Istanbul the majority of migrants go to Germany. Their crossing of the frontier is officially organized. They go to the Recruitment Centre. There they are medically examined and undergo tests to prove that they possess the skills which they claim to have. Those who pass, sign a contract immediately with the German firm which is going to employ them. Then they get into a labour train and travel for three days. When they arrive they are met by representatives of the German firm and taken to their lodgings and the factory.

He strips and lines up with many hundreds of other novice migrants. They glance hastily (to stare would be to show their astonishment) at the implements and machines being used to examine them. Also hastily at one another, each trying to compare his chances with those around him. Nothing has prepared him for this situation. It is unprecedented. And yet it is already normal. The humiliating demand to be naked before strangers. The incomprehensible language spoken by the officials in command. The meaning of the tests. The numerals written on their bodies with felt pens. The rigid geometry of the room. The women in overalls like men. The smell of an unknown liquid medicine. The silence of so many like himself. The in-turned look of the majority which yet is not a look of calm or prayer. If it has become normal, it is because the momentous is happening without exception to them all.

The fit are being sorted from the unfit. One in five will fail. Those who pass will enter a new life. The machines are examining what is invisible inside their

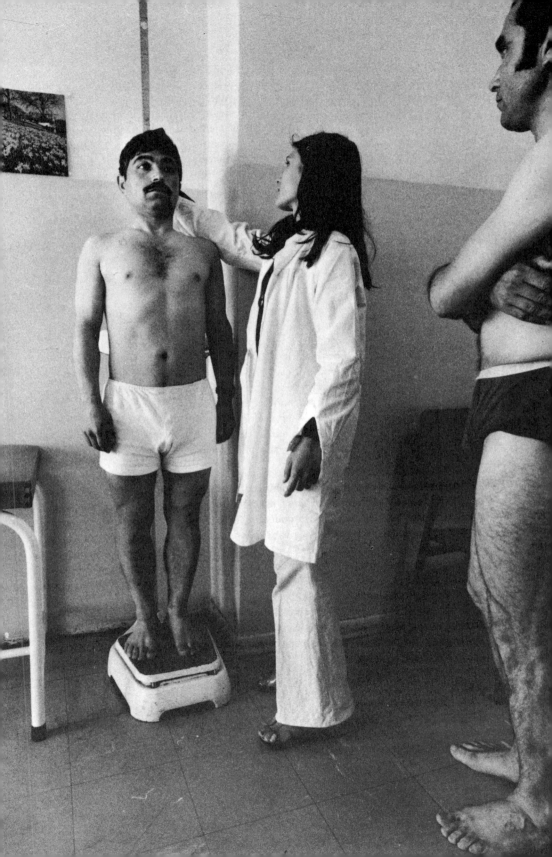

bodies. Some have waited eight years for this chance of crossing.

A man asks him if there is a machine which can reveal what he fears is a kind of disease in his head: the disease of not being able to read.

When the medical tests are finished, there are tests of skill to qualify for the job. Show how strong you are, a friend had advised, answer slowly, and show how strong you are. Some sit to wait for the results. Others pace. The expression on many faces is reminiscent of another situation: the expression of a father waiting outside whilst his child is being born. Here he awaits his own new life.

John Berger
The Seventh Man (Penguin)

WAYS OF WORKING

• During the early stages of a course on documentary, students could divide into groups of three and go out to a busy public place. Each group would observe a special area, and the individuals in the group then choose a viewing place and record what goes on during a specified 10—15 minutes. You might note down word portraits of people seen, jot down any overheard comments and describe the location and setting. A comparison later of the three versions of the same events may help you to begin to perceive the limitations of language for describing an eye-witness account and the linked opportunities for deception, both of the observer-reporter and of a potential audience. Much will be learned, too, of the skills required for accurate recording, and of how members of the public react to students' presence.

• Much can be learned about documentary by working with a partner and helping each other to perceive and articulate the stages of learning. Using a recorder and camera, pairs of students could try collecting interviews from people in markets, shopping precincts, stations, etc. Questions would need to be prepared in advance, e.g. older people could be asked about changes in the area, about local amenities, traffic or a current local talking point. Both students can use the recorder and camera, and later, when the interviews have been played back and the slides viewed, two different documentaries could be compiled. These would depend on devising different sequences, linking tape to different slides, using contrasting views, editing out questions, and so on. What is learnt about the process of editing and the collecting of material without a pre-determined stance?

• A log book is essential in making a documentary, to record all that is planned and thought about, what changes are made, what setbacks occur, first-hand impressions of people and places and so on (see George Orwell's diary for *The Road to Wigan Pier* and Janette Bushell's journal for a documentary in our other volume, *The Process of Writing*). Because a documentary is an in-depth study, sometimes taking months to complete, the log book can be used to help make decisions about the final shape of the presentation. Try keeping a log book for a short documentary on a topic that is easily accessible and which can be sustained over a long period of time (e.g. it could be on allotment holders, a local youth club, an old people's home, a nearby factory, etc.). Present a 20–30 minute documentary on tape, and then, using your log, explain to others how you decided to edit the material in that particular way.

● Sometimes there is an opportunity for a student of 16–19 to be placed on attachment for a week or more to a local firm, public institution, etc. This would be the ideal time to set about a detailed study of the place with a view to presenting a short documentary to other students, or the people concerned, on attachment. The student would need to take an active role in enlisting the co-operation of all concerned so that a full range of interviews could be carried out. Some research could be carried out in the local library, using newspaper archives etc., into the history and development of the place. Personal, first impressions could be noted in detail for use in the documentary, offering a different perspective from the final, more informed one.

● With the help of a friend, neighbour or one of the family, a student could try to make a short documentary on that person's work, referring to the George Wood extract as a possible model. That is, a series of taped interviews would be supplemented by later comments and the completed text would be edited in accordance with the subject's wishes. Notes could be kept by the compiler on the editorial choices, for reporting back to fellow students.

● It may be that a student knows people who are unemployed and who would be willing to talk about their problems. Could such interviews be placed in a wider perspective (c.f. Jeremy Seabrook's *Unemployment*) by investigating the recent pattern of work in the area or in a particular firm? Who else would need to be consulted? How could the resources of a firm or job centre help?

● When photographs have been taken during any of the above activities, the way they are to be used alongside the written text should be fully explored. It might help at that stage to examine the sequence of text and photograph in John Berger's books. What is added by particular juxtapositions? Would anything of significance be lost if the photographs were left out? What viewpoints does Jean Mohr explore?

FURTHER REFERENCES

Books

The Other Britain ed. Paul Barker, Routledge and Kegan Paul
A Seventh Man John Berger and Jean Mohr, Penguin
Let Us Now Praise Famous Men James Agee and Walker Evans, Peter Owen
Working for Fords Huw Beynon, Penguin
Down and Out in Paris and London George Orwell, Penguin
Dispatches M. Kerr, Picador

Lighthouse Tony Parker, Hutchinson
Journal of the Plague Year Daniel Defoe, Penguin
Nicaragua Susan Meiselas, Writers and Readers Cooperative
City Close-up Jeremy Seabrook, Allen Lane
Gypsies Jeremy Sandford, Secker & Warburg
Down and Out Tony Wilkinson, Quartet Books
The Classic Slum Robert Roberts, Penguin
Round About a Pound a Week M. Pember Reeves, Virago
Hard Work and No Consideration A. Paul, Queens Park Books
The Road to Wigan Pier George Orwell, Penguin
Pig Earth John Berger, Writers and Readers Cooperative
Condition of the Working Classes in Manchester Frederik Engels, Granada
Hiroshima John Hersey, Penguin
Akenfield Ronald Bythe, Penguin
Working Studs Terkel, Allen Lane and Penguin
Schindler's Ark Thomas Keneally, Carcanet
Unemployment Jeremy Seabrook, Paladin

Photography

Worktown People: Photographs from Northern England 1937–38 Humphrey
   Spender, Falling Wall Press
Walker Evans: Photographs The Museum of Modern Art, New York
Nicaragua Susan Meiselas, Writers and Readers Cooperative
The English Ian Berry, Allen Lane and Penguin
A Day Off: an English Journal Tony Ray-Jones, Thames and Hudson
A Fortunate Man Photographs by Jean Mohr, Writers and Readers Cooperative
Living Like This: Around Britain in the Seventies Daniel Meadows, Arrow Books
Camerawork No. 15 *Documenting Clydeside;* No. 11 Special issue on Mass Obser-
   vation, a documentary project started in the thirties; No. 22 *Women and
   documentary photography in Northern Ireland.*

Films

Man of Aran Robert Flaherty
Drifters John Grierson
Housing Problems Edgar Anstey
Culloden Peter Watkins
Cathy Come Home Jeremy Sandford
Days of Hope Ken Loach/Tony Garnett
The Gamekeeper Ken Loach
The Life and Times of Rosie the Riveter Connie Field
The Creggan Mary Holland
'A Television Documentary Course' S. Bennett from *Screen Education* no. 25
   (Winter 1977–78)

4
Letters

INTRODUCTION

Readers can often best enter into the inner spirit of a writer through a close contact with his or her letters. Whereas biographies and autobiographies can sometimes be about arranging an acceptable, public face (think of Thomas Hardy's calculated, over-directed attempts) letters can frequently present writers at their most unguarded and open. Through the writer's more casual handling of relationships, incidents, cameos, atmospheric flavours in the letter form they occasionally allow more of their true beliefs, values, and attitudes to come through, unchecked, to the reader. Of course there are exceptions to this; some writers' letters can be self-conscious and studied, like the letters of Henry James, but, in the main, there is often more chance of a relaxed, intimate style of presentation in this particular mode.

A sense of audience plays a crucial part in letter writing. The style, tone, mood of the different letters varies considerably according to the writer's awareness of how his message might be received. D.H. Lawrence's two letters are revealing in this context; they are both about the same incident but whereas his letter to Frieda is passionately engaged, not stopping to weigh the exact effect of his words, his letter to Ernest Weekley, Frieda's husband, is much more measured because of the uncertainty about how it will be received.

The writer's comparative position and place is also an important aspect of letter writing. George Jackson, in a position of increasingly alienated loneliness, devoted all his time in prison to an attempt to 'understand his surroundings' through reading, studying and thinking. And his letters, emotionally committed though they are, sometimes read like political or historical essays rather than communications with his parents. His attempt to make sense of his position in his own way through the act of putting his thoughts down on paper is at least as important as sharing his experiences with his parents.

A deliberately wide range of letter writing has been attempted in this selection. Starting with the more nakedly personal letters of Lawrence, through the rather awkward confession of Robert Frost, isolated in Scotland with an embarrassing situation on his hands, there is a progression from personal to public. Of course it isn't as simple as that. There are subtleties within the entire spectrum, such as the e.e. cummings piece that appears, on first reading, to be spontaneously racy until you look again and realise the element of conscious artifice that underlies it.

Van Gogh's letters show the preoccupations of a working painter aroused by new sights and new feelings from his excursion to the Drenthe area. The detailed observation of the painter's eye is found in the accuracy of remarks like, 'dashes of more or less glaring lilac, grey, white, a single rent through which the blue gleamed' in describing the sky.

The war letters, besides bringing up contrasts between social position and rank, reveal an intermediary stage combining fact and feeling. Both Fielder and Owen are trying to pass on actual information but both letters are coloured by emotional purposes. Owen's is to puncture the bubble of complacency back in Britain as well as to tell his mother how he is getting on, while Fielder seems to be caught between the need to share the actual horror of war with a loved one back home and, at the same time, to soften the hard edges of the experience for a nervous listener.

At the end of the section there are more open, public letters (e.g. 'Letter to a teacher', 'My dungeon shook', 'Sonny's lettah') that carry with them the impression of intimacy within a public mode. James Baldwin's 'My dungeon shook' is both a personal attempt to 'strengthen [his nephew] against a loveless world' and a 'public dispute' with the white attitudes and assumptions to be found in his country. Simultaneously the letter is for an individual and for a wider public and even for posterity. The School of Barbiana write searchingly and urgently to their teacher but also to everybody in their country who has produced such a repressive system.

Letter writing often puts the reader into a peculiar position. Some of the more personal letters exist against a private, unknown background making the reader feel like a trespasser. The power of the letter is in whether the reader is made willing or is able to reconstruct for him or herself something of that assumed context of meaning and experience. However the public letter is written with the knowledge that there will be other readers glancing over the shoulder of the individual or group that the letter professes to be addressed to. It is written with the more deliberate purpose of making its context explicit for the needs of a wider audience. The reader is invited in rather than left feeling like an interloper.

TWO LETTERS BY D.H. LAWRENCE

(The first is to the husband of the woman he has just run away with, explaining his reasons)

To Ernest Weekley, (7 May 1912)

[Hotel Deutscher Hof, Metz]

You will know by now the extent of the trouble. Don't curse my impudence in writing to you. In this hour we are only simple men, and Mrs Weekley will have told you everything, but you do not suffer alone. It is really torture to me in this position. There are three of us, though I do not compare my sufferings with what yours must be, and I am here as a distant friend, and you can imagine the thousand baffling lies it all entails. Mrs Weekley hates it, but it has had to be. I love your wife and she loves me. I am not frivolous or impertinent. Mrs Weekley is afraid of being stunted and not allowed to grow, and so she must live her own life. All women in their natures are like giantesses. They will break through everything and go on with their own lives. The position is one of torture for us all. Do not think I am a student of your class – a young cripple. In this matter are we not simple men? However you think of me, the situation still remains. I almost burst my heart in trying to think what will be best. At any rate we ought to be fair to ourselves. Mrs Weekley must live largely and abundantly. It is her nature. To me it means the future. I feel as if my effort of life was all for her. Cannot we all forgive something? It is not too much to ask. Certainly if there is any real wrong being done I am doing it, but I think there is not.

D.H. Lawrence

To Frieda Weekley, (7 May 1912)

[Hotel Deutscher Hof, Metz]
Tuesday

Now I can't stand it any longer, I can't. For two hours I haven't moved a muscle – just sat and thought. I have written a letter to Ernest.* You needn't, of course, send it. But you must say to him all I have said. No more dishonour, no more lies. Let them do their – silliest – but no more subterfuge, lying, dirt, fear. I feel as if it would strangle me. What is it all but procrastination? No, I can't bear it, because it's bad. I love you. Let us face anything, do anything, put up with anything. But this crawling under the mud I cannot bear.

I'm afraid I've got a fit of heroics. I've tried so hard to work – but I can't. This situation is round my chest like a cord. It *mustn't* continue. I will go right away, if you like. I will stop in Metz till you get Ernest's answer to the truth.

---

* DHL enclosed the previous letter with this and gave Frieda the responsibility of deciding to send it or to incorporate its message in a letter of her own to Weekley.

Letter from D. H. Lawrence to Frieda Weekley, 7 May 1912

But no, I won't utter or act or willingly let you utter or act, another single lie in the business.

I'm not going to joke, I'm not going to laugh, I'm not going to make light of things for you. The situation tortures me too much. It's the situation, the situation I can't stand – no, and I won't. I love you too much.

Don't show this letter to either of your sisters — no. Let us be good. You are clean, but you dirty your feet. I'll sign myself as you call me.

— Mr Lawrence

Don't be miserable — if I didn't love you I wouldn't mind when you lied. But I love you, and Lord, I pay for it.

The Letters of D.H. Lawrence
Vol. 1 (CUP)

LETTER TO HIS MOTHER

c/o Huene, Hammamet, Tunisie. Afrique du Nord
fullmoon
September
[September 13, 1933]

Dear Mother!

here we are. The sea lives a few hundred feet away; this palace is built around a court; we wear handkerchiefs-on-head and bathingsuits-to-beach; the beach — uninhabited save for occasionally goats — outdoes any I've seen; the Mediterrané's warmer than to be imagined; about 20 minutes walk away lies Hammamet (meaning 'City of Doves', they say) and patter donkeys and lurch camels (the worstput-together of all creatures?) and howls a trumpetting phonograph and loll ay-rabz galore (with occasionally a wedding); behind us, a range of mountains borrowed from the Sandwich line, and not excluding a simulacrum of Chocorua; the land here is full of cactus and low shrubbery and Bedoins whose mansions consist of shelters slightly larger than a bananaskin; heat equals somethingtobegotusedto, almost everyone (alias I) sleeps from noon till afternoon (3 PM); the first evening Huene and Marion and I all sampled some cactusfruit, becoming full-of-thorns inside our faces and outside — without dire results; when people wish to punish people people throw people into people's cactuses, it seems; camels placidly nibble the whole shebang, not merely the smallish but the spike thorns; have already made many sketches and 1 watercolour; our host is Kindness Personified, offers me sanguine and easel and space and time; chameleons are splendid models; Marion's sunburn is becoming tan (you burn while you watch yourself burn and tan almost as quickly) of the premier order — as for me, shall shortly ressemble The Spirit Of Bronze; * * * today is the baron's birthday and a German lad who's visiting has constructed an imposing centrepiece from seashell and sand and snails . . . there are lots of snails; we lunch every day about noon very lightly and enjoy citronade at 5 and dine — also outdoors — facing la mer — about 8 and retire circa 10:30 and rise at 9 sharp (the master gets up at 6 to assist his Arab workmen in the completion of this palace, as I insist it is); Djeedee (?) and Muhammed (?)

are the principal plus only servants; everyone does exactly as everyone likes, including the sun and a full moon! * * *

e.e. cummings
Selected Letters of e.e. cummings
ed. F. Duprée and George Stade (Andre Deutsch)

LETTER TO JOHN T. BARTLETT

30 August 1913
Kingsbarns, Fifeshire

Dear John,

To relieve my feelings just a word from Scotland on the funny holiday we are having with the Professor Gardiners. They are a family I got entangled with at the opening of the Poetry Shop in High Holborn last winter. It was not my fault at all. I want you to know one thing: I have thrust myself and book on no one here. I have made my way partly on my merits, mostly on my luck, but I have never forced my way one inch. These Gardiners are the kind that hunt lions and they picked me up cheap as a sort of bargain before I was as yet made. I ought not to draw them too unsympathetically, for they have meant to be kind and I count it to their credit that they have embraced the whole family in their attentions. But, but! There is a string to it all, I find. They are a one-hoss poet and artist themselves and at the present moment they are particularly keen on lions as creatures who may be put under obligations to review them in the papers. *Sic ad astra itur* in London town. It would make you weep. The Missus Gardiner is the worst. Nothing would satisfy her but we must all pack up and come to Scotland (Firth of Tay) to be near them for two weeks. So we let ourselves be dragged. Now the question is what do we think of their book. Well, I haul off and start to say what I don't think with appropriate sops to my conscience. But such integrity as I have is all literary. I make a poor liar where the worth of books is concerned. I flounder and am lost. Thus much in the historical present. The Gardiners don't like me any more. They despise my judgement and resent my tactlessness. But here I am on their hands. They are a gentleman and must carry it off with manners. Himself being an archaeologist (London University) he proposes to entertain us of an afternoon by conducting us to a cave near St Andrews for a look at an elephant a horse and an ass done by paleolithic man on the walls. These are the first drawings (or cuttings) of cavemen discovered in the British Isles and as Gardiner discovered them and the discovery is going to make a stir when it is announced presently naturally we were expected to feel the honour of being taken into what is as yet a profound secret. But, but! Same old hoodoo of my too critical mind. I wanted to see the animals and I saw them. There were many marks on the cave wall, some wavy grooves due to water, some sharp edged depressions due to the flaking off of the sandstone strata. It would have been strange if some of the marks hadn't accidentally looked like something. The sandstone was so soft and moist that a little rubbing easily made them look more like something. Animals are always the better for rubbing. And think of it – tracery like that and in such a substance assumed to have lasted for ten – twenty thousand years. Why I'd be willing to leave it to the cave men as to whether they had anything to do with the elephant the horse or the ass. I'll bet the layer of sandstone they are on hasn't been uncovered five hundred years if it has been a hundred. I begin to think I must be some archaeologist myself, I doubted the authenticity of this prehistoric menagerie so easily. The beasts left me cold. I tried to rise to the moment, but the cave was clammy and there were other things, principally the literary literature. Still I have no doubt a rumpus will be raised over Gardiner's discovery. *Sic ad astra itur* in highbrow circles. Let's see didn't you dig up a Neanderthal man in the Vancouver city dump?

Not a word to your city editor about all this. I am betraying a confidence in consigning it to paper. But damn –

St Andrews is old enough anyway without the cave drawings . . .

Robert Frost
Selected Letters of Robert Frost
ed. Lawrence Thompson
(Jonathan Cape)

TO DEREK HAWES

Swaffham Prior
7 July, 1958

Dear Mr Hawes,*

Forgive me for being so long in replying. I have been ill with water on the lung, ordered to rest, and undergoing injections to draw off the water. I am now slowly recovering.

I agree with much that you say about my poem, and am very glad that it moved you so much. I am still not well enough to write at any length. I think the poem is to some extent 'engagé': it began as that anyway, and then developed of itself. I think you have gone wrong in thinking of the horses as wild horses, or as stampeding. It is less than a year since the seven days' war happened. So the horses are good plough-horses and still have a memory of the world before the war. I try to suggest that they are looking for their old human companionship. As for the 'tapping': have you ever listened, on a still evening, to horses trotting in the distance? the sound is really a pretty tapping. The drumming sound indicated

---

* Derek Hawes, then a student, had sent Muir an essay on his poem 'The Horses'.

137

that they were drawing nearer: the hollow thunder when they turned the corner meant that they saw the village or farmstead and found their home. I think I am right in the choice of verbs here. And the apparent contradiction between the lines you quote afterwards is not a real one. For the horses are seeking the long lost archaic companionship, accepted in former times by man as an obvious right, so that it never occurred to them that there was anything surprising in using and owning horses. It is the surprise of the return that makes them realise the beauty of that free servitude. I wonder if I have explained myself.

The many fine things you say about the poem I feel very grateful for. I think there is genuine understanding there. I hope you will go on with your criticism, and I hope these few remarks of mine will be of help.

Yours sincerely,
Edwin Muir

Selected Letters Edwin Muir
ed. P.H. Butter (Hogarth Press)

THE DRENTHE LETTERS

Dear Theo,   [Drenthe, Holland, mid September 1883]

Now that I have been here a few days, and have strolled about in different directions, I can tell you more about the neighbourhood where I have taken up my quarters. I enclose a little scratch of my first painted study in these parts: a cottage on the heath. A cottage made only of sods and sticks. I saw also the interior of about six of that kind, and more studies of them will follow.

How the outside of them appears in the twilight, or just after sunset, I cannot express more directly than by reminding you of a certain picture by Jules Dupré, which I think belongs to Mesdag, with two cottages, the moss-covered roofs of which stand out very deep in tone against a hazy, dusky evening sky.

So it is here. Inside those cottages, dark as a cave, it is very beautiful. In drawings of certain English artists who worked in Ireland on the moors I find shown most realistically what I observe here.

Alb. Neuhuys gives the same effect, but a little more poetically than the actual first impression on the eye, but he never makes a thing that is not fundamentally true.

I saw splendid figures out of doors – striking in terms of their sobriety. A woman's breast, for instance, has that heaving movement which is quite the opposite of voluptuousness, and sometimes, when the creature is old or sickly, arouses pity or respect. And the melancholy which things in general have here is of a healthy kind, like in the drawings of Millet. Fortunately the men here wear short breeches, which show off the shape of the leg, and make the movements more expressive.

Est ce qu'ils ont lu le livre de Silvestre sur Eug Delacroix ainsi que l'article sur la _couleur_ dans la grammaire des arts du dessin de Ch. Blanc.

Demandes leur donc cela de ma part et sinon s'ils n'ont pas lu cela qu'ils le lisent. J'épense moi à Rembrandt plus qu'il ne peut paraitre dans mes études.

Voici croquis de ma dernière toile en train encore en demeur. Immense disque citron comme soleil. Ciel vert jaune à nuages roses. le terrain violet le semeur et l'arbre bleu de prusse, toile de 30

Letter of Vincent Van Gogh written at Arles in 1888

In order to give you an idea of one of the many things which gave me new sensations and feelings on my excursions, I will tell you that one can see here peat barges in the *very middle of the heath,* drawn by men, women, children, white or black horses, just as in Holland, for instance, on the Rijswijk towpath.

The heath is splendid. I saw sheepfolds and shepherds more beautiful than those in Brabant.

The kilns are more or less like the one in Th. Rousseau's 'Communal Oven'. They stand in the gardens under old apple trees or between cabbages and celery. In many places there are beehives too. One can see on many faces that the people are not in good health; it is not exactly healthy here, I believe; perhaps because of foul drinking water. I have seen a few girls of seventeen, or younger still, perhaps, who look very brisk and beautiful, but generally they look faded very early on. But that does not interfere with the great noble aspect of the figures of some, who, seen from nearby, are already very faded.

In the village there are four or five canals to Meppel, to Dedemsvaart, to Coevorden, to Hollands Veld.

As one sails down them one sees here and there a curious old mill, farmyard, wharf, or lock, and always a bustle of peat barges.

To give you an idea of the character in these parts – while I was painting that cottage, two sheep and a goat came to browse *on the roof* of this house. The goat climbed on the top, and looked down the chimney. Hearing something on the roof, the woman rushed out, and threw her broom at the said goat, which jumped down like a chamois.

The two hamlets on the heath where I have been, and where this incident took place, are called Sanddrift and Blacksheep. I have been in several other places too, and now you can imagine the originality here, as after all Hoogeveen is a town, and yet quite nearby already there are shepherds, those kilns, those peat huts, etc.

I often think with melancholy of the woman and the children, if only they were provided for; oh, it is the woman's own fault, one might say, and it would be true, but I am afraid her misfortunes will prove greater than her offence. That her character was spoilt I knew from the beginning, but I hoped she would improve, and now that I do not see her any more, and ponder over some things I saw in her, it seems to me more and more that she was too far gone for improvement.

And that just makes my feeling of pity the greater, and it becomes a melancholy feeling, but it is not in my power to redress it.

Theo, when I meet on the heath such a poor woman with a child on her arm, or at her breast, my eyes get moist. It reminds me of her, her weakness; her untidiness, too, contributes to making the likeness stronger.

I know that she is not good, that I have a complete right to act as I do, that I *could not* stay with her over there, that I really could not take her with me, that what I did was even sensible and wise, whatever you like; but, for all that, it pierces right through me when I see such a poor little figure feverish and miserable, and it makes my heart melt within me. How much sadness there is in life, nevertheless one must not become melancholy, and one must seek distraction in other things, and the right thing is to work; but there are moments when one only finds rest in the conviction: 'misfortune will not spare me either.'

Adieu, write soon. Believe me,

Yours,
Vincent

Dear Theo,   [New Amsterdam, end of September 1883]

This once I write to you from the very remotest part of Drenthe, where I came after an endless long voyage on a barge through the moors. I see no chance of describing the country as it ought to be done; words fail me for that, but imagine the banks of the canal as miles and miles of Michels or Th. Rousseaus, van Goyens or Ph. de Konincks.

Level planes or strips of different colour, getting narrower and narrower as they approach the horizon. Accentuated here and there by a peat shed or small farm, or a batch of meagre birches, poplars, oaks – heaps of peat everywhere, and one constantly goes past barges with peat or bulrushes from the marshes. Here and there lean cows, delicate in colouring, often sheep – pigs. The figures which now and then appear on the plain are generally of an impressive character; sometimes they have an exquisite charm. I drew, for instance, a woman in the barge with crape over the gold plates on her headdress, because she was in mourning, and afterwards a mother with a baby; the latter had a purple shawl over her head. There are a lot of Ostade types among them: physiognomies which remind one of pigs or crows, but now and then a little figure that is like a lily among thorns.

Well, I am very pleased with this excursion, for I am full of what I have seen. This evening the heath was inexpressibly beautiful. In one of the Boetzel Albums there is a Daubigny which exactly gives that effect. The sky was of an indescribably delicate lilac white, no fleecy clouds, for they were more compact and covered the entire sky, but dashes of more or less glaring lilac, grey, white, a single rent through which the blue gleamed. Then at the horizon a glimmering red streak, under which ran the very dark stretch of brown moor, and standing out against the brilliant red streak a number of low-roofed little huts. In the evening this moor often shows effects which the English call 'weird' and 'quaint.' Don Quixote-like mills, or curious great hulks of drawbridges, stand out in fantastic silhouettes against the vibrating evening sky. Such a village in the evening, with reflections of lighted windows in the water, or in the mud puddles, looks sometimes very cosy.

Before I started out from Hoogeveen, I painted a few studies there, among others a large moss-roofed farm. For I had had paint sent from Furnée, as I thought on the subject like you wrote in your letter, that by absorbing myself in my work, and quite losing myself in it, my mood would change, and it has already greatly improved.

But at times – like those moments when you think of going to America – I think of enlisting for the East Indies; but those are miserable, gloomy moments, when one is overwhelmed by things, and I could wish you might see those silent moors, which I see here from the window, for such a thing calms one down, and inspires one to more faith, resignation, steady work. In the barge I drew several studies, but I stayed a while here to paint some. I am quite near Zweeloo, where, among others, Liebermann has been; and besides, there is a part here where you still find large, very old turf huts, that have not even a partition between the stable and the living room. I intend first of all to visit that part one of these days.

But what tranquillity, what expanse, what calmness in this landscape; one feels it only when there are miles and miles of Michels between oneself and the ordinary world. I cannot give you a permanent address as yet, as I do not exactly know where I shall be for the next few days, but by 12th October *I shall be at Hoogeveen,* and if you send your letter at the usual time *to the same address,* I shall find it there, on the 12th, at Hoogeveen.

The place where I am now is New Amsterdam.

Father sent me a postal order for ten guilders, which, together with the money from you, makes me able to paint a little now.

I intend to settle for a long time at the inn where I am now, if I can easily reach from there that district with the large old turf huts, as I should have better light and more space there. As to that picture you mention, by that Englishman, with the lean cat and the small coffin, though he got his first inspiration in that dark room, he would hardly have been able to paint it in that same spot, for if one works in too dark a room, the work usually becomes too light, so that when one brings it out to the light, all the shadows are too weak. I just had that experience when I painted from the barn an open door and a glimpse into the little garden.

Well, what I wanted to say is that there will be a chance to remove that obstacle too, for here I can get a room with good light, that can be heated in winter. Well, lad, if you do not think any more about America, nor I of Harderwijk* I hope things will work themselves out.

I admit your explanation of C. M.'s** silence may be right, but sometimes one can be careless purposely. On the back of the page you will find a few scratches. I write in haste, it is already late.

How I wish we could walk here together, and paint together. I think the country would charm and convince you. Adieu, I hope you are well and are having some luck. During this excursion I have thought of you continually. With a handshake,

Yours,
Vincent

Vincent van Gogh
The Letters of Van Gogh ed. Mark Roskill
(Fontana/Collins)

---

* Place where Volunteers enlisted.
** His uncle C. M. van Gogh.

THREE LETTERS FROM THE FIRST WORLD WAR

Bert Fielder to Nell Fielder

[21 July 1915]

My Dearest Nell,

I think I may be able to keep here a few weeks yet, anyhow I've got hopes of staying until the Dardanelles job is over . . . You ask me when the war is going to be over. Well, I will just tell you, only keep it secret. *In October.* You say we don't seem to be getting on very well out here; My Word if you only knew what a job we've got before us, just try to imagine a hill called Achi Baba, just fancy yourself at the bottom of a big hill with trenches and trenches piled on top of one another, made of concrete with thousands of Turks and machine-guns, five of these trenches we took one morning one after the other, but before we got to the first trench we left a good many of our chums behind, but it's no good stopping and the faster you can run the better chance you have of getting through the rain of bullets, and our boys went mad.

I have thought just lately what a lot of savages war turns us into, we see the most horrible sights of bloodshed and simply laugh at it. It seems to be nothing but blood, blood everywhere you go and on everything you touch, and you are walking amongst dead bodies all day and all night, human life seems to be of no value at all – you are joking with a chap one minute and the next minute you go to the back of the trench to do a job for yourself and then you see a little mound of earth with a little rough wooden cross on it with the name of the man you had been joking with a short time before. My dear Scrumps, I don't know whether I'm right in telling you this, because you worry so but I would not mention it only for the reason that I don't think I shall have any more of it, but I certainly *do* thank the One Above and you for your prayers at night together with our Boy for keeping me safe throughout it all.

Always you are both in my thoughts, I think of you both in that little kitchen by yourselves and know that you are thinking of me and wondering perhaps if you will ever see me come back again, every night at nine o'clock out here which is seven o'clock in England, I think that it is the Boy's bedtime and I always can picture him kneeling in his cot saying his prayers after Mummy. But 'Cheer up', my Scrumps, this will all end soon and we shall be together again and carry on the old life once more.

My dear Scrumps, I wonder if the Boy still thinks of the gun I promised to bring him home, I got hold of two Turks' guns to bring home and after keeping them for about two weeks, I got wounded and then of course I lost them as I did everything else. I might also say that the Deal Battalion have all lost their bags again, they were coming from the ship in a barge and a Turk shell hit the barge, so they sank to the bottom of the Dardanelles. The Naval Division is pretty well cut up, especially the Marines, they can only make 3 btns out of 4 even after the last lot came out from England. I think there is some move on to withdraw the Marines and Naval Division from the Dardanelles also the other troops which were in the first part of the fighting as they are in a bad state and I expect we'll get a quiet job as garrison for some place. I expect by this time you have got General Hamilton's report of the fighting here, my dear Scrumps I think I will wind up now as I've just looked at the watch and its a quarter to eleven. I've been writing ever since nine o'clock, so Night Night and God Bless you.

PS Please don't cry so much when you write next, as it makes them in an awful mess.

A Place Called Armageddon (David & Charles)

Wilfred Owen to Susan Owen

Tues: 16 January 1917   [2nd Manchester Regt., B.E.F.]

My own sweet Mother,

I am sorry you have had about 5 days letterless. I hope you had my two letters 'posted' since you wrote your last, which I received tonight. I am bitterly disappointed that I never got one of yours.

I can see no excuse for deceiving you about these last 4 days. I have suffered seventh hell.

I have not been at the front.

I have been in front of it.

I held an advanced post, that is, a 'dug-out' in the middle of No Man's Land.

We had a march of 3 miles over shelled road then nearly 3 along a flooded trench. After that we came to where the trenches had been blown flat out and had to go over the top. It was of course dark, too dark, and the ground was not mud, not sloppy mud, but an octopus of sucking clay, 3, 4, and 5 feet deep, relieved only by craters full of water. Men have been known to drown in them. Many stuck in the mud & only got on by leaving their waders, equipment, and in some cases their clothes.

High explosives were dropping all around out, and machine guns spluttered every few minutes. But it was so dark that even the German flares did not reveal us.

Three quarters dead, I mean each of us ¾ dead, we reached the dug-out, and relieved the wretches therein. I then had to go forth and find another dug-out for a still more advanced post where I left 18 bombers. I was responsible for other posts on the left but there was a junior officer in charge.

My dug-out held 25 men tight packed. Water filled it to a depth of 1 or 2 feet, leaving say 4 feet of air.

One entrance had been blown in & blocked.

So far, the other remained.

The Germans knew we were staying there and decided we shouldn't.

Those fifty hours were the agony of my happy life.

Every ten minutes on Sunday afternoon seemed an hour.

I nearly broke down and let myself drown in the water that was now slowly rising over my knees.

Towards 6 o'clock, when, I suppose, you would be going to church, the shelling grew less intense and less accurate: so that I was mercifully helped to do my duty and crawl, wade, climb and flounder over No Man's Land to visit my other post. It took me half an hour to move about 150 yards.

I was chiefly annoyed by our own machine guns from behind. The seeng-seeng-seeng of the bullets reminded me of Mary's canary. On the whole I can support the canary better.

In the Platoon on my left the sentries over the dug-out were blown to nothing. One of these poor fellows was my first servant whom I rejected. If I had kept him he would have lived, for servants don't do Sentry Duty. I kept my own sentries half way down the stairs during the more terrific bombardment. In spite of this one lad was blown down and, I am afraid, blinded.

This was my only casualty.

The officer of the left Platoon has come out completely prostrated and is in hospital.

I am now as well, I suppose, as ever.

I allow myself to tell you all these things because *I am never going back to this awful post.* It is the worst the Manchesters have ever held; and we are going back for a rest.

I hear that the officer who relieved me left his 3 Lewis Guns behind when he came out. (He had only 24 hours in). He will be court-martialled.

In conclusion, I must say that if there is any power whom the Soldiery execrate more than another it is that of our distinguished contryman.* You may pass it on via Owen, Owen.

Don't pass round these sheets but have portions typed for Leslie etc. My previous letter to you has just been returned. It will be too heavy to include in this.

Your very own Wilfred x

Wilfred Owen to Susan Owen

Friday, 19 January 1917   [2nd Manchester Regt., B.E.F.]

We are now a long way back in a ruined village, all huddled together in a farm. We all sleep in the same room where we eat and try to live. My bed is a hammock of rabbit-wire stuck up beside a great shell hole in the wall. Snow is deep about, and melts through the gaping roof, on to my blanket. We are wretched beyond my previous imagination – but safe.

---

* David Lloyd George of Dwyfor, 1st Earl (1863–1945), Minister for War before becoming Prime Minister 1916–22.

Last night indeed I had to 'go up' with a party. We got lost in the snow. I went on ahead to scout – foolishly alone – and when, half a mile away from the party, got overtaken by   GAS

It was only tear-gas from a shell, and I got safely back (to the party) in my helmet, with nothing worse than a severe fright! And a few tears, some natural, some unnatural.

Here is an Addition to my List of Wants:

Safety Razor (in my drawer) & Blades

Socks (2 pairs)

6 Handkerchiefs

Celluloid Soap Box (Boots)

Cigarette Holder (Bone, 3d. or 6d.)

Paraffin for Hair.

(I can't wash hair and have taken to washing my face with snow.)

Coal, water, candles, accommodation, everything is scarce. We have not always air! When I took my helmet off last night – O Air it was a heavenly thing!

Please thank Uncle for his letter, and send the Compass. I scattered abroad some 50 Field Post Cards from the Base, which should bring forth a good harvest of letters. But nothing but a daily one from you will keep me up.

I think Colin might try a weekly letter. And Father?

We have a Gramophone, and so musical does it seem now that I shall never more disparage one. Indeed I can never disparage anything in Blighty again for a long time except certain parvenus living in a street of the same name as you take to go to the Abbey.

They want to call No Man's Land 'England' because we keep supremacy there.

It is like the eternal place of gnashing of teeth; the Slough of Despond could be contained in one of its crater-holes; the fires of Sodom and Gomorrah could not light a candle to it – to find the way to Babylon the Fallen.

It is pock-marked like a body of foulest disease and its odour is the breath of cancer.

I have not seen any dead. I have done worse. In the dank air I have *perceived* it, and in the darkness, *felt*. Those 'Somme Pictures' are the laughing stock of the army – like the trenches on exhibition in Kensington.

No Man's Land under snow is like the face of the moon: chaotic, crater-ridden, uninhabitable, awful, the abode of madness.

To call it 'England'!

I would as soon call my House (!) Krupp Villa, or my child Chlorina-Phosgena.

Now I have let myself tell you more facts than I should, in the exuberance of having already done *'a Bit.' It is done,* and we are all going still farther back for a long time. A long time. The people of England needn't hope. They must agitate. But they are not yet agitated even. Let them imagine 50 strong men trembling as with ague for 50 hours!

Dearer & stronger love than ever. W.E.O.

Wilfred Owen
Collected Letters (OUP)

146

LETTERS FROM PRISON

December 1964

Dear Father,

Everything was in order, concerning the package that is. They brought it right in front of the cell and opened it.

Mama sent me a card with a picture of some white people on the front of it. I guess she just can't perceive that I don't want anything to do with her white god.

I am still confined to this cell. It is nine by four. I have left it only twice in the month I've been here for ten minutes each time, in which I was allowed to shower. Did I tell you? They have assured me that I have not been given a bad-conduct report. It is just that they felt I was about to do some wrong. It's always suspicions. What I was supposed to have done or was about to do, never, never what they caught me doing as it should be. The last time I was in a cell like this three months, from February to May (1964) for reasons that are not altogether clear yet! I have had no serious infraction in almost three years now. You know I had at least $125 on me when I was arrested in 1960 and they took it. I assume it was to cover the $70 that was missing as the result of the robbery. So I'm thinking that I shouldn't owe them too much more. You know in fact I'm fast awakening to the idea that I may not owe anyone anything and that they even might owe me. I have given four-and-a-half years of life, during which I have had to accept the unacceptable, for $70 that I didn't take — I protest. I protest.

If you knew how much I protested, how seriously I felt about the matter, you and Mother and anyone who has a natural affinity with me would surely be trying to convince me that you were on my side.

The events of the Congo, Vietnam, Malaya, Korea, and here in the US are taking place all for the same reason. The commotion, the violence, the struggles in all these areas and many more spring from one source, the evil and malign, possessive and greedy Europeans. Their abstract theories, developed over centuries of long usage, concerning economics and sociology take the form that they do because they suffer under the mistaken belief that a man can secure himself in this insecure world best by ownership of great personal, private wealth. They attempt to impose their theories on the world for obvious reasons of self-gain. Their philosophy concerning government and economics has an underlying tone of selfishness, possessiveness, and greediness because their character is made up of these things. They can't see the merit in socialism and communism because they do not possess the qualities of rational thought, generosity, and magnanimity necessary to be part of the human race, part of a social order, part of a system. They can not understand that 'From each according to his abilities, to each according to his needs' is the only way men can live together without chaos. There is a species of fly that lives only four hours. If one of these flies (June fly I believe they are called), if one of these flies was born at twelve o'clock midnight in darkness and gloom, there would be no way possible for him in his lifetime to ever understand the concept of day and light. This is the case with the Europeans.

They are small men with their petty intrigues and prejudices. 'In shallow men the fish of small thoughts cause much commotion, in magnanimous oceanic minds the whales of inspiration cause hardly a ruffle' (Mao Tse-tung).

George

Dear Mother,

I promised myself that I wouldn't write you again from here. I only take pen in hand when feeling moves me to do so. My feeling seems to be wasted on you. You know beyond question what my feelings are, I never think of anything trite or inconsequential anymore. I've forgotten the feeling of joy. I've long since had my last smile wrung unceremoniously from my hollow soul. I write home to you people, my people, the closest of my kind for understanding and advice. I attempt to advise you in areas of which experience has made me better informed. I get no understanding. If I followed the advice I receive it would only serve to enslave me further to this madness of our times. My advice falls upon deaf ears!

This is my reason for not wanting to write. What can I say further? It is clear you don't love me when you refuse to aid me the only way you can, the only way I expect! By telling me I am right and that I have your blessings. You see I am being frank: though I care about your feelings, I care more for your well-being. There are things brewing now that could ruin you completely if, when they break, you are in sympathy with wrong. Robert* is the same way, he pretends or he may earnestly not feel the effects of the circumstances I attempt to explain. He is sympathetic to wrong. But I can overlook him more readily because of his almost complete lack of mental training. His past experiences have been very limited regarding the stimulus of academic learning, he is innocent. But not so with you, though your exposure was not all that it should have been, you are equipped with the basic fundamentals needed to guide one to the truth, should it be truth one favours. When I consider my own experience bought at the cost of these terrible years, supplemented in love and concern by your own experience and learning, what am I to think but that something is radically wrong, that I am being betrayed and have been betrayed. The question is one of grave proportions to me. I cannot stress this point too clearly. I mean to make sure this doesn't happen to me again or to my seed. If a person doesn't stand with me, he stands against me to my way of thinking. I feel that you have failed me Mama. I know that you have failed me. I also know that Robert has never held an opinion of his own. You have influenced his every thought ever since you have known him. You have always had the running of things. You have done him a disservice. You are doing Jon** a disservice now. You are a woman, you think like a bourgeois woman. This is a predatory man's world. The real world calls

---

* Jackson's father, Robert Lester Jackson, whom he sometimes calls Robert, sometimes Lester.
** Jonathan, George Jackson's younger brother.

148

for a predatory man's brand of thinking. Your way of viewing the world is necessarily bourgeois and feminine. How could I, Robert, Jon, or any of the men of our kind accomplish what we must as men if we think like bourgeois women, or let our women think for us. This is what's happening all over this part of the world! Robert should have been stronger, should have had more time and freedom of movement. So should Grandfather, and Great-Grandfather.

But they didn't and it isn't their fault. The cruelest and most suppressive treatment has always fallen to the males because they have not that tender defence the woman is born with. So understand me once and for all. I speak no further on the matter. You conceived and Robert sired a man. Nothing can turn me from my resolve. Make no further attempts. I am going to give my all to this thing, and if the victory is to fall to me, you and people like you must stand beside me, not lean or lie on me.

Robert tells me you are sick. I am writing to ask about the nature of your illness. I know a hope will not aid you any, but by whatever gods there be I hope and wish you well. There is much sickness and tears to come, some will fall to me also I guess, but my condition can only improve from where I stand now.

Fare you well.

Son

16 March, 1965

Dear Father,

I've been going through final examinations at school. Had to use all of my available time in study and have not been able to write like I should, but forgive me. They are over now and I did well.

I go before the board next week.

I didn't know about L.'s husband. That is too bad. She seems to be extremely unlucky in that area. She told me that the last husband she had was worse. Since that is the case I can feel nothing against her, but as you said, she should have explained. People are odd indeed, about money that is. The best method of testing a person's character is through money. The shocks and strains of this money-mad society are enough to ruin the purest of minds. Men are so deeply engaged in making a living that their very existence is shaped and dominated by the system of production. I'm thoroughly tired already, Pop. When I obtain what I need to work with, nothing could stop me from going home. That is where I will invest my money, resources, and talents. My labor shall be expended where it will be appreciated. My taxes will go to an order and system of government that will in turn protect me and my interests. I shall not, as long as I call myself a man, compromise with tyranny. There are a few things that mean more to me than life. Though I must think of and plan for tomorrow, I cannot, I must not surrender for tomorrow all that I possess today. I can repair this loss, this morbid depression that owns a little more of my mind each day that passes. The pale and almost indistinguishable glow of the future may yet materialize to disperse the gloomy stupor that has encompassed me completely. I have been purposely kept ignorant, I have been taught *what* to think, instead of *how* to think. I have been subjected to the ordeal of hunger, thirst, name-calling, and other uncountable indignities. Danger comes even from those of my own kind. Their lack of response and unyielding adherence to ineffectual thought and action is an obstacle to my plans. I may yet surmount it, but only if I follow my call. I must obey the dictates of my mind.

Give my regards to all.

30 March, 1965

Dear Father,

I haven't read anything or studied in a week now. I have been devoting all my time to thought. I trust you are all in health. I think of my personal past quite often. This is uncomfortable sometimes but necessary. I try not to let my past mistakes bother me too much, though some seem almost unpardonable. If it were not for the few intermixed little victories, my confidence in my ability would be irreparably shaken.

Though I know I am a victim of social injustice and economic pressure and though I understand the forces that work to drive so many of our kind to places like this and to mental institutions, I can't help but know that I proceeded wrong somewhere. I could have done a lot worse. You know our people react in different ways to this neoslavery, some just give in completely and join the other side. They join some christian cult and cry out for integration. These are the ones who doubt themselves most. They are the weakest and hardest to reach with the new doctrine. Some become inveterate drinkers and narcotic users in an attempt to gain some mental solace for the physical depravity they suffer. I've heard them say, 'There's no hope without dope'. Some hire on . . . thinking that as it has always been this way it must always remain this way; these are the fatalists, they serve and entertain and rationalize.

Then there are those who resist and rebel but do not know what, who, why, or how exactly they should go about this. They are aware but confused. They are the least fortunate, for they end where I have ended. By using half measures and failing dismally to effect any real improvement in their condition, they fall victim to the full fury and might of the system's repressive agencies. Believe me, every dirty trick of deception and brutality is employed without shame, without honour, without humanity, without reservation to either convert or destroy a rebellious arm. Believe me, when I say that I begin to weary of the sun. I am by nature a gentle man, I love the simple things of life, good food, good wine, an expressive book, music, pretty black women. I used to find enjoyment in a walk in the rain, summer evenings in a place like Harrisburg. Remember how I used to love Harrisburg. All of this is gone from me, all the gentle, shy characteristics of the black men have been wrung unceremoniously from my soul. The buffets and blows of this have and have-not society have engendered in me a flame that will live, will live to grow, until it either destroys my tormentor or myself. You don't understand this but I must say it. Maybe when you remember this ten or twenty years from now you'll comprehend. I don't think of life in the same sense that you or most black men of your generation think of it, it is not important to me how long I live, I think only of how I live, how well, how nobly. We think if we are to be men again we must stop working for nothing, competing against each other for the little they allow us to possess, stop selling our women or allowing them to be used and handled against their will, stop letting our children be educated by the barbarian, using their language, dress, and customs, and most assuredly stop turning our cheeks.

George

June 1965

Dear Mother,

Even though I have plenty of time now, I don't write more regularly because of my studies. I get involved in some aspect of the subjects that interest me and before I can extract myself the lights are going off and it is twelve o'clock. You know the last thing we discussed just before you people left me when you were up here last, well I've decided to go into it – now.

My life here is slowly becoming one of complete alienation. I talk to fewer convicts every day. Just one lieutenant here has tried to do anything for me. He got me out of segregation twice last year. The die is cast now though, I guess, thumbs down on me. My future is about as sound as a three-dollar bill. I thank whatever forces there are working for me that I'm still able to write you. I'm joking of course, it isn't that serious.

Nothing will help me now though but patience and I have developed plenty. There is nothing left to me now but to await whatever may come. I go back to the board October or is it December. Nine months from March would be December. Yes! Perhaps the fog will lift and I will see some ray of hope by then. You know the thing which they have locked me up for now could mean spending my next few years in confinement here. It would be merely a flight from reality to think that I could get a date this year. I would be happy though to just know how long I will be held, even if it was 10 years. I'd feel better knowing.

Take care of yourself.

Son

June 1965

Dear Father,

One of those tall ultrabright electrical fixtures used to illuminate the walls and surrounding area at night casts a direct beam of light in my cell at night. (I moved to a different cell last week.) Consequently I have enough light, even after the usual twelve o'clock lights-out, to read or study by. I don't really have to sleep now if I choose not to. The early hours of morning are the only time of the day that one can find any respite from the pandemonium caused by these the most uncultured of San Quentin inmates. I don't let the noise bother me even in the evenings when it rises to maddening intensity, because I try to understand my surroundings. I've asked myself, as I do about *all* the other aspects of life, why – why do white cons act and react as if they were animals of a lower order than we black men (some blacks get foolish also but we don't refer to them as 'men')? Why just because they look like shaved monkeys must they also act like them? It's frayed nerves, caused by the harsh terms that defeat brought when they went against the system, the same system that runs this place. I must ask myself why did they go against the system and why are the terms so harsh? Could it be that a man will most always pursue his interests, system or no? But why should so many people's interests lie outside the system? Why doesn't the system encompass the needs and requirements of all or, to be realistic, the majority. We now come to the part of the question around which the whole contention pivots: Why are the terms so harsh, the price of defeat so high? What is it that causes a man to become power-mad, to deify exploitation and mendacity and vilify the compatible, harmonious things of nature, how many times have you heard that 'everyone should help fight the evils of communism', etc.?

George

July 1965

Lester,

I write this letter to inform you that the people who hold me here read that letter you sent them. They read it and smiled with satisfaction and triumph. You are under a grave illusion, I must now admit. You didn't think they would inform me of it, did you? But you are in serious error. They let me read it. Apparently every petty official in the prison has read it, all to my embarrassment. For it sounded like something out of Stowe's *Uncle Tom's Cabin*.

It didn't just cause me embarrassment. It also has caused me to be put in a cell that has the lock welded closed. Can it possibly be? Is it within the scope of feasibility that you did not know that to tell these people I was 'bent on self-destruction' (to use your reference) would cause me harm? Are you so feeble of mind as to 'report', after a visit with me, that I am bent on violent self-destruction and think it would cause me no harm!

I have always respected and loved you people, and hated myself, cried bitter tears of remorse, when, because of circumstances and conditions, which I didn't understand, I let you down. Even after I discovered the true cause of my ills, when I found that this social order had created, through its inadequacies and its abandonment of our interest, the basis for my frustrations, I forgave you for not preparing me; for not warning me, for pretending that this was the best of all possible worlds. I forgave you for misleading me. I forgave that catholic school thing. I tried to understand your defeat complex and your loyalty to institutions contrary to the blacks' interest.

I've traveled widely over this country and some in Mexico. I've met and have had exchanges with hundreds of thousands of people. I've read extensively in the fields of social-economic and political theory and development, all of this done against serious resistance from all sides. But because I knew one day that I would find what I'm after, and answer some of the questions that beset my mind with confusion and unrest and fear, I pushed ahead in spite of the foolish conformity that I saw in you people. Now I have arrived at a state of awareness that (because of the education system) few Negroes reach in the US. In my concern for you, I try to share the benefits of my experience and my observations, but am rewarded by being called madman. Thank you for the vote of *confidence* you displayed in that letter to the warden. I'll never forget it! All my younger life you betrayed me. Like I said, I could forgive. At first you may not have known any better, but over the last two years I've informed you of many things. I've given you my best and you have rejected me for my enemies. With this last act, you have betrayed my bosom interest, even though I warned you not to say anything at all. I will never forgive you this. Should we live forever I'll never trust you again. Your mind has failed you completely. To take sides against your son! You did it in '58 and now again. There will not be a third time. The cost to me is too great. Father against son, and brother against brother. This is truly detestable. You are a sick man.

George

George Jackson
Soledad Brother: Letters from Prison (Cape)

LETTER TO A TEACHER

Dear Miss
You won't remember me or my name. You have failed so many of us.

On the other hand I have often had thoughts about you, and the other teachers, and about that institution which you call 'school' and about the boys that you fail.

You fail us right out into the fields and factories and there you forget us.

While giving a test you used to walk up and down between the rows of desks and see me in trouble and making mistakes, but you never said a word.

I have the same situation at home. No one to turn to for help for miles around. No books. No telephone.

Now here I am 'in school'. I came from far away to be taught. Here I don't have to deal with my mother, who promised to be quiet and then interrupted me a hundred times. My sister's little boy is not here to ask me for help with his homework. Here I have silence and good light and a desk all to myself.

And over there, a few steps away, you stand. You know all of these things. You are paid to help me.

Instead, you waste your time keeping me under guard as if I were a thief.

You know even less about men than we do. The lift serves as a good machine for ignoring the people in your building; the car, for ignoring people who travel in buses; the telephone for avoiding seeing people's faces or entering their homes.

I don't know about you, but your students who know Cicero — how many families of living men do they know intimately? How many of their kitchens have they visited? How many of their sick have they sat with through the night?

How many of their dead have they borne on their shoulders? How many can they trust when they are in distress? . . .

A thousand motors roar under your windows every day. You have no idea to whom they belong or where they are going.

But I can read the sounds of my valley for miles around. The sound of the motor in the distance in Nevio going to the station, a little late. If you like, I can tell you everything about hundreds of people, dozens of families and their relatives and personal ties.

Whenever you speak to a worker you manage to get it all wrong: your choice of words, your tone, your jokes. I can tell what a mountaineer is thinking even when he keeps silent, and I know what's on his mind even when he talks about something else.

This is the sort of culture your poets should have given you. It is the culture of nine-tenths of the earth, but no one has yet managed to put it down in words or pictures or films.

Be a bit humble, at least. Your culture has gaps as wide as ours. Perhaps even wider. Certainly more damaging to a teacher in the elementary schools.

At the gymnastics exam the teacher threw us a ball and said, 'Play basketball.' We didn't know how. The teacher looked us over with contempt: 'My poor children.'

He, too, is one of you. The ability to handle a conventional ritual seemed so vital to him. He told the principal that we had not been given any 'physical education' and we should take the exams again in the autumn.

Any one of us could climb an oak tree. Once up there we could let go with our hands and chop off a two-hundred pound branch with a hatchet. Then we could drag it through the snow to our mother's doorstep.

I heard of a gentleman in Florence who rides upstairs in his house in a lift. But then he has bought himself an expensive gadget and pretends to row in it. You would give him an A in physical education.

The School of Barbiana *Translated from the Italian by Nora Rossi and Tom Cole*

MY DUNGEON SHOOK

(James Baldwin's letter to his nephew on the one-hundredth anniversary of Emancipation)

Dear James:

I have begun this letter five times and torn it up five times. I keep seeing your face, which is also the face of your father and my brother. Like him, you are tough, dark, vulnerable, moody — with a very definite tendency to sound truculent because you want no one to think you are soft. You may be like your grandfather in this. I don't know, but certainly both you and your father resemble him very much physically. Well, he is dead, he never saw you, and he had a terrible life;

he was defeated long before he died because, at the bottom of his heart, he really believed what white people said about him. This is one of the reasons that he became so holy. I am sure that your father has told you something about all that. Neither you nor your father exhibit any tendency towards holiness: you really *are* of another era, part of what happened when the Negro left the land and came into what the late E. Franklin Frazier called 'the cities of destruction'. You can only be destroyed by believing that you really are what the white world calls a *nigger*. I tell you this because I love you, and please don't you ever forget it.

I have known both of you all your lives, have carried your Daddy in my arms and on my shoulders, kissed and spanked him and watched him learn to walk. I don't know if you've known anybody from that far back; if you've loved anybody that long, first as an infant, then as a child, then as a man, you gain a strange perspective on time and human pain and effort. Other people cannot see what I see whenever I look into your father's face, for behind your father's face as it is today are all those other faces which were his. Let him laugh and I see a cellar your father does not remember and a house he does not remember and I hear in his present laughter his laughter as a child. Let him curse and I remember him falling down the cellar steps, and howling, and I remember, with pain, his tears, which my hand or your grandmother's so easily wiped away. But no one's hand can wipe away those tears he sheds invisibly today, which one hears in his laughter and in his speech and in his songs. I know what the world has done to my brother and how narrowly he has survived it. And I know, which is much worse, and this is the crime of which I accuse my country and my countrymen, and for which neither I nor time nor history will ever forgive them, that they have destroyed and are destroying hundreds of thousands of lives and do not know it and do not want to know it. One can be, indeed one must strive to become, tough and philosophical concerning destruction and death, for this is what most of mankind has been best at since we have heard of man. (But remember: *most* of mankind is not *all* of mankind.) But it is not permissible that the authors of devastation should also be innocent. It is the innocence which constitutes the crime.

Now, my dear namesake, these innocent and well-meaning people, your country-men, have caused you to be born under conditions not very far removed from those described for us by Charles Dickens in the London of more than a hundred years ago. (I hear the chorus of the innocents screaming, 'No! This is not true! How *bitter* you are!' – but I am writing this letter to *you*, to try to tell you something about how to handle *them*, for most of them do not yet really know that you exist. I *know* the conditions under which you were born, for I was there. Your countrymen were *not* there, and haven't made it yet. Your grandmother was also there, and no one has ever accused her of being bitter. I suggest that the innocents check with her. She isn't hard to find. Your countrymen don't know that *she* exists, either, though she has been working for them all their lives.)

Well, you were born, here you came, something like fifteen years ago; and though your father and mother and grandmother, looking about the streets through which they were carrying you, staring at the walls into which they brought you, had every reason to be heavyhearted, yet they were not. For here you were, Big James, named for me – you were a big baby, I was not – here you were: to be

155

loved. To be loved, baby, hard, at once, and for ever, to strengthen you against the loveless world. Remember that: I know how black it looks today, for you. It looked bad that day, too, yes, we were trembling. We have not stopped trembling yet, but if we had not loved each other none of us would have survived. And now you must survive because we love you, and for the sake of your children and your children's children.

This innocent country set you down in a ghetto in which, in fact, it intended that you should perish. Let me spell out precisely what I mean by that, for the heart of the matter is here, and the root of my dispute with my country. You were born where you were born and faced the future that you faced because you were black and *for no other reason*. The limits of your ambition were, thus, expected to be set for ever. You were born into a society which spelled out with brutal clarity, and in as many ways as possible, that you were a worthless human being. You were not expected to aspire to excellence: you were expected to make peace with mediocrity. Wherever you have turned, James, in your short time on this earth, you have been told where you could go and what you could do (and *how* you could do it) and where you could live and whom you could marry. I know your countrymen do not agree with me about this, and I hear them saying, 'You exaggerate.' They do not know Harlem, and I do. So do you. Take no one's word for anything, including mine – but trust your experience. Know whence you came, there is really no limit to where you can go. The details and symbols of your life have been deliberately constructed to make you believe what white people say about you. Please try to remember that what they believe, as well as what they do and cause you to endure, does not testify to your inferiority but to their inhumanity and fear. Please try to be clear, dear James, through the storm which rages about your youthful head today, about the reality which lies behind the words *acceptance* and *integration*. There is no reason for you to try to become like white people and there is no basis whatever for their impertinent assumption that *they* must accept *you*. The really terrible thing, old buddy, is that *you* must accept *them*. And I mean that very seriously. You must accept them and accept them with love. For these innocent people have no other hope. They are, in effect, still trapped in a history which they do not understand; and until they understand it, they cannot be released from it. They have had to believe for many years, and for innumerable reasons, that black men are inferior to white men. Many of them, indeed, know better, but, as you will discover, people find it very difficult to act on what they know. To act is to be committed, and to be committed is to be in danger. In this case, the danger, in the minds of most white Americans, is the loss of their identity. Try to imagine how you would feel if you woke up one morning to find the sun shining and all the stars aflame. You would be frightened because it is out of the order of nature. Any upheaval in the universe is terrifying because it so profoundly attacks one's sense of one's own reality. Well, the black man has functioned in the white man's world as a fixed star, as an immovable pillar: and as he moves out of his place, heaven and earth are shaken to their foundations. You, don't be afraid. I said that it was intended that you should perish in the ghetto, perish by never being allowed to go behind the white man's definitions, by never being allowed to spell your proper name. You have, and many of us have, defeated this intention; and, by a terrible law, a terrible paradox, those innocents who believe that your imprisonment made them safe are losing their grasp of reality. But these men are your brothers — your lost, younger brothers. And if the word *integration* means anything, this is what it means: that we, with love, shall force our brothers to see themselves as they are, to cease fleeing from reality and begin to change it. For this is your home, my friend, do not be driven from it; great men have done great things here, and will again, and we can make America what America must become. It will be hard, James, but you come from sturdy, peasant stock, men who picked cotton and dammed rivers and built railroads, and, in the teeth of the most terrifying odds, achieved an unassailable and monumental dignity. You come from a long line of great poets, some of the greatest poets since Homer. One of them said, *The very time I thought I was lost, My dungeon shook and my chains fell off.*

You know, and I know, that the country is celebrating one hundred years of freedom one hundred years too soon. We cannot be free until they are free. God bless you, James, and Godspeed.

Your uncle,
James

James Baldwin
The Fire Next Time (Michael Joseph)

SONNY'S LETTAH

(Anti-Sus poem)

Dear Mama,
Good Day.
I hope dat wen
deze few lines reach y'u,
they may find y'u in di bes' af helt.

Mama,
I really doan know how fi tell y'u dis,
cause I did mek a salim pramis
fi tek care a lickle Jim
an' try mi bes' fi look out fi him.

Mama,
Ah really did try mi bes',
but none-di-les',
mi sarry fi tell y'u seh
poor lickle Jim get arres'.

It woz di miggle a di rush howah
wen everybady jus' a hus'le an' a bus'le
fi goh home fi dem evenin' showah;
mi an' Jim stan-up
waitin' pan a bus,
nat causin' no fus',
wen all an a sudden
a police van pull-up.

Out jump t'ree policeman,
di 'hole a dem carryin' batan.
Dem waak straight up to mi an' Jim.
One a dem hol' an to Jim
seh him tekin him in;
Jim tell him fi let goh a him
far him noh dhu not'n',
an him naw t'ief,
nat even a but'n.
Jim start to wriggle.
Di police start to giggle.

Mama,
mek Ah tell y'u whey dem dhu to Jim;
Mama,
mek Ah tell y'u whey dem dhu to him:

dem t'ump him in him belly
an' it turn to jelly
dem lick him pan him back
an' him rib get pap
dem lick him pan him he'd
but it tuff like le'd
dem kick him in him seed
an' it started to bleed

Mama,
Ah jus' could'n' stan-up deh
an' noh dhu not'n':

soh mi jook one in him eye
an' him started to cry;
mi t'ump one in him mout'
an' him started to shout
mi kick one pan him shin
an' him started to spin
mi t'ump him pan him chin
an' him drap pan a bin

an' crash
an de'd.

Mama,
more policeman come dung
an' beat mi to di grung;
dem charge Jim fi sus;
dem charge mi fi murdah.

Mama,
doan fret,
doan get depres'
an' doun-hearted
Be af good courage
till I hear fram you.

I remain,
your son,
Sonny

Linton Kwesi Johnson
Inglan is a Bitch
(Race Today Publications)

WAYS OF WORKING

Letters are perhaps best approached through other sections in this book, like
authentic letters in a documentary project asking permission to go round a factory,
or to get things done. But here are a few possibilities that can be developed by the
student and teacher considering them and taking them further.

● Through responding to the different tones and voices of the letters included
in this section decide which person you would most like to meet and the kinds
of questions you would like to ask him/her.

● Listen to Linton Kwesi Johnson's reggae-backed version of 'Sonny's lettah'
on *Forces of Victory*, Virgin Records. How differently do you receive these spoken
and written versions as a listener/reader?

● In small groups talk through the differences in Bert Fielder's and Wilfred Owen's
reactions to the First World War. Which view do you believe in most? Also you
might like to follow up the other letters of the period, e.g. those by Robert Graves,
Edmund Blunden, Isaac Rosenberg, Siegfried Sassoon, and visit the Imperial War
Museum where they also have collections of letters from ordinary soldiers.

● The letter from the School of Barbiana is an open one to a public audience
about an issue that the students feel deeply concerned about. Are there any
subjects in your school, college, local area that you feel strongly enough about

to want to make a case through an open letter, to be published in your local newsletter, magazine, community newspaper? Possible subjects might be: Would you send your child to a Comprehensive school, Grammar school or Public school: A review of your own education; Unemployment among teenagers; Exploitation of youth styles (music, clothes, hair etc.) by people who want to make money out of them.

● Look carefully at examples of letter stories (like 'Computers don't argue' by Gordon Dickson in *Story 3* (Penguin) and 'Too many funerals' by David McRobbie in *The Blue Storyhouse* (OUP). Try to write your own on an experience that means something to you, e.g. an exchange of love letters, an attempt to claim your full rights from the DHSS, an argument with a mail order firm, a misunderstanding with the local police, etc. Before you start, talk through in groups how you might explore different styles in the letters according to different audiences and contexts.

● Perhaps you would like to follow up the other work of one of the letter writers included here. For instance try and track down, through your school or local library, volumes 1 and 2 of the collected letters of D.H. Lawrence, (Cambridge University Press), Robert Frost's poems, Edwin Muir's poem 'The Horses' to go with a reading of Derek Hawes' letter, Wilfred Owen's biography by Jon Stallworthy and Dominic Hibberd's edition of Wilfred Owen's work called *War Poems and Others* (Chatto and Windus), where the poems are interwoven with the letters, and the complete version of George Jackson's prison letters, *Soledad Brother* (Jonathan Cape and Penguin).

● In small groups talk through how you might have responded to and answered George Jackson's letters from prison if you had been one of his parents.

FURTHER REFERENCES

Soledad Brother George Jackson, Jonathan Cape
Letters Home Sylvia Plath, Faber
Letters from the Great War ed. Michael Moynihan, David and Charles
The Letters of Van Gogh ed. Mark Roskill, Fontana/Collins
The Selected Letters of Robert Frost ed. Lawrence Thompson, Jonathan Cape
The Collected Letters of D.H. Lawrence: volumes 1 and 2, CUP
Love Letters ed. Antonia Fraser, Weidenfeld and Nicholson/Penguin
The Letters of John Keats ed. Maurice Forman, OUP
Lucy's Letters from *Cut-Way Feelings Loving and Lucy's Letters* James Berry, Strange Lime Fruit Stone, Stafford and London
The Selected Letters of Edwin Muir ed. P.H. Butter, The Hogarth Press
The Collected Essays, Journalism and Letters: Volumes 1–4, George Orwell, Penguin
The Collected Letters of Byron ed. Marquand, John Murray

The Mark Twain-Howells Letters (2 volumes) ed. Smith and Gibson, Belknap Press, Harvard

Selected Prose Gerard Manley Hopkins ed. G. Roberts, OUP

War Poems and Others Wilfred Owen, Chatto and Windus

The Letters of James Joyce ed. Richard Ellman, Faber

'Letters of a Crewe Factory Girl to the Crewe Chronicle' from *The Life and Writings of a Working Woman* Ada Nield Chew, Virago

A Message from the Falklands David Tinker, Penguin

5
Journalism

INTRODUCTION

Journalism arises from a need to satisfy a popular hunger for information about daily public events. (It is also worth adding that this need can be artificially stimulated by commercial interests.) Journalism tells us what it felt like to be there, as with the report from the Argentinian soldier in the Falkland Islands, experiencing the events as they occurred. That is why journalism as a form can often connect most directly with students' everyday habits of looking around them and wanting to record what they see. Community, school/college newspapers can valuably emerge from the students' inquisitiveness and need to make sense of the daily happenings that occur with bewildering complexity around them.

News is never a neutral account. It always expresses a viewpoint that reflects the overall editorial control and direction of a particular agency. So Pilger's version of the Vietnam war makes revealing reading alongside the two angles on the Falklands. Pilger's view is one from the bottom up, a treatment of the underdog's perspective as suits an article originally published in the *New Statesman.* But the *Daily Mirror* article shows how inflammatory news reporting can be in war-time. The Waind piece is also worth considering in detail in this context.

It is the need for instant appeal in journalism that often produces problems; banner headlines punch out at us one day, fade away the next, and by the end of the following week are forgotten completely. And it is this transience of journalism, allied to its constant need to grab the limited attention of a busy reader, that leads to the peculiar difficulties of choice and selection in this section.

We haven't wanted to linger on the ephemeral product of much popular journalism, nor have we wanted to set up a detailed exploration of what is wrong with the popular press (see *The Manufacture of News* by S. Cohen and J. Young, Constable, for an example of that kind of approach); but we have wanted to stress some of the more constructive examples of what can be done within the constraints indicated above. That has proved hard. In such a changing world one cannot predict with total certainty that Polly Toynbee, Andrea Waind, Keith

Waterhouse will last, but they do offer examples of some of the more positive possibilities.

What are the special qualities of this kind of writing? Dramatic surprise is one of the main, initial prerequisites. Look at the unexpectedness of an opening like John Pilger's 'Fats was shot in 1967–', or Andrea Waind's 'The apprentice millionaire glues two pieces of wood together'. Often this effect works through a shockingly bizarre contrast, like the ending of John Hersey's piece: 'There, in the tin factory, in the first moment of the atomic age, a human being was crushed by books.'

The sense of urgency can come through dialogue or interviews, as in the examples here. Also important is a strong eye for arresting, physical detail or the sudden, graphic image, as in the Pilger reference to 'portable electric flush lavatories, all puce coloured'. Another necessary feature is the line of argument, which when misused can actually be given a spurious legitimacy through the allusive use of uncredited opinion polls or alarmist statistics.

Effective humour is not so easy to achieve when you are up against a deadline, but the Keith Waterhouse and Alan Coren pieces seem to us to work well. The 'Talking turkey' piece is built around the contrast between long-winded 'gobbledygook' and a direct, plain use of language, and as such embodies much of the general argument Waterhouse puts forward in his 'Writing for the *Daily Mirror'* extracts.

Coren works more urbanely, creating a collision between the spiritual associations of 'Genesis' and estate agents' blurbs, in a witty example of how to make comic use of mixed forms.

In terms of the language of journalism, Keith Waterhouse gives specific advice on adjectives, jargon and clichés and general comments on how to improve the popular press: 'It can throw out much of its cliché-ridden, pun-barnacled vocabulary and invest in a good, modern supply of plain English. It can dismantle ancient, cor-blimey headlines which have become as familiar as the neon signs in Piccadilly Circus. It can re-examine the stereotyped news values that encourages stereotyped observation.'

It is this challenging of stale, second-hand, news values and attitudes, as found in the best writing of Hersey, Mayhew, Orwell, Pilger, that leads to some of the most searching journalism.

There is a wide difference in this selection of writing between those journalists who see their job primarily in terms of conveying news and those mainly concerned with commenting on it. In practice the perception of newsworthy facts is always influenced by an ideological stance, as we have noticed above. So fact and opinion are always working in relation to each other. Nevertheless there are particular emphases to be observed in the writing of all these articles. Toynbee can see her approach to the news as one of standing back and making considered comments on general tendencies emerging from the daily events. But Hersey, although clearly holding his own opinions, views his main task as one of describing what he sees.

TALKING TURKEY

An American airline steward, apparently educated, civilised and sober, delivered himself of the following as my Boeing 747 touched down.

'Ladies and gentlemen, for your further safety at this time, please arrange to remain in your seats until the aircraft has finalised completal at the arrival point.'

Since we were in a jumbo jet, I suppose it was in order for him to speak mumbo-jumbo.

But also, or further, an American student – upon hearing that I was a journalist (or 'into the media', as he put it) – asked me how, Unitedstateswise, I assessed the downward readjustment gig. He meant, what did I think about the depression.

An American taxi-driver told me that transportation in the City of New York was reaching totality. He meant the traffic jams were bad.

An American hotel man told me that the new name of the game is prime-comfort indoctrination, because of the need to maintain accommodations in premium condition. He meant – but who the hell knows what he meant?

It is a mistake – a communicative oversimplification, as an American might say – to believe that we speak the same language. We get burgled – they get burglarised. We take medicine – they are on medicaments, or under medication.

It is a sign of the times – a signalment of the epoch – that an American Ambassador has just gone home after five-and-a-half years, remembered for nothing except that he experienced some discomfiture as a result of a need for elements of refurbishing.

When I first visited the United States over twenty years ago, they said tomayto and we said tomahto. That was all right by me. I didn't even mind when we said tomahto and they said a king-sized California sun-kissed breakfast-fresh juicy-fruity tomayto sliced like mother used to make and served with the dressing of your choice.

I began to object when a tomayto became a gourmet-connoisseur nourishment-guaranteed food in nature's own pack, sold at a retail outlet and weight-computerised for your convenience.

The American phrase 'for your convenience' is one that fills me with terror. It means that something is going to go wrong. I saw it at Boston airport and immediately had no wish to come home.

TWA, 'for your convenience', had computerised their boarding-passes. Wives were separated from husbands in the mad scramble to get aboard, non-smokers coughed in the smoking section and smokers fumed in the non-smoking seats – which were introduced, incidentally, 'for your further enjoyment'.

The American phrase 'for your further enjoyment' means that you are going to be stopped from doing something you were doing quite happily until an overall consumer assessment was made by young men in dark suits.

What has happened to the American language is that it is now more or less owned by business concerns. They run it, 'hopefully', at a profit or at least on a break-even cost basis, in order to facilitate their operability. And somehow, it's like putting fluoride in the water.

The gobbledygook is processed by the business colleges and the advertising agencies and the legal offices and the computer workshops (both hardware and software divisions) and somehow – in a high-density communication situation – it's transmitted to the ordinary American citizen.

Thus my hotel waiter promises me a 'failsafe' in the way of a vodka-and-tonic if my 'vodki down' (that's a vodka martini on the rocks, being the opposite of a vodka martini not on the rocks, or straight up) is 'not viable'. Thus the hero of my favourite TV soap opera, on finding his wife in the bedroom with another man, tells her: 'There's got to be some attempted justification, a rationale, some kind of scenario, for your behavioural pattern of late.'

I heard a sales executive, explaining why a certain customer service (consumer facilitation) no longer existed, say that it had been mediated to an upper-cut point.

H.L. Mencken, who was the custodian of the American language as Dr Fowler and Eric Partridge were the custodians of ours, must be turning in his grave. Or do I mean that current probabilities suggest he would be contemplating taking up a resumed position in his finalised accommodatiory container?

I must say I enjoyed American more when it was the bee's knees and the cat's pyjamas.

Keith Waterhouse
Rhubarb, Rhubarb (Sphere Books)

THE OTHER ARGENTINA

Fabián is a guitarist in a rock group. He lives with his parents and a younger sister in a simple, but spacious house, with a beautiful garden. He completed his national service on March 8 1982. On April 9, they called him up again, and, on the 13th, he was moved to the Falklands. His platoon, on Mount Longdon, was in the most advanced position of the whole regiment, and it suffered the heaviest losses.

The tremendous English attack on the night of June 11 surprised Fabián as he was doing guard duty. He heard voices, distant at first, but soon much closer. He woke his colleagues just at the moment that hundreds of tracer bullets began raining down on them. They tried, in vain, to reach the cannon for which they were responsible. Alone, with no orders, without even the most elementary of weapons, there was nothing they could do. Except scramble back to their trench. And wait. They spent the whole night in hiding. Miraculously, the advancing English actually trod on the roofing of the trench, but did not discover them. The next morning, they came out into the open. They were taken prisoners.
Fabián describes the experience.

It was the worst night of my life. I spent the whole night trembling, praying that we wouldn't be found, that a grenade wouldn't hit us. At first, grenades were exploding all around us, and then, by the sound of the voices that grew

MIRROR Comment

THE HARLOT OF FLEET ST.

THE Sun

THE SUN, a coarse and demented newspaper, yesterday accused The Daily Mirror, The Guardian and Mr Peter Snow of the BBC of being traitors to Britain.

What The Sun means by treachery is a refusal to twist, distort and mangle the truth about the fighting in the South Atlantic.

No one could accuse The Sun of failing to do that.

There have been lying newspapers before. But in the past month it has broken all records.

It has long been a tawdry newspaper. But since the Falklands crisis began it has fallen from the gutter to the sewer.

Anyone who dares question Mrs Thatcher—in the Press, in politics, in television or on the radio—is a coward, according to The Sun.

ANYONE who fails to urge the immediate sending of troops into battle is denounced for treason.

For its part, The Sun has exulted at the death of Argentine sailors. "Gotcha!" it shrilled when the cruiser General Belgrano, with over 1,000 men aboard, was torpedoed.

Proudly it boasted it had sponsored a missile which brought down an Argentine warplane. With a crudity which sickens other journalists, its reporter with the task force wrote, "Up yours, Galtieri" on the side of the missile. The Sun is the harlot of Fleet Street.

It has been seen on American TV as an example of how British newspapers cover the crisis. Far from helping our cause, it shames it.

From behind the safety of its typewriters it has called for battle to commence to satisfy its bloodlust. The Sun today is to journalism what Dr Josef Goebbels was to truth. Even Pravda would blush to be bracketed with it.

The Daily Mirror does not believe that patriotism has to be proved in blood. Especially someone else's blood.

We have said that in the last resort, if all else fails, force would have to be used to eject Argentina from the Falklands.

We also know that but for the bungling of the Government to which The Sun gives such hysterical support this crisis need never have arisen.

If force has finally to be used it must be to retrieve the freedom of the islanders. Not to save Mrs Thatcher's reputation. Nor to secure military revenge for a political defeat.

We do not want to report that brave men have died so that The Sun's circulation might flourish.

THOUGH such is the temper of the British people that they are as likely to be repelled by The Sun's treatment of the fighting as is every decent British journalist.

The Daily Mirror believes that there should be a ceasefire now so that the diplomats can search again for peace.

That is not only our view. It is what the Foreign Secretary, Mr Francis Pym, has been working for.

If that is treachery, then Mrs Thatcher has just recruited a traitor to No. 10 Downing Street.

For the new head of the unit which advises her on policy is a distinguished political journalist, Mr Ferdinand Mount. And in this week's Spectator he calls for a ceasefire.

How long before the proprietor of The Sun, Mr Rupert Murdoch, an Australian who lives in New York, adds Mr Mount to his blacklist?

A Labour MP yesterday called for The Sun to be prosecuted for criminal libel. There is no point in that. It has the perfect defence: Guilty but insane.

What would be more useful would be if The Sun was compelled to carry an official Government announcement on each copy: "Warning : reading this newspaper may damage your mind."

The Sun's crude handling of the Belgrano attack.

The Sun features a Jumbo airlift. It never took place.

The Sun's flip response to an Argentine peace move.

The Sun's "dawn attack" told before it happened.

Thatcher's new adviser says:

Ferdinand Mount

Spectator
Time for a cease fire
Ferdinand Mount

Front cover of The Spectator

louder, we could tell that the English army was moving off. I was lying on the ground, clinging to my helmet, as if that would give me more protection. I had Carlos and Gustavo on either side of me. There was complete silence. No one wanted to breathe too deeply in case they discovered us. It was a terrifying moment. We didn't know how they'd react if they found us. Our guns were all broken, and so, unarmed, we had no way of defending ourselves. We heard voices on all sides of our position. It was still dark, and, surrounded by rocks, we weren't easy to find. The hours went by. We were still flat out on the ground, and we didn't say a single word. There was one moment when we almost died of fright: some English, running past and shouting, passed right over our heads. They trod on the roof of our position but, somehow, didn't discover us. I thought I was going to die; my heart felt like it was going to explode. 'Why can't they find us?' I thought. They had passed directly over our heads and we heard the crunch of their boots on the metal sheet we had put up as a roof. It was a miracle that they didn't find us.

Dawn came. We thought we were the only survivors from the whole company. We had no idea what had happened to the rest. We began to talk in whispers. 'What do we do now?' we asked each other. 'If we get out, maybe they'll kill us.' We eventually decided that we couldn't hide for ever. It would soon be nine o'clock in the morning. We heard a few English talking near by. I suppose they didn't even consider looking inside our position because they thought that there couldn't be anyone left at that time of day. Suddenly we heard the familiar voice of one of our officers. 'They've taken him prisoner,' we said. 'Let's take our chance while we can and get out.' Carlos was closest to the exit. 'I'll go first,' he said. He took everything off – his helmet, his belt, and left only his 9mm pistol. 'Cover me,' said Carlos. 'If they shoot kill at least one of them.' He left. Gustavo and I held our breath in the trench. Carlos stepped out right in front of an Englishman. I think the chap asked him how many there were of us and Carlos signalled three with his fingers. We got out of the trench, with our hands above our heads. I saw the light again: it was a sunny day.

Daniel Kon
Los Chicos de la Guerra
(New English Library)

HEROES

'Fats' was shot in 1967, and I feel ashamed that I have long since forgotten his name. He lay with his stunned, bleached face and his sergeant, trying to stem a crescendo of screams, which were heard through the night and dawn and remain as memorable as the place where he fell: a trench in which were stacked boxes of toothbrushes, thousands of them, and party balloons and portable electric flush lavatories, all puce coloured, and New York cut steaks packed in dry ice. Fats was a United States Marine, a 'grunt' in a Combined Action Company, better known as a 'hearts and minds' unit. The toothbrushes, balloons and lavatories were to win the hearts and minds of Vietnamese villagers in 'Indian country': the steak was for the next day's barbecue in honour of a colonel who had promised to bring out beer for 'my boys who never say die'. In the colonel's office in Danang were the framed words: 'Grab 'em by the balls and their hearts and minds will follow'. Lyndon Johnson is alleged to have coined that.

One year later I looked up Fats's sergeant in upstate New York and found him on a porch, coming out of a bender. He had uttered barely a word about the war since his return home with a piece of shrapnel, knife-shaped, in his neck because nobody wanted to listen. To former friends in the peace movement he was a pariah or a dupe or a child-killer; to his own community he was obsolete; to his family he was an embarrassment, though they never said as much.

He came home just as the Vietcong were storming the American embassy in Saigon and Walter Cronkite was handing down a televised tablet to the nation: 'Thou shalt no longer support this war, for it is lost'. Fats, he reported, was 'in some bad VA hospital, dead up to his neck'. Both men had volunteered for the Marines, having been weaned on John Wayne, to whom Jimmy Carter felt moved to give some ridiculous posthumous medal and who never saw action in any war. Both men were decorated and given a disability allowance that would keep them in Kentucky fried chicken and little else. Both men had fussed protectively over me, a terrified civilian in their midst, when half the village turned into Vietcong and had come over the wire, bearing hearts and minds and AK-47s.

When they left for Vietnam they were American winners − the kind John Wayne evangelists were proud of; now they were losers and among the first to be drafted into a great invisible army assigned to a purgatory of silence, shame, indifference. In 1979 a national poll found that 62 per cent of American people believed that veterans of Vietnam 'fought in the wrong war, in the wrong place, at the wrong time, and were suckers'.

Vietnam was the longest war this century, in which more Marines died than during all of World War Two, and 80 per cent of all those who served were volunteers. There is not a single national monument to the dead of that war, nor has there been a great parade of the kind America relishes; of the kind given to the 52 American 'heroes' held hostage in Iran and then celebrated relentlessly, although their faces were unzapped by the 'friendly fire' of Napalm and their testicles were intact and their body cells undisturbed by cancers resulting from chemical warfare. When a group of disabled Vietnam veterans took their hurt to the White House, President Carter was 'unavailable'. One of his media men, in a loud aside, said. 'You have got to understand these guys are a no-votes situation'. Bob Muller, in his wheelchair, heard that.

I never met Bob Muller in Vietnam, but I vividly remember him being thrown out of the Republican Party's nomination circus for Richard Nixon in 1972 − in his wheelchair. Bob Muller, a Marine lieutenant, having lost the use of his legs and gained a chest-load of ribbons and medals, was a Grade-A hero: but, alas, there he was spoiling it all by bellowing at Nixon that the war was unwinnable and genocidal. Seven years later I saw this hero again, shrunken and more fragile now, on the steps of New York's City Hall.

It was a Memorial Day and there were uniforms and salutes and dignitaries, although Bob Muller's was the only broken body in view. He had hold of a microphone and within seconds had silenced even the construction site beyond the crowd. 'Listen to me!' he commanded, 'there are 280,000 veterans of Vietnam in New York alone, and a *third* of them can't find jobs. Throughout America *sixty per cent* of all black combat veterans are unemployed. Almost *half* of all combat veterans are either alcoholics or addicted to drugs, or in pain in the head and just as many are probably dying now from the poisons we dumped over there as died in the battlefield. You people out there ran a number on us, right? Your guilt, your hangups make you walk away from us; we wear artificial legs so *you* won't know we're disabled veterans. Why do we feel like we just held up a bank when someone asks us about our wounds? Why do we feel that, if we believe in America, we must be guilty for letting America down or, if we're critical of America, we can't explain even to ourselves why we went over there and needlessly killed civilians? Eight of my friends, with legs like these, killed themselves when they got home; we've got the *highest* suicide rate in America . . . and that's all I want to say to you today'.

Bob Muller now runs Vietnam Veterans of America from an almost bare office adjacent to a wholesaler of dolls, at the seedy end of Fifth Avenue. There is seldom enough money to pay the telephone bill, in contrast with the Government Veterans Administration, which devotes much of its powerfully-lobbied budget to the running of a chain of nursing homes, mostly for veterans of the two world wars and Korea: the 'winners'. The statistics Bob Muller punched at the Memorial Day assembly included those borne out by a five-volume study by the Centre for Policy Research in New York and commissioned by the Veterans Association. The results made such a mockery of previous official estimates of the distress of Vietnam veterans that the government 'lost' the report until Muller's organisation forced its release under the Freedom of Information Act. The study found that more than a third of Vietnam veterans were suffering from 'delayed stress syndrome' – a slow-fuse psychological disturbance quite distinct from the 'shell shock' and 'combat fatigue' of the world wars, and unique to the Vietnam experience of terror, atrocities and guilt sustained in the cause of nothing.

Alonza Gibbs, whom I met in Philadelphia, was blown up by mortar fire and suffered multiple gunshot wounds. He said that a third of his company had been wiped out by inept air strikes ordered by the company commander. (This was not uncommon: thus the term 'friendly fire'.) He watched Vietnamese prisoners interrogated, then thrown out of helicopters and others laced together with a detonating cord which, when pulled, blew their heads off. 'We had a battalion commander who is a general now', he said. 'I believe he's a cissy. He issued all of us with hatchets and offered a case of whisky to the first man to chop somebody's head off. And, sure enough, a head got chopped off. Some of his boys are right here now, crazier than bed bugs'.

Decorated for trying to save the life of a comrade, Alonza Gibbs now seldom sleeps, is in constant pain from his wounds, drinks too much and suffers, almost certainly, from delayed stress syndrome. 'His personality is completely changed', says his sister, with whom he lives. He fought in Vietnam in 1965 and says that a

Veterans Administration doctor told him, 'There is nothing wrong with you that a young man won't snap out of'. In the last two years he has received about £20 a month. 'I didn't like to face up to it at first,' he said, 'but the fact is if I go for a job and tell the man I was in Vietnam, I don't get the job'.

This rejection by employers is also part of the 'Vietnam syndrome'. After World War Two it was deemed a 'patriotic duty' to employ a returned soldier. By comparison, most of the Vietnam veterans I interviewed spoke of not getting a job, regardless of their qualifications, whenever they listed their service record – 'in the time honoured way', as one veteran put it, 'that blacks are politely turned down'. One veteran was told outright: 'This plant is not taking on any Vietnam dope addicts'. Mike Sulsona, a New York double amputee, wears artificial legs, with pain, chiefly because he wishes to disguise the fact he is a disabled Vietnam veteran. 'When I'm in the wheelchair', he said, 'I'm asked about my legs and if I say "Vietnam" the embarrassment and at times hostility is too much to take.'

World War Two and Korea veterans were 'rewarded' with the GI Bill which Lyndon Johnson reluctantly re-introduced in 1966, but with a catch: it gave Vietnam veterans £1500 a year *less* than their fathers received more than 30 years earlier. In 1972 Nixon vetoed the Veterans Medical Care Expansion Act, calling it 'fiscally irresponsible and inflationary'. The United States then had spent some $165 billion pursuing its task of human and environmental vandalism in Southeast Asia, which Ronald Reagan was to call, in 1980, 'our noble cause'.

'I was an infantry officer', said Bob Muller, 'I had the battleship *New Jersey* fire in support of me in the DMZ. I had jet strikes one after the other. I had an hour and a half of heavy artillery many, many times. It was *routine* for me to spend £100,000 a day to kill people. Then I get shot in the process, come back home and my government tells me it's fiscally irresponsible and inflationary to provide adequate medical care in the hospital! Can you imagine what that does to us?'

What that does to them is to punish them for losing and, worse, for *admitting* failure and for shouting the secret of Vietnam: that it was a war of rampant, experimental technology against a peasant people who were, from the beginning, racially expendable. Not a 'mistake' as the tribunes of the American liberal consensus, now gone to ground, used to say; but a crime without the finale of a Nuremberg. The veterans 'punishment' continued under Jimmy Carter who, in his first fireside chat as President, promised 'top priority' to creating jobs for disabled veterans. Out of 21,000 seriously disabled veterans, 500 were offered work. During last year's Presidential election campaigns, Ronald Reagan said: 'To me it's the height of hypocrisy for the Carter administration to repeatedly tell us how much we owe our Vietnam veterans, then recommend a stingy ten per cent increase in the GI Bill. They deserve pure gratitude, our respect and our continuing concern . . .'

Last March, President Reagan asked Congress to cut the few programmes designed to help Vietnam veterans find jobs, finish their education and be treated for drug addiction and alcoholism. Ninety-one 'Outreach' programme counselling centres, many of them in the poorest parts of cities and towns, have become a small salvation to many veterans. David Stockman, who runs Reagan's Office of

Management and Budget, who evaded the draft by confining himself to divinity school, wants to close them all down.

Reagan's elevation of the Vietnam war as a 'noble cause' which 'ought to have been won' and the relegation of those who bear the war's truth to the boweries of the nation fits nicely into the 'gameplan' for the next 'noble cause'. And if that one fails it, too, can be absolved as a 'tragic mistake.' Vengeance for the humiliation in Vietnam has dominated American global strategy since the day, six years ago, when Ambassador Graham Martin and his poodle were lifted by helicopter out of the US embassy in Saigon. Since then, three administrations have worked to restore the United States from Nixon's memorable 'pitiless giant' to Reagan's 'shining house on the hill'. Reading the newspapers now, deleting Vietnam and writing in El Salvador, the stories seem uncannily similar. In a front page report in the *New York Times* of 28 July 1964, headlined 'US To Enlarge Vietnam Force by 5000 Advisers', there is this gem: 'There was still no sign of a United States decision to carry the war into North Vietnam or throw American units into combat'. In the *Daily Telegraph* of 5 March 1981, under the headline 'No Combat Troops for Salvador,' there is the news that Congress will not block the sending of additional military advisers to El Salvador and that President Reagan sees 'no likelihood' of US troops going into combat.

Like Kennedy, Johnson, Nixon and Ford then, Haig and Reagan now see the world in the same obsessional and obtuse terms, speaking of dominoes as if nations were mere blocks of wood, not complex societies riven with profound differences and cultural animosities. 'It isn't just El Salvador', said Reagan. 'That happens to be the target at the moment. Our problem is this whole hemisphere and keeping this sort of thing out'. Johnson and Nixon spoke almost precisely those words; only the geography changed.

Perhaps the lies that power the escalator going up to the inevitable are more obvious now, but the escalator keeps moving. Indeed, the fabled 'line' that was drawn in Vietnam 'to stop the advance of Chinese communism' is being drawn once again, this time to keep out the forces of 'Soviet-backed international terrorism' in Central America which mysteriously threaten the most powerful nation on earth.

No matter that armed and battle-ready exiled foreign 'freedom fighters' — surely international terrorists by the White House's standards — are training openly, and illegally, in Florida. No matter that even the CIA, in common with other US intelligence groups, has questioned the catch-all charge against Moscow that it is running the international terrorist show, because the Soviet Union is as much beset by 'terrorism' as any other adventurous imperial power: for example, in Afghanistan and Eritrea where it is using weapons and tactics studiously copied from the Americans in Vietnam — yet another brutal irony. No matter that the former American ambassador in El Salvador, Robert White, has told a Congressional hearing that the war in that country is caused by social injustice and that the real terrorists are the regime backed by Haig and Reagan. 'The security forces in El Salvador have been responsible for the deaths of thousands and thousands of young people', said White, 'and they have executed them on the mere suspicion that they are leftists or sympathise with leftists. Are we *really* going to be part of all that . . .?' No matter that the Reagan administration's real aim is to be seen 'hanging tough', as Nixon used to say, in a little country where the options are soft and the fodder is plentiful.

The policy of hanging tough, partly to justify a war economy and partly in the cause of vengeance, is double-handed: while adventure is pursued in El Salvador (and, less obtrusively, in much of Central America) revenge is exacted in Vietnam itself. The Reagan administration's commitment to 'another Vietnam' is deeper than those Americans who oppose it realise; and it is not purely American. According to the excellent Center for International Policy in Washington, $523 million will go to the El Salvador junta after Washington applies its persuasive powers to the World Bank, the Inter-American Development Bank and the International Monetary Fund and after it 'harnesses' the European donors, regardless of their public utterances of distaste for the new adventure. Not that the Thatcher government has uttered any such distaste. Indeed, which government is likely to give more money than any European government, more than Canada, more than Argentina and Brazil, to a regime patently guilty of murdering its own people? Margaret Thatcher's government, of course.

Half a world away, in Vietnam, about which we hear little these days, there is the beginning of famine. Six million Vietnamese are faced with 'serious malnutrition', according to a UN Food and Agricultural Organisation group. Rations are now less than ever during the war years: less than half the daily amount of food needed for a healthy survival. General Haig has now said publicly that the United States intends to 'squeeze' Vietnam in every way: 'de-stabilisation' once more. The Japanese and the EEC have sent no relief: Britain long ago cut off its piddling humanitarian aid.

In May 1981 China carried out a 'punitive' action against Vietnam's northern border, similar to its attack in 1979 which had prior American approval. Last week the 'landbridge' from Thailand to Cambodia was re-opened, allowing Western, chiefly American sustenance to flow more conveniently to Pol Pot's Khmer Rouge and thus to accelerate the 'de-stabilisation' of Cambodia and Vietnam and to push both countries deeper into the arms of the Soviet Union, which neither wants. In Cu Chi, near Saigon, which I remember as thick forest, there is today a shimmering horizon of wilderness which has been poisoned, perhaps for generations. Eleven million gallons of the herbicide Agent Orange were dumped on Vietnam; its chief ingredient, dioxin, is estimated to be a thousand times more destructive than thalidomide. Blind and deformed babies are now common in those areas sprayed during Operation Hades, later re-named Operation Ranch Hand.

Charlie Hartz, a Vietnam veteran who was exposed to Agent Orange, is going blind and is dying from cancer. His four children were born deformed. He is one of many veterans similarly afflicted, and none of them has been compensated. In Beallsville, Ohio, Betty Rucker still has the telegram which told her that her son, Rick, was killed by 'a friendly rocket'. When Rick went off to war, Mrs Rucker thought Vietnam was 'somewhere near Cuba or Panama, real close and threatening'. Considering events today, her remark, made to me a decade ago, is searing in its irony.

Indeed, as we now know, US 'advisers' have arrived in that very region, and more are to follow, but of course they will only shoot their guns in self-defence, just as it was in Vietnam, in the beginning. And if they do find themselves shooting their guns, they will need to be 'protected'; and then there is the 'likelihood' if not the certainty that a new generation of heroes, the Ricks and Bobs, the Charlies and Fats, will be on their way.

John Pilger
Aftermath (New Statesman)

HIROSHIMA

After an alarm, Father Kleinsorge always went out and scanned the sky, and this time, when he stepped outside, he was glad to see only the single weather plane that flew over Hiroshima each day about this time. Satisfied that nothing would happen, he went in and breakfasted with the other Fathers on substitute coffee and ration bread, which, under the circumstances, was especially repugnant to him. The Fathers sat and talked a while, until, at eight, they heard the all-clear. They went then to various parts of the building. Father Schiffer retired to his room to do some writing. Father Cieslik sat in his room in a straight chair with a pillow over his stomach to ease his pain, and read. Father Superior LaSalle stood at the window of his room, thinking. Father Kleinsorge went up to a room on the third floor, took off all his clothes except his underwear, and stretched out on his right side on a cot and began reading his *Stimmen der Zeit*.

After the terrible flash – which, Father Kleinsorge later realized, reminded him of something he had read as a boy about a large meteor colliding with the earth – he had time (since he was 1400 yards from the centre) for one thought: A bomb has fallen directly on us. Then, for a few seconds or minutes, he went out of his mind.

Father Kleinsorge never knew how he got out of the house. The next things he was conscious of were that he was wandering around in the mission's vegetable garden in his underwear, bleeding slightly from small cuts along his left flank; that all the buildings round about had fallen down except the Jesuits' mission house, which had long before been braced and double-braced by a priest named Gropper, who was terrified of earthquakes; that the day had turned dark; and that Murata-*san*, the housekeeper, was near by, crying over and over, *Shu Jesusu, awaremi tamai!* Our Lord Jesus, have pity on us!'

On the train on the way into Hiroshima from the country, where he lived with his mother, Dr Terufumi Sasaki, the Red Cross Hospital surgeon, thought over an unpleasant nightmare he had had the night before. His mother's home was in Mukaihara, thirty miles from the city, and it took him two hours by train and tram to reach the hospital. He had slept uneasily all night and had wakened an hour earlier than usual, and, feeling sluggish and slightly feverish, had debated

173

whether to go to the hospital at all; his sense of duty finally forced him to go, and he had started out on an earlier train than he took most mornings. The dream had particularly frightened him because it was so closely associated, on the surface at least, with a disturbing actuality. He was only twenty-five years old and had just completed his training at the Eastern Medical Univeristy, in Tsingtao, China. He was something of an idealist and was much distressed by the inadequacy of medical facilities in the country town where his mother lived. Quite on his own, and without a permit, he had begun visiting a few sick people out there in the evenings, after his eight hours at the hospital and four hours' commuting. He had recently learned that the penalty for practising without a permit was severe; a fellow-doctor whom he had asked about it had given him a serious scolding. Nevertheless, he had continued to practise. In his dream, he had been at the bedside of a country patient when the police and the doctor he had consulted burst into the room, seized him, dragged him outside, and beat him up cruelly. On the train, he just about decided to give up the work in Mukaihara, since he felt it would be impossible to get a permit, because the authorities would hold that it would conflict with his duties at the Red Cross Hospital.

At the terminus, he caught a street-car at once. (He later calculated that if he had taken his customary train that morning, and if he had had to wait a few minutes for the street-car, as often happened, he would have been close to the centre at the time of the explosion and would surely have perished.) He arrived at the hospital at seven-forty and reported to the chief surgeon. A few minutes later, he went to a room on the first floor and drew blood from the arm of a man in order to perform a Wassermann test. The laboratory containing the incubators for the test was on the third floor. With the blood specimen in his left hand, walking in a kind of distraction he had felt all morning, probably because of the dream and his restless night, he started along the main corridor on his way toward the stairs. He was one step beyond an open window when the light of the bomb was reflected, like a gigantic photographic flash, in the corridor. He ducked down on one knee and said to himself, as only a Japanese would, 'Sasaki, *gambare!* Be brave!' Just then (the building was 1650 yards from the centre), the blast ripped through the hospital. The glasses he was wearing flew off his face; the bottle of blood crashed against one wall; his Japanese slippers zipped out from under his feet – but otherwise, thanks to where he stood, he was untouched.

Dr Sasaki shouted the name of the chief surgeon and rushed around to the man's office and found him terribly cut by glass. The hospital was in horrible confusion: heavy partitions and ceilings had fallen on patients, beds had overturned, windows had blown in and cut people, blood was spattered on the walls and floors, instruments were everywhere, many of the patients were running about screaming, many more lay dead. (A colleague working in the laboratory to which Dr Sasaki had been walking was dead; Dr Sasaki's patient, whom he had just left and who a few moments before had been dreadfully afraid of syphilis, was also dead.) Dr Sasaki found himself the only doctor in the hospital who was unhurt.

Dr Sasaki, who believed that the enemy had hit only the building he was in, got bandages and began to bind the wounds of those inside the hospital; while outside, all over Hiroshima, maimed and dying citizens turned their unsteady steps toward the Red Cross Hospital to begin an invasion that was to make Dr Sasaki forget his private nightmare for a long, long time.

Miss Toshiko Sasaki, the East Asia Tin Works clerk, who is not related to Dr Sasaki, got up at three o'clock in the morning on the day the bomb fell. There was extra housework to do. Her eleven-month-old brother, Akio, had come down the day before with a serious stomach upset; her mother had taken him to the Tamura Pediatric Hospital and was staying there with him. Miss Sasaki, who was about twenty, had to cook breakfast for her father, a brother, a sister, and herself, and – since the hospital, because of the war, was unable to provide food – to prepare a whole day's meals for her mother and the baby, in time for her father, who worked in a factory making rubber earplugs for artillery crews, to take the food by on his way to the plant. When she had finished and had cleaned and put away the cooking things, it was nearly seven. The family lived in Koi, and she had a forty-five-minute trip to the tin works, in the section of town called Kannon-machi. She was in charge of the personnel records in the factory. She left Koi at seven, and as soon as she reached the plant, she went with some of the other girls from the personnel department to the factory auditorium. A prominent local Navy man, a former employee, had committed suicide the day before by throwing himself under a train – a death considered honourable enough to warrant a memorial service, which was to be held at the tin works at ten o'clock that morning. In the large hall, Miss Sasaki and the others made suitable preparations for the meeting. This work took about twenty minutes.

Miss Sasaki went back to her office and sat down at her desk. She was quite far from the windows, which were off to her left, and behind her were a couple of tall bookcases containing all the books of the factory library, which the personnel department had organized. She settled herself at her desk, put some things in a drawer, and shifted papers. She thought that before she began to make entries in her lists of new employees, discharges, and departures for the Army, she would chat for a moment with the girl at her right. Just as she turned her head away from the windows, the room was filled with a blinding light. She was paralyzed by fear, fixed still in her chair for a long moment (the plant was 1,600 yards from the centre).

Everything fell, and Miss Sasaki lost consciousness. The ceiling dropped suddenly and the wooden floor above collapsed in splinters and the people up there came down and the roof above them gave way; but principally and first of all, the book-cases right behind her swooped forward and the contents threw her down, with her left leg horribly twisted and breaking underneath her. There, in the tin factory, in the first moment of the atomic age, a human being was crushed by books.

John Hersey
Hiroshima (Penguin)

THE CONCRETE ELEPHANT

The apprentice millionaire glues two pieces of wood together.

'It was a gamble actually. I saw the ad in the paper for managers of small businesses to take a tenancy here. It was either gambling or staying on the dole. I thought, if I'm going to be on the dole for the rest of my life, I'd like to have *tried*. Now I'm on my way to being a millionaire!'

Dave Thomas is Cameo Acoustics Engineers. He makes speakers, assembles them from kits and runs a disco and PA hire service. He is a 31 year old six foot three West Indian with a jaunty cap and matching grin, dwarfing unit No. 7 of the Hyson Green workshops in Nottingham. Speaker units crowd what was once parking space for two cars – or, more likely, dumping space for local industry.

Six hundred garages were built under the main concourse of the Hyson Green flats complex – 31 council blocks, built in 1969. Only 19 of these garages were occupied. Tenants called it the concrete elephant.

'People dumped tellies, cars and mattresses – which dossers then slept on. Business dumped stuff you wouldn't care to investigate,' says Brian Sweet, the fulltime manager of Hyson Green Workshops. 'Kids were molested, doors vandalised. The fire engines were always here.'

Now a section of the garages has been turned into 28 self-contained workshops. Fifteen have been occupied since the opening last May; the Manpower Services Commission is taking six more as youth training workshops. Tenants, behind doors either side of the driveway, include a printer, a joiner, a wrought-iron worker, engineers, a building design draughtsman, language laboratory equipment maker and surgical instruments repairer. They are on the ground floor, but there is no natural light. It is like working in an underground car park.

'Most are first-time ventures,' says Brian Sweet, 'so some are having cash-flow problems. But we've had our first successes. The printer has taken on the first employee and he's expanding into the next unit.'

Hyson Green Workshops is a limited share company which runs the workshops on a 'non profit-making and socially useful basis.' The company leases the property from the city council and sublets the units. Hyson Green tenants' association holds 74 of the 100 £1 shares to the council's 26.

The initiative came from the tenants of the flats. In 1978, their association ran a survey asking what they would most like to change. 'The garages,' they said. Stan Starkey is an original association member:

'There was always a stigma to Hyson Green,' he says. 'A woman's magazine called it Murder Mile. Any crime for miles around is reported as in Hyson Green. A stabbing in Aspley was reported as Hyson Green and that's an hour's walk away. We wanted to reverse the image.'

They organised a garages committee and contacted Brian Moore, a Trent Polytechnic planning department lecturer, who checked for structural defects. 'He called it "redundant space" and knew there was a shortage of small premises. You can get 2000 square feet, but not 250.'

Rob Robinson, a wiry fighter who was the first committee chairman, said:

'In the early days, the council [then Tory] didn't want to know. There was a lack of vision. We had to take councillors to see some London workshops, as they just couldn't imagine it.' Now councillors from Battersea, the Isle of Wight and Llanelli come here.

It was an expensive idea. Conversion cost £250 000, provided under the inner urban area programme and there was a £6000 one-off city grant. 'But the council was paying out £20 000 a year putting out fires, policing and maintaining empty garages,' says Brian Sweet. 'And it's providing jobs, starting the economy from the bottom.'

Dave Thomas plans to take on one or two hi-fi salesmen. He came into disco via an NCB electrical engineering apprenticeship. They gave him a golden hand-shake – 'Well, not *golden*. I was a DJ, then I went into servicing disco equipment. I'm a bit old now to stand there impressing the young people.' Dave was one of six tenants to attend a Trent Polytechnic Small Business Unit course sponsored by the MSC. 'Very useful, especially the book-keeping.'

A couple of doors along, Derek Brown, bundled in jumpers, is finishing a batch of 100 party invitations. It is draughty when the door opens. Down by his feet is a pile of thermal insulation ads.

'Jim [his new boss] wanted his own business. He has plenty of contacts, because he worked for a big printing company. He got fed up because there wasn't much work coming in.' He switches off Radio Trent. This, he says, is much better than his last job: 'A bit crowded, mind.' There are stacks of paper, a large black press, strong ink smells. They'll be glad to spread out next door. Notices and pamphlets cover the door, including *Pink Pages*, the polytechnic Small Business Club magazine. 'We advertise services and have meetings. It's the poor man's Freemasons.'

Contact with the Small Business Unit and the county council-funded Action Resource Centre – which sends a community worker to advise on marketing – comes with the rent (£83.75 a month for a 16 X 16 foot unit, including rates). 'If anyone wants help, we can get it,' says Brian Sweet. He provides office help. 'I do typing and I'm always here to take messages. If the joiner's out joining when his client rings, he'd be in trouble without this phone.'

Brian Sweet, middle-aged, in green tweeds, is an unlikely typist. He was a British Steel personnel manager until he was made redundant. 'We'll probably tart up the tea machine room next door and get an MSC secretary.' He is also the advertising man, arranging group ads at good rates.

The rent also includes background heating ('Not front lounge level, sit-down people like the draughtsmen need a fire'), water, fire sprinkling, security, waste disposal and communal area cleaning. 'The all-in rent means you aren't budgeting away for five months, then wallop. We'll break even in the first year, though next year, with MSC, there'll be a profit to plough back. Hundreds, not thousands.'

Lloyd, the builder who has filled one of the larger units with planks and window frames, calls in the office. He is 25, started ten years ago as an apprentice brick-layer, and has worked for himself for five.

'I use the shop as an office.' It's convenient – 'I work on site locally, do improvements and alterations' – but not ideal. The fire regulations and 8 pm lock-up restrict him: 'I sometimes turn out in the middle of the night.' But he is glad of the double lock system on the gates. 'I had my last place broken into.'

Security is a strong feature. 'We've had no break-ins and the wrought-iron man has started making security grilles. Ironic, for Hyson Green.' The Nottingham summer riot started just outside. 'That set our image back a bit.'

Tenants fit out their own units. The benches of No. 12 are loaded with forceps and syringes. Bill, the assistant, is regrinding hairdressing scissors. His boss is on the road, taking samples round local hospitals.

'We both worked for a surgical firm and he took the chance of starting his own business. Mostly repairing, a bit of manufacturing. We've just started wheelchair repairs.' Above are two sphygmomanometer clocks for testing the motors on ripple beds — which prevent bedsores. 'Our prospects are better now we're on our own.'

Brian Sweet hopes the project will expand. 'I'm a big cost,' he said. 'We need 40 units to support a manager, so I want to see expansion on these premises by 1983, or even this year. And we're looking for similar projects round the city to share costs. Our third aim is to provide something for the community here.' Like a social centre.

'It's very much a model,' says Stan. 'We want to plug into the unemployed skills knocking about. If we do all that we'll run up a flag and declare UDI.'

They are starting with Brian Sweet's first aim. Two engineers are fitting out their units. A man in soft drinks has applied; another wants to open a poodle parlour.

'The lemonade king and the poodle man,' muses Brian Sweet. 'One does like to see a bloke with a lathe rather than a comb, beautifying poodles. I don't know if I'll let him in.'

Andrea Waind
New Society 18.2.82

EXAMINATIONS

If we really want to do something dramatic to improve the lives of our children for this International Year of the Child, we should free their childhood from exams and selection.

At the tender age of 13 or 14 children are weeded out and thrust into O level or CSE classes that will, to all intents and purposes, seal their futures. Then, at the age in their lives when most of them are least receptive to learning, they are forced to sit exams where the penalties for failure are truly momentous.

The lives of secondary school children are dominated by these exams. Comprehensives do of course offer a wide range of enticing subjects, but only for those who are deemed incapable of passing O levels. So parents continue to push, pull, bully and worry their children through exams, or search anxiously for schools with 'high standards' to do the pushing and bullying for them, because that is what our universities demand.

But is there any need for all that? What's the hurry? The labour market is not exactly crying out for very young newly qualified people. Why do we put such pressure on our adolescents? What do they want? Between the ages of 13 and 16 a great many adolescents feel less like studying and learning than at any other time in their lives. The business of growing up is enough. For a lot of the time nothing preoccupies their minds, or they are busy coming to terms with sex, God and socialism. They need time, and space. Often highly motivated children who have read libraries of books suddenly come to a stop at adolescence. It doesn't mean they'll stop forever. With any luck after about 16 or 17 they come out of that phase, but under our present system, that's too late. If they took the wrong course at 14, then they've had their chips. Parents can easily despair at children who given the chance spend half the day in bed, and the other half getting dressed, but it doesn't last for ever. So why do we choose this period in their lives as the time to make or break them?

If the pressures of selection at 16 were removed, secondary education could become a different process altogether. From about 13 onwards children should be free to study if they choose, as obsessively as they like. Or they could choose to study part of the time. They could spend exactly as long as they wanted doing the subjects they wanted to do. Or otherwise they would be free to do nothing. Schools would have sitting space for them to do nothing in. If they wanted to spend half the day in the art rooms, or doing drama that would be their decision. Since the 1930s such progressive schools have existed, but while the present exam system exists, the penalties for encouraging a child to develop its own interests and talents and not satisfy matriculation requirements can be severe.

To torment and terrify recalcitrant adolescents with threats of failure seems to me a scarcely better way to teach than the old methods of beating education into them.

When I consider that between the ages of 5 and 18 at school I was subjected to 17,745 lessons at a time when the brain is biologically at its most receptive, and how little I knew at the end of it all, I am astounded by the waste of time, money and effort. The school day itself is hardly conducive to teaching serious application and concentration, divided up into those arbitrary 40 minute gobbets of learning. Classes shunt along school corridors like cars on a conveyor belt to have a bit of French welded on here, and a bit of geography there, a rivet of algebra hammered on top of a nugget of community studies.

Children bear the brunt of the whole society's aspirations. Standards in education is such an emotive subject because we invest our sense of identity and success in how many A grades at A level the nation can squeeze out of its children. If they do badly then hysterical statements get tossed around the Houses of Parliament declaring that society is rotten, decadent, collapsing. If we are assured that children are still being sufficiently battered with theorems, ablative absolutes, and dates, people breathe easier and feel that society is still on its feet. Ultimately, of course we do have to turn out plenty of highly educated people, but we don't have to cram reluctant adolescents in order to do so. People can learn later, when they are more able and willing to do so.

Most children cannot concentrate under these oppressive conditions. The very act of being taught all day by people who know better is enough to make any but the most highly motivated rebel. The only point of the system is that it makes organisational and administrative sense but it can hardly be called efficient. Why, for instance does it take five years of lessons to get children up to a paltry O level standard French? If someone really wanted to teach an eleven-year-old French and the child actually wanted to learn, it could be done in a matter of months.

The voice of the children themselves is rarely heard, and all too often, when they do write about education, they merely parrot what their teachers and parents have said. But one clear, articulate and reasoned view comes from the National Union of School Students.

John Munford, one of the NUSS's two full-time organisers, is 16 and has just left a Harlech comprehensive. He is now studying for his A levels in London at the same time as working for the NUSS.

The NUSS is still in its infancy, with a membership of only 10 000 and an income of £7000 a year. Its offices are inside those of the NUS. It has just produced a magazine, *Blot*, which is financed by the Gulbenkian Foundation and violently criticised by many teachers. At the moment its policies centre around those issues most immediately popular with its membership, campaigning against school uniform, and caning, and opposing petty rules like forcible eviction into the playground at break times and compulsory games.

If John Munford had his way school would not be compulsory, boring teachers would get few pupils, and many more people from ordinary jobs would take turns teaching in schools. If jobs were available pupils would be able to do some work outside. Adults would be encouraged to come and learn as well, to try to break down the barriers between school and the community.

John Munford believes that under some such free system pupils would be likely to learn more. With coercion removed they would have no need to rebel against being taught. He says that children who hang around the streets all day have a miserable time, for the most part, and would choose to be in school.

I have no idea whether he is right, and children would actually learn more. But I am sure they would be happier. I very much doubt whether they would end up learning less, and we shouldn't have to spend so much time threatening 13 and 14 year olds that if they don't eat up their theorems they will end up on the scrap heap.

Polly Toynbee
The *Guardian*

MAN'S ESTATE

1   In the beginning, God acquired the heaven and the earth.
2   And the earth was without form, and void, and represented a wonderful opportunity for the imaginative developer; and darkness was upon the face of the deep, but scheduled for major structural alteration at an early date.

3 And God said, Let there be light: and the darkness was tastefully converted at the developer's own expense.

4 And God made the light the subject of his personal inspection, that it was good: and God divided the light from the darkness, to the highest specifications.

5 And God called the light Day, and the darkness he called Night. And the evening (which was within a stone's throw of the Night) and the morning (which was most convenient for easy reach of the Day) together constituted a virtually detached unit.

6 And God granted outline planning permission for a prestige firmament in the midst of the waters, so that the entire project would enjoy full waterside frontage.

7 And God erected the firmament: and to underline the extremely high quality designed to appeal to the most discriminating taste in homes, he called it Heaven.

8 And God said, Let the waters under Heaven be gathered together unto one place, to constitute a substantial area for recreation, yet one with considerable industrial potential for the discerning businessman seeking to diversify; and let the dry land appear. And it was so.

9 And God called the dry land Earth; and the gathering together of the waters called he Seas: and at those points where the Seas lapped against the Earth, he called it nothing to worry about.

10 And God said, Let the earth bring forth attractive lawns needing a minimum of attention, and borders offering a wealth of mature flowering shrubs, and numerous climbing plants including clematis, wisteria and a veritable riot of honeysuckle, plus good-size plots for the keen vegetable enthusiast.

11 And it was so.

12 And God said, Let there be carriage drives.

13 And God saw that not all of the earth faced South; and where it faced South, called he it South-facing; and where it faced East, called he it partly South-facing; and where it faced West, called he it largely South-facing; and where it faced North, called he it Enjoying-broad-outlook-all-round.

14 And when God looked upon his work, and the countless charming plots, and the countless convenient plots, and the countless exclusive plots, and the countless substantial plots, and the countless spacious plots, and the countless quality plots, and the countless valuable plots, and the countless enviable plots, and the countless ideal plots, and the even more countless unique plots, all of which were just in the market, he found them good.

15 And God said, Let us make man in our image, after our likeness, quietly traditional and yet containing the ultimate in modern features; and let him have dominion over all the plots on earth.

16 So God created man in his own image; male and female created he then, similar in basic design but differing in details according to individual taste.

17 And God planted a lovely, but manageable, garden eastward (though South-facing) in Eden; and there he put the man whom he had formed.

18 And out of the ground made the LORD God to grow every tree that is pleasant for the sight, and good for food, including a very old apricot which could be counted on to produce at least two or three fruit a year and looked truly fabulous against the wall down by the ample parking space for up to three vehicles.

19 And a river went out of Eden to water the garden; which also represented an attractive investment, since fishing rights went with the property. There was also more than enough space for a swimming-pool, if required, plus a hard tennis court, the whole extending to some two-and-a-ninth acres to form a truly delightful self-contained leisure area.

20 And the LORD God took the man, and put him into the garden of Eden to dress it and to keep it; and to build thereon a detached residence in keeping with the truly salubrious environment, after the nature of the planning permission, and to hold it against a 999-year lease, at a peppercorn rent.

21 And the man, who was called Adam, enquired in his wise as to whether the freehold was available for purchase; and there was thunder about that place for a goodly time.

22 And Adam erected himself an executive property of distinction in a much sought after position over-looking a favoured reach of the Eden, completely secluded, yet within five minutes walk of all the beasts of the field and all the fowls of the air.

23 He split the level, so that the dining recess was three gracious steps up from the elegant lounge, the two combining to form a truly impressive entertainments area. It would have suited a diplomat, or film person.

24 He installed a dream kitchen; it had countless fabulous features.

25 And above, reached by a staircase that was a feature of the property built he a magnificent bedroom, fully fitted; and, en-suite, a bathroom. And there yet remained ample space.

26 And God saw the residence; and saw that it was exclusive. And he noted the ample space above, more than enough for two more bedrooms plus lavish space for storage, or maid.

27 And the LORD God said, It is not good that the man should be alone; I will make him an help meet for him. And he caused a deep sleep to fall upon Adam, and he slept: and he took one of his ribs, and closed up the flesh instead thereof, and made good.

28 And the rib, which the LORD God had taken from the man, made he a woman, despite being up to here with work; and brought her to the man.

29 And the man took her into the house; and said, In celebration I shall call this attractive residence Adeve.

30 And the woman said, Evam.

31 And the woman looked about her; and said, It may be executive to you, but it is not executive to me. And she caused the man to build an extension in cedarwood upon that which had been built before, and she caused him to convert the loft space into a play area. And above the extension, there was erected a granny flat.

32 And God came to Adam, and waxed exceeding wrath, and said, What is that wooden thing stuck on the delightful brick elevations to side and rear? And what is that thing on top of it?

33 And Adam replied in this wise: the thing is a room extension, a charming suntrap throughout the year, and the thing on top of it is a granny flat.

34 And God said, a GRANNY flat?

35 And Adam thought awhile.

36 And replied, All right, then, how about a sauna?

37 And the LORD God waxed terrible in his fury. And he said, Hast thou ignored the planning permission? Hast thou flouted all the requirements and stipulations of the lease that I granted unto you?

38 And the man said, The woman whom thou gavest to be with me, she has persuaded me to this.

39 And God said unto the woman, What is this that thou hast done?

40 And the woman replied, The property was ripe for extension, there was no point staying stuck in two rooms with all that space going begging, I wanted somewhere with a bit of tone. Didn't I?

41 And God said, I will greatly multiply thy sorrow and thy conception; in sorrow thou shalt bring forth children. They shall fill those rooms that thou has built, contrary to mine of the 15th ultimo; they shall write on the walls, and break the windows, and get their heads caught in the banisters, and scream. They shall block the plugs and the drains, they shall knock the tiles from the roof, they shall pull up the shrubs and make waste the velvet lawns. They shall kick the skirtings to pieces.

42 And Adam cried, Before we know it, this will be a property in need of some minor decoration, despite being basically sound.

43 And God looked about him, and saw that the situation and the dwelling were indeed second to none; and that a substantial price could be expected for the freehold.

44 Therefore the LORD God sent them forth from the garden of Eden. He drove out the man; and he placed at the east of the garden Cherubims, and a flaming sword which turned every way; and the approach to the house alone made it worth easily six figures.

Alan Coren
The Rhinestone as Big as the Ritz
(Robson)

WRITING FOR THE 'DAILY MIRROR'

Standfirst

When the *Daily Mirror* first gave voice it spoke in the celluloid-collar English then common to all newspapers.

In those penny-a-lining days, policemen were upholders of the law, criminals were denizens of the underworld, goalkeepers were custodians of the citadel —

and journalists were gentlemen of the Press. They wrote like counting-house clerks forging their own references.

Long after the times had changed, the language of the newspapers had not. This headline tells us that the period is the Twenties: SHORT-LIVED ROMANCE OF WELL-TO-DO WIDOW AND A COCKTAIL SHAKER. But the accompanying report could have been written in the eighteen-nineties: 'In the Divorce Court yesterday, Mr Justice Hill granted a decree nisi to Mrs Ellen O'Connor, residing at Lancaster Gate, W., in consequence of the misconduct of her husband . . .'

Not many years later, the *Daily Mirror* became the first British newspaper to revolt against such strangulated prose. The story of how it did so has been well told in Hugh Cudlipp's *Publish and be Damned* and doesn't need to be re-summarised here. It is enough to say that in the mid-thirties the *Mirror* spat the plum from its mouth and began to speak in its own voice (although the voice was not averse to the occasional imitation, as a blurb for the Beezlebub Jones strip shows: 'Zeke was plumb kayoed by the bonk on the cabeezer which Davy done give him with his wooden laig . . .' Several decades after Beezlebub's demise, expressions of the *plumb loco* variety are to be found only in old dictionaries of American slang – and in current newspaper headlines).

The *Mirror* – to borrow some favourite expressions from its new, robust vocabulary – ceased to be fuddy-duddy and became brash and cheeky. Or so it seemed at the time: from a distance of forty years, its snappy captions now have the wistful charm of old sepia photographs:

WELL, OF ALL THE LUCK

On the hottest day of the year, these two girls set out for a day's work in a film studio at Denham.

And found that their job was to be photographed in their undies for the film 'Ten Days in Paris'.

And if that isn't luck on a blazing day, we'd like to know what luck is.

Sometimes, it has to be said with hindsight, the paper's efforts to be bright and breezy had all the desperation of a fixed smile, and on occasion it could be so trivial as to appear feather-brained. The self-conscious, over-staccato language, striving to be up-to-date and down-to-earth at the same time, oscillated wildly between the slangy and the streamlined, between the homely and the Hollywood. But at its best it was good, plain, refreshing, vigorous English. It was not, as has sometimes been claimed, 'the language of the people,' for just as the people had never called criminals denizens of the underworld nor goalkeepers custodians of the citadel, neither did they now call psychiatrists mind-doctors nor drop the definite article from the beginning of sentences ('Box with documents buried 64 years ago has been unearthed during repairs at . . .'). But it was language the people could understand.

What was just as important: it was language that had a profound effect on journalism. When reporters stopped calling policemen upholders of the law and started calling them cops (in the movie-slang of the day) it was not only Fleet Street's musty terminology they were beginning to question.

The Uriah Heep approach typified by the *Mirror's* coverage of the 1929 election

– 'A further succession of Socialist gains was the unhappy tale of yesterday's election results . . .' – had now gone for ever. Authority was no longer kow-towed to. Institutions were challenged. Emperors wearing new clothes were told unkind home truths. Applecarts were upset. Cassandra, the *Mirror's* great columnist, was billed as 'the terror of the twerps.' Sledgehammer text accompanied pile-driver headlines. And when not engaged in its favourite pastime of taunting the 'fuddy-duddies', the paper was indulging in its other celebrated preoccupation of having Fun. (The *Daily Mirror* periodically pursued Fun with the dedication of an alcoholic on a three-day jag.)

Excitable, exuberant, always vigorous, sometimes vitriolic, the prose style that the *Mirror* evolved in the course of inventing British tabloid journalism was to remain for several decades its virtual copyright. Few could imitate it (not many wanted to) and those who tried were usually misled by its apparent simplicity into 'writing down' to the reader.

Today the *Mirror* is so widely imitated, or anyway emulated, that there is no longer anything exclusive about its brand of English. When not only other newspapers but television newsreaders speak fluent Tabloidese ('Good evening. The dollar takes a pounding'), the copyright may be said to have lapsed. The once unique style is in such general use, indeed, that casual observers may sometimes mistake the copy for the original. But is the original ever mistaken for the copy?

The *Daily Mirror* has better operators than any of its competitors or would-be competitors. It still has original, sometimes brilliant ideas. Its pages remain fresh and lively. Its pictures continue to lead the field. Why, then, has it not always kept ahead of the pack (though the pack has never been ahead of the leader) in its use of words?

Popular journalism – as H. L. Mencken acknowledges in his scholarly *The American Language,* even though his stuffier counterparts on this side of the Atlantic may not – used to be one of the great invigorating influences on the language (there is a plaque in Times Square to the sports cartoonist who coined *hot dog*). Today it is one of the most deadening influences. With some notable exceptions – not all of them the star writers who have carte blanche to use words like 'carte blanche' – the popular newspapers give us, in the immortal words of Ernest Bevin, 'clitch after clitch after clitch.' And this in an age when ordinary street English grows ever more expressive and colourful.

It is tempting to quote fancy theories about what has gone wrong. One is that we no longer live in a black-and-white world tailor-made for crusading tabloids and that as the issues of the day grow ever more complex, the newspapers retreat into trivia, with a resultant trivialisation of their once trenchant style. Another is that competition has raised the tabloid voice to such a monotonously shrill level that it has lost its impact. (Note that raising the voice is not the same as raising the tone.)

While there is probably something in both these notions, there could be a more mundane explanation. Tabloid journalism is no longer doing anything new. The pioneer days are long over. When journalists arrive on a tabloid paper they no longer have to rethink their reporting or subbing style to its very basics, with that resultant jolt to the creative system that has produced some of Fleet Street's finest writers and editorial technicians over the years. They already know tabloid style, or what they have been told is tabloid style, backwards. They learned it on their very first suburban weeklies. There is not a junior reporter in the land who cannot churn out, 'Feathers really flew the night a chicken-sexer got the bird,' or 'Smoky the cat went on the tiles yesterday – and used up most of her nine lives.' Recruits to Fleet Street are entitled to ask what need there is of learning new tricks when the old ones are still so much in demand.

What can be done? The *Mirror* transformed the language of journalism in or around November 1934. It was as different from the language once used by newspapers as that of commercial radio is from the BBC English of the Reith era. But what is done first can be done only once. Revolutions do not go on happening. There can be only one real revolution, and everything that follows (as the *People's Daily* of Peking would probably agree) is merely revision.

No Harry Guy Bartholomew, and certainly no Rupert Murdoch, is likely to shake up the popular newspaper as thoroughly as it was shaken up over forty years ago. Someone may invent a totally new kind of paper, but invention is something more than transformation. While the popular, Fleet Street-based, nationally-distributed daily lasts, it will be in something pretty well approximate to its present form.

What it can do is to get better. It can take stock of itself. It can spring-clean. It can throw out much of its cliché-ridden, pun-barnacled vocabulary and invest in a good, modern supply of plain English. It can dismantle ancient, cor-blimey headlines which have became as familiar as the neon signs in Piccadilly Circus. It can re-examine the stereotyped news values that encourage stereotyped writing – and the stereotyped writing that encourages stereotyped observation. It can, in sum, stop selling itself short.

Clichés

When Sam Goldwyn advised that clichés should be avoided like the plague, he forgot that the plague, by its very nature, is almost impossible to avoid. That is what gave the Black Death such a bad name.

Journalism has been contaminated by clichés since the profession began. It always will be. But not, mercifully, the same ones. Old clichés, like old soldiers, may not die but they do eventually fade away – to be replaced by new clichés.

Manuals of journalism published only a few years ago seem quaintly dated when they come to their lists of newspaper clichés – *burning issue, beggars description, like rats in a trap, limped into port, news leaked out, fair sex, speculation was rife* and so on.

Most such phrases would not be given house-room in a modern newspaper. But when we notice what *is* given house-room, it is evident that the cliché-plague is not only still with us but that it is all the time developing powerful new strains resistant to any known antidote.

Clichés should be avoided by writers in general because reach-me-down phraseology has no place in original prose. They should be avoided by journalists in particular because it is the tendency of clichés to generalise, approximate or distort. The day will never arrive when newspapers are cliché-free, but the following cross-section of words and phrases could vanish at once without any loss to journalism.

Angels (for nurses)	Dashing
Alive and well and . . .	Dropped a clanger
And that's official	Dream holiday
Billy Bunters	Fashion stakes
Clampdown	Feathers really flew
Clown prince	Flushed with shame
Curvy	Fair cop
Cheeky	Good buys
Giantkillers	Purrfect (for cats)
Hammered	Pinta
Hurtle	Rampage
Helluva	Rapped
Hello sailor	Sin-bin
Inch war	Slammed
Knickers in a twist	Slapped a ban
Love-tug	Sweet smell of success
Love-child	Soccer clash
Merry widow	Spree
Nationwide hunt/search	Sir (for teachers)
Oo-la-la (this foreign-desk	Take a letter, Miss Smith
phrase, believed to be	There's an awful lot of coffee
extinct, was sighted	Tragedy struck when
recently in *The Sun*)	Trouble flared when
Petite	Vivacious
Pay bonanza	Writing on the wall

Note: In an era of radical change, clichés are now vulnerable not only to old age but to technological and social progress. *Gymslip mums*, for example, must have given way to *jeans and T-shirt mums* by now, and today's *carbon-copy deaths* are surely *photocopies*.

Miracle is also over-used. The *Mirror* has vouchsafed so many miracle wives, miracle mums, miracle babies, miracle cures and miracle escapes that an apposite consolation prize for competition runners-up not qualifying for a luxuriant week on palm-fringed sands could well be a year's supply of loaves and fishes, at no cost to the management.

Jargon

In the *Guardian* (but not in the *Mirror*) we may read: 'Derbyshire is into high-speed transport.'

In the *Observer* (but not in the *Mirror*) we may read: 'Journalism input comes almost entirely from agency reports.'

This is the kind of journalism input that is appearing daily in American papers: 'PanAm reported no upturn in traffic flow yesterday. "There's been no onrush." A PanAm spokeswoman said.'

Business corporations, in particular, want everyone to speak their unspeakable 'in-house' Dalek language. It is steadily insinuating itself into newspapers, but not, it is to be hoped, into the *Mirror.*

PS But are the Daleks as appalled by our jargon – *bid, probe, mercy dash,* etc. – as we are by theirs?

Adjectives

Adjectives should not be allowed in newspapers unless they have something to say.

Red-haired tells us that a person has red hair. *Vivacious* – a word belonging to the lost world of Marcel waves and cocktail cherries – tells us nothing except that someone has sat down at a typewriter and tapped out the word 'vivacious.'

An adjective should not raise questions in the reader's mind, it should answer them. *Angry* informs. *Tall* invites the question, how tall? The well-loved phrase *His expensive tastes ran to fast cars* simply whets the appetite for examples of the expensive tastes, and the makes and engine capacity of the fast cars.

Adjectives used for effect should not be too clapped-out to evoke anything in the reader's mind: *grim* timetable of death, *vital* clues, *brutal* murder, *hush-hush* inquiry, no longer add very much to the nouns they accompany.

Smothering an intro in an HP sauce of adjectives does little to improve its flavour:

> Manchester City are poised to sign Wolves' *brilliant* midfield man Steve Daley and Wrexham's *impressive* striker Bobby Shinton in a *massive* £1 million *double* deal.

Massive, like *double,* is tautology, and remains so when we learn later that 'the Maine Road club' are determined to push through the *massive* deal that would involve £850 000 for Daley and £350 000 for Shinton. Then we are told that other clubs have been keen on the *impressive* Shinton. The repetition of an already inessential adjective is lame.

For a profession that is supposed to be hard-boiled, journalism is remarkably chivalrous with its adjectives. Models are *attractive* or *stunning,* or they are given the accolade of *top,* or they are *curvy* – which seems to have come into vogue when someone realised that *curvaceous* was getting long in the tooth. (So is *curvy,* by now.) Small young women are *petite.* Small old women are *tiny.* Young men are often *dashing* – an anyone-for-tennis word from the same era as *vivacious.* There are few ordinary housewives, but *model* housewives abound. The *Mirror* has even given us a *model* soldier:

> Model soldier John Jones is being made homeless – by the army.

Long experience of the *Mirror's* weakness for model housewives arouses suspicions that this is not a story from Toytown.

Model, of course, is strictly speaking not an adjective but a noun. A glance at any day's paper (*MIRACLE* WIFE WHO 'DIED'. *DANGER* FOOD FIRMS

RAPPED. *DREAM* TRIP TO PARADISE) will show that nouns are used as adjectives far more than adjectives proper. There is nothing wrong with that: a considerable acreage of pulp forest must have been saved over the years by the use of *flight chaos* as shorthand for *chaos caused by a strike of air traffic controllers*. But the cautions expressed at the beginning of this section still apply. Bearing in mind that an adjective by any name still has to earn its keep, a noun used as an adjective should ideally make a statement rather than raise a question.

Dawn swoop, though a choice example of Tabloidese, makes a statement: it tells us roughly at what time of day the swoop was made. *Surprise swoop* raises the question, who was surprised? (It is also tautology, since swoops are not usually made by appointment.) *Shock swoop* is as bad as surprise swoop, with the bonus fault that *shock* is a much-over-used noun-adjective (*shock* report, *shock* move, etc.).

Another over-used noun-adjective is *luxury*. Is it worth mentioning that a Saudi Arabian prince lives in a *luxury home?* We would hardly expect him to live in a barrel (which would be worth a line or two). But his *25-bathroom home* or his *£250 000 home* would be informative. (*Luxury* has been for so long used as an adjective that we have forgotten the proper meanings of its legitimately adjectival offshoots. The Mirror invited competition winners to relax *luxuriantly* for a week on palm-fringed sands. *Luxuriant* means abundant or exuberant in growth. A *luxurious* week would have been a better offer.)

Our readers in Wigan

The question, 'Will our readers living in Wigan understand this?' is not always a legitimate one.

Where the question is genuinely and literally asked about an obscure word or passage, it should not be in any spirit of superiority. ('Even *I* can't understand it,' is a rider often heard in the cloisters and quadrangles of the *Daily Mirror*.) If any line of the paper cannot be understood, it is not because of the limited education or intelligence of the reader but because of the limited ability or effort of the writer.

But 'Will our readers living in Wigan understand this?' may as often as not be translated as, 'Will newspapermen living in Petts Wood appreciate this?' The matter is frequently one of editorial taste and judgement — or what the questioner supposes editorial taste and judgement ought to be — rather than of clarity.

It should never be assumed, as the only yardstick, that any topic is outside the spectrum of interest of *Mirror* readers. Popular journalism was founded on the belief that ordinary people have an unquenchable thirst for information of all kinds. When the range of a typical saloon-bar discussion is more limited than that of the *Mirror's* usual editorial content (it never is) Northcliffe will have been proved wrong at last.

This is not to say that the *Mirror* is in the market for 2000-word articles on porcelain. Its content is largely governed by its style, and its style is that of a tabloid newspaper, not of a learned journal. This extract from a front-page manifesto by Silvester Bolam (Editor 1948–53) is still the best summary of what the *Mirror* is about:

The *Mirror* is a sensational newspaper. We make no apology for that. We believe in the sensational presentation of news and views, especially important news and views, as a necessary and valuable public service in these days of mass readership and democratic responsibility.

We shall go on being sensational to the best of our ability . . .

Sensationalism does not mean distorting the truth. It means the vivid and dramatic presentation of events so as to give them a forceful impact on the mind of the reader. It means big headlines, vigorous writing, simplification into familiar everyday language, and the wide use of illustration by cartoon and photograph . . .

Every great problem facing us – the world economic crisis, diminishing food supplies, the population puzzle, the Iron Curtain and a host of others – will only be understood by the ordinary man busy with his daily tasks if he is hit hard and hit often with the facts . . .

As in larger, so in smaller and more personal affairs, the *Mirror* and its millions of readers prefer the vivid to the dull and the vigorous to the timid.

No doubt we make mistakes, but we are at least alive.

Readers living in Wigan – and elsewhere – would still approve of that philosophy.

Keith Waterhouse
The Mirror's Way with Words
(Mirror Books)

WAYS OF WORKING

● Look closely at Keith Waterhouse's detailed advice on writing good popular journalism, especially his comments on the use of adjectives, jargon, clichés and audience. Select several articles from daily newspapers (a spread of papers would be helpful) and, in small groups, apply Waterhouse's guidelines for judgement. Decide which articles you think are well written and explore reasons with the other members of the group.

● Investigate the journalism of music. Bring in a range of musical papers (like the *NME, Melody Maker, Rolling Stone,* etc.). Select several articles of common interest (e.g. different reviews of the same record or live performance) and talk through your reactions to the style, tone and implied sense of audience of the articles. Then try and write your own reviews and articles to be put in your own school/college magazine.

● Make your own newspaper, booklet or pamphlet explaining how your current course of study differs from how you worked when you were younger. This could take the form of an introduction for those about to join your course, or a summary aimed at parents. Form editorial groups and decide together how you are going to make your selection of items and how they are going to be presented. You will need to sort out your general viewpoint on the details being presented, e.g.

are you going to write it through the eyes of a student, or in a more distanced manner?

Some of the possible ways of presenting your material might be in terms of photographs, a 'day in the life of' diary, interviews, striking images, a list of points to look out for, etc.

● How do the pieces included in this section reflect the wider editorial control and direction of the newspapers and magazines that they originally appeared in? Look carefully at the slanting and organisation of the material. Who is each aimed at and how is this achieved?

● Try your own comic journalism. But first find a subject that you genuinely feel that you want to make a comment on through a satirical approach (like personal liberties 16–19 or the absence of them, CB radio, a micro-chip way of life, sex education, authoritarian teaching styles, exam factories, the pop world, muzak, tourists abroad, etc.) You can often get intriguing subjects from small snippets of newspaper information, as Alan Coren does (see *The Rhinestone as Big as the Ritz* – Alan Coren, Robson Books). Decide exactly what you are trying to debunk and then choose a suitable style and voice that will do justice to your intentions.

● Are there any community initiatives in your local area (like Andrea Waind's piece on 'The Concrete Elephant') that people outside your district ought to hear about? Examples might be the community working together to build an adventure playground on an old tip, a Help the Aged scheme that really works, a tenants' association speaking out for their rights, a street festival or outing. Write about one such operation in clear, plain English and send it to your local newspaper. Or investigate the possibility of starting your own community or school/college newspaper. Remember that the most telling journalism relies upon exact detail, the carefully placed interview or dialogue, the apt, summarising quote or statistic and the dramatic surprise of the unexpected image.

● Find out about the journalism of writers like George Orwell, Mayhew in his *Morning Chronicle* pieces, John Hersey, Jonathan Swift, James Cameron, John Pilger, Keith Waterhouse. Take the Further references as a starting point.

● Contrast the quality of the journalistic coverage of the Falklands War. First track down some of the following books from your local or school/college libraries. (Remember there is always the effective inter-library loan postal service at your disposal.)

The Falklands War The Sunday Times Insight team, Sphere Books
The Winter War Patrick Bishop and John Witherow, Quartet Books
Eye-Witness Falklands Robert Fox, Methuen
I counted them all out and I counted them all back Robert Fox and Brian Hanrahan, Methuen
Los Chicos de la Guerra Daniel Kon, New English Library

Pin-point key passages from several of the books that illustrate your general argument. Try to make clear to yourself and others what it is exactly in the

writing that makes you approve or disapprove, and be able to give reasons for
your views.

● Try to separate the elements of fact and opinion from some of the pieces
included in this selection. (A possible classroom approach might be to divide a
piece of plain paper into two and collect on one side of the paper hard information,
and on the other, the writer's comments or opinions.) Is it possible? Can you do
it for random articles taken from the daily press? Argue with the points made in
the introduction on the journalist as a purveyor of and commentator on the news.

FURTHER REFERENCES

Rhubarb, Rhubarb and other noises Keith Waterhouse, Sphere Books
The Way we Live Now Polly Toynbee, Eyre Methuen
The Unknown Mayhew ed. E.P. Thompson and Eileen Yeo, Merlin Press
The Best of Cameron James Cameron, New English Library
The Fight Norman Mailer, Pan Books
The New Journalism Tom Wolfe and E.W. Johnson, Picador
By-line (Selected articles and dispatches of four decades) Ernest Hemingway,
    Penguin
Aftermath: The struggle of Cambodia and Vietnam John Pilger and Anthony
    Barnett, New Statesman
The Mirror's Way with Words Keith Waterhouse, Mirror Books
The First Casualty Phillip Knightley, Quartet Books
The Collected Essays, Journalism and Letters of George Orwell: Volumes 1–4,
    Penguin (especially the 'As I Please' column)
Here to Stay John Hersey, Hamish Hamilton
Journey into Journalism Arnold Wesker, Writers and Readers Cooperative
The Other Britain ed. Paul Barker, Routledge & Kegan Paul
Nothing Sacred Angela Carter, Virago
Los Chicos de la Guerra Daniel Kon, New English Library

6
Responses

INTRODUCTION

Authentic response comes from an openness to experience, and from having the time, the right context and the space to allow further stages of response to develop out of that initial encounter. Despite the occasional evidence of lively, engaged approaches, too often students are told what to think and feel about what they read, or are nudged into playing safe because of examination pressure and end up borrowing a stock orthodoxy of response.

The first step towards enabling a broader sense of response may be to encourage the student to trust in her/his own insights. Doris Lessing in 'The training of a critic/reader' shows how the educational system often persuades students to hide behind other people's opinions rather than '(making) up your own mind about what you think, testing it against your own life, your own experience. Never mind about Professors White and Black.'

To value the first encounter, rather than to scurry prematurely into final products, is crucial to this more open type of response. Because of the unexpectedness of the first response, we often react more immediately and vulnerably, as in the early childhood reading experiences recorded by Fred Inglis, where the memories of comics stuck in the mind, their 'primary colours blazing with excitement to come', and where the adventures of Desperate Dan and Alf Tupper produced an intensity of experience that we can hardly do justice to later on.

If later critical reflection and commentary are to be genuinely based, then we must start from those first impressions. We must not be afraid to state them publicly as Pauline Kael does in her frank reaction to Peter Brook's film of *King Lear*. She allows herself to bare her first antipathy to the ashy, sterile atmosphere of the film, and that momentum then carries her on to a more detailed, considered argument where commentary, intelligence and feeling can inform each other.

It is not an easy journey; sometimes these first encounters appear to collapse in blockages and dead ends, but persistence and a constructive approach to the reading process can often move us on to a more solid position.

We have included the student reactions to Seamus Heaney's poetry in order to map out the possible stages of developing a response: from the first impressions and coming to terms with other perspectives in small group talk, through to the synthesising, more carefully reflective stage of making a statement. The important point about response is that the 'Making a statement' stage (usually over-valued by schools and colleges) grows out of the early stages. Through trying out and exchanging initial impressions and ideas, a future line of enquiry might emerge that carries with it the first flavour of the experience but is modified by the more considered discovery of more generalised patterns of meaning.

Not only can the expression of the response be expanded but also the possible modes of response. Tape recordings, collage work, answering in role, improvised drama, strip cartoons — all these are legitimate ways of working in the classroom so that students can have a greater variety of choice in selecting the best form for their response. We have included two examples: Elizabeth Gladwin writing in the style of Ken Kesey; and John Berger reacting to the social and historical development of Hals' painting by inventing his own appropriate form of response — a dramatic projection of some of Hals' scenes brought to life by the workings of an historical imagination.

It would have been too limiting to restrict this section to responses to books, so, as a way of suggesting the possibilities for broadening the activities of English studies' courses of the future, we have selected a range of responses to comics, photographs, the theatre, television, film, architecture and painting. We have also tried to show that reviewing does not have to be a dry, academic 'critic talk', but can be a much more full-blooded activity, with personal attack. The examples we have chosen are by Ted Hughes on 'Poems of the First World War', Edward Thomas on Cobbett and, from a different angle, a *Camerawork* review which also includes an interview with the photographer.

Finally, we wanted to investigate how responses are also products of a specific time and place. Berger's art criticism sets Hals' personal development against a background of free enterprise and vicious acquisitiveness in the Holland of his time: 'A new energy has been released and a kind of metaphysic of money is being born.' And John Pilger's piece on Cimino's *The Deer Hunter* shows how the public response to a traumatic event (in this case Vietnam) can easily be manipulated through slick camerawork, while actually misrepresenting the facts: 'That the same cynical mythmaking is now being applied to Vietnam . . . induces more melancholy than anger in those like myself, who saw whole Vietnamese communities used as guinea pigs for the testing of a range of 'anti-personnel' military technology, and who saw demoralised, brutalised, often mutinous and doped American teenagers lying in their own blood and shit, for the purposes of some pointless, sacrificial siege staged in the cause of nothing . . .'

In the end, the very term 'response' is inadequate, implying a passively routine reaction, triggered off by a stimulus. Meaning comes through the creative interaction of the learner and the experience and, in the future, we will probably need a tauter, more dynamic image to do fuller justice to the vitality of this learning process.

READING COMICS

Begin with comics. When we turn back to those immortal figures, Korky the Cat, Desperate Dan, Lord Snooty, we are returning to moments of irrecoverable vividness and joyfulness, against which the present can only seem banal. Lord Snooty and his pals belong to the age of radical innocence, which moves in and out of the fabulous at will and without its even being clear which of two worlds is more real. There never were such teachers in mortar-boards carrying such thick canes, there never was a paradise in which Lord Snooty was at one with the working class: Scrapper Smith, Happy Huggins, Skinny Lizzie, the two weird baby twins Snitchy and Snatchy and, even more brilliantly improbable, Gertie the Goat. There could never be such cow-pies as Desperate Dan ate, pudding-basin and all, nor such a bristly jaw as could ignite whole forests, nor such a fist as struck down walls and houses (but never other men). Dilly Dreeme, the lovable duffer, Lettice Leefe, Hungry Horace, Dennis the Menace, Weary Willie and Tired Tim join the throngs of these shades in a busy, insubstantial and immortal limbo, where souls wait for ever. Their ancestors walk the tall tales of a millennium, making a brief bow in Shakespeare and Dickens at a time when the opportunity was there for an imagination of genius to seize upon everything in popular culture, and then going back to haunt comics, and music halls, and animated cartoons.

These characters offered an extraordinary pleasure. It was one of many striking insights in that remarkable film *Kes* to note that a comic was and is taken in by children in complete gravity. Billy Casper reads the *Dandy* with utter absorption and an expressionless face.

I remember the flatness of Mondays and Fridays when no comic was delivered for my sisters and me. We were a comfortably off family, and my parents strikingly tolerant as well as generous: they encouraged us to read as much as we could and while, as parents should, they screened what came into the house, they were admirably and lightheartedly liberal in what they gave us to read. *Dandy* and *Beano* came out on alternate Tuesdays, as they still do, and were delivered with the morning paper. On Wednesday, so were *Knockout* and *School Friend;* on Thursday, *Girl* and the *Rover* or the *Adventure,* depending which football or cricket serial I was following – I changed loyalties to the Thursday comic as often as I did from cornflakes to Weetabix; but all the others were fixed points in the changeless landscape in which my mother and father were such solid, fixed, and living proof that the world was uniform, harmonious, and untouched by time. That is why my sisters and I went on reading comics when an outsider might have thought they were too childish for us. The experience of living within the solidities of my family made us unconscious, as children naturally are, of change and the marks of time. More mature reading came along with the comics, and happily co-existed with them. I read *Dandy* and *Knockout* beside *Kidnapped* with no sense of incongruity. We fell upon the comics and squabbled over precedence because they were the margins of an organized day which remained magic and separate. We knew what was in them, and yet anything might be in them.

Not only that. We could master their strangeness and surprises immediately. In a world subject to the arbitrary proscriptions of adult legislation, we read the comics fast, and they magically debarred the incomprehensibility of boredom.

Perhaps television has done the same for children born, let us say, since the IBA charter was granted in 1954, and a TV became part of the accepted furniture of every household. I don't know. I do know that I came down to read the comics at breakfast time (the only meal at which we could read at table) with a sense of delicious expectation. My sisters wrangled about who should read which on the bus to school. I kept the boys' comics, and when I turned to the long prose stories, I took off into a world which captured and held me, staring-eyed and focused only upon the unbroken columns of tight print until I came out at the end. Reading Nick Smith, the Incredible Wilson, Rockfist Rogan, and the rest was hardly *like* reading Korky the Kat or Big Eggo (the ostrich, for heaven's sake). We read the comic-strip stories in a different spirit. It's hard to catch now, but I think that the crazy banality of those serials, their endless release of the forces of misrule, marked out a secret garden to which the comics guaranteed entrance and in which a trivial riotous pointlessness eternally obtained. There is nothing intended here about the provision of 'security' which some of the gentler, goofier spirits amongst primary teachers sometimes claim for comics. Korky is not so much a security against the inanity of the world as he is both circumscribed and unpredictable, like an early Disney character or a quantum particle. You never know what he will do, but he will do it according to his own laws of motion, which are held in by the frames of the pictures.

It was quite different with Wilson, Alf Tupper, Nick Smith, and Baldy Hogan. I wanted so much to believe in the reality of the football stories that I quarrelled quite passionately on the top deck of a bus with a sceptical friend who insisted there was no such person as Nick Smith. Like the other heroes, Nick Smith, who was captain of one of those blankly named, non-existent Midland towns which have disfigured the map of literary England since Barchester (Ambridge is with us yet), was, rightly and unironically, a footballer and sportsman of complete probity and honour. The core of the week's episode was always announced in the single illustration, itself (like the stories) rather in the style of Socialist Realism, with broad-shouldered, heavy-muscled, expressionlessly handsome giants scoring impossible goals with whizz-marks behind the ball.

One week Nick Smith was being sent off in the illustration! It transpired that, partly concussed in a collision, he subsequently couldn't see an opponent whom he unintentionally fouled. His good name was only cleared when the referee saw him walk heavily into the edge of a dressing-room door which was straight in his line of vision, and realized that the hero's excuse was entirely truthful. The point is that his good name had to be cleared, for as in all these stories, the hero remains consistently and unselfquestioningly admirable. Like Roy Rogers on Trigger and the Lone Ranger on Silver, the sportsmen are excellent by virtue of their actions, not their motives. The essential structure is assertive – the hero tensed against the events. In himself he is finite and circumscribed – unconscious, so to speak, but all-powerful. He stands in the line of the chivalrous and knightly men who have embodied the central virtues of the West in its stories since the

196

Provençal troubadours first took to the road. Nick Smith and the Lone Ranger have no need to be gentlemen any more than they are knights: their honour is synonymous with their manhood.

It is a tricky point. But a structural strength of these simple tales is that role and identity are one. There is no strain or gap between how a footballer (or cowboy or fighter pilot) ought to be and how this man behaves. Individual integrity is perfectly satisfied by the definition of the role and its duties. A main shift in the values we live by has, in real life, made this definition often a breaking strain for many people. Their sense of themselves insists upon its own claims as paramount – 'I have a duty to myself.' While the fact of this struggle, and the battles won or lost in the name either of individual integrity or of loyalty and duty to an institution, is present in so much adult experience and its fictions, it is fitting that the simple, single structure of what we tell children should hold out the chance of beatitude. A fortunate man may be able to hold together his pictures of himself and his responsibility to the world. The heroes of popular culture have no difficulty in doing so.

Alf Tupper, the tough of the track, was an interesting example of this effortless unity of desire and actuality. For he was an exaggeratedly working-class hero, who lived in dreadful squalor in a derelict home with smashed windows beside a railway bridge, and ran through the wet nights across broken tarmac, under the black shadow of the dockside hulls, along the canal behind the gasworks. He was a prophetic figure. Many real working-class runners have followed him on the same harsh and lumpy cinders. Alf Tupper could only run well on fish and chips, that evocative class emblem, although the sporting accuracy demanded by the reader of *Rover, Wizard, Adventure, Hotspur* also required that he train properly and do believable times on the track. He was constantly put down by the snobberies of those who ran athletics (much truth there!) and unfailingly put them down in his turn by winning. All his readers, in and out of private schools, were on his side because the snobs were obviously awful and in the wrong, and his toughness simply confirmed his integrity by its lack of fancy frills. It was never in question, to himself or anyone else; he was as innocent and independent as Tom Jones.

Fred Inglis
The Promise of Happiness
(CUP)

ON PETER BROOK'S FILM OF 'KING LEAR'

Peter Brook's *King Lear* is gray and cold, and the actors have dead eyes. I didn't just dislike this production – I hated it. The fact that it's *intentionally* gray and cold and dead doesn't redeem it; a slob of a director might have let the actors take over and some of *King Lear's* emotional poetry might have come through, but Brook has a unified vision and never lets go of the reins. There are no accidental pleasures in this movie – and, as I see it, no deliberate ones, either. I think I understand why Gloucester's eyes are plucked out in giant closeup (though I averted my own eyes); I guess I know why the black-and-white cinematography is predominantly dark gray and pale gray and why everyone is lighted in a flat, *unlighted* way, and why Cordelia is sullen and mechanical – a walking corpse, like the others. One can glimpse the intention to make Lear himself less centrifugal and to use the icy, empty landscapes (the film was shot in northern Denmark) as a metaphor for the unyielding, ungoverned universe, in which all men are pawns and there is no hope for anyone. There are no apparent light sources, and surely the dead eyes are metaphorically linked to this blind, godless desolation. The movie is all nightmare images of blindness and nothingness; Brook has retained the metaphors of *Lear* and thrown out the play. Ideas in theatre are rare, but to have a conception is not the same as having a good conception. The world's exhaustion and the light's having disappeared may open up new meanings in Shakespeare's play to us, but as the controlling metaphors in this production they don't enlarge the play, they cancel it out.

The performances are kept so dry and rigidly mannered that you don't get involved in who is who in time to catch hold of the plot strands, which are clipped short and presented in a loony, egalitarian manner, as if all the elements were of equal importance. Obviously, Brook intends to make them so, because when the several subplots have the same weight as the story of Lear and his daughters the action of the play tends to become meaningless and the characters are drained of emotional force. If Lear is not allowed to be a titanic unreasonable man, a vain, impetuous old fool who stands for all of us when he brings torment upon himself – if he is cut down to life-size, so that he no longer represents supreme human rashness – then he is merely one of us, and what happens to him becomes part of a generalized meaninglessness and despair.

Pauline Kael
Deeper into Movies
(Calder)

ON A DISTANT PROSPECT . . .

. . . three perfectly regular spheres in the middle of nowhere. Everyone knows vaguely that they are somewhere up in that part of Yorkshire, but no one seems quite to expect them to appear at that moment on that particular piece of road. The A169 has been climbing into true (though fenced) moorland for some miles out of Pickering, and just after it turns and plunges down at Gallows Dyke you see the huge square dishes of the forward-scatter antennae on the skyline, and the three white domes of the early-warning radar setting like paper suns behind the ridge as your viewpoint drops with the dropping road.

Your next view of Fylingdales, half a mile further along, will be more complete though still distant, but it won't have the impact of the first encounter, which is a visual happening of the first order and a textbook demonstration of the downright *unfairness* of our aesthetic responses. Unfair, because however much you may disapprove of lunatic foreign policies that make the construction of such things necessary, however much you may disapprove their construction in the teeth of National Parks legislation and local protests, I can pretty well guarantee your helplessness to do anything but approve when you see them in that setting.

Nor does the availability of at least partial explanations of their power exorcise their impact on second or third viewing. Attempts at explanation tend, rather, to explain why their effect is sustained. Simple they may be in geometrical form, but even their verbally accessible meanings are of a complexity that goes far beyond the 'absolute' beauty that Plato supposed to lie in elementary geometrical solids. For instance, our first sight of them was greeted by a scholarly query on Paul Nash in the front passenger seat, and a delighted shout of 'They've landed!' from the younger generation in the back.

Both responses check out as equally valid. For people who survived the progressive aesthetics of the thirties and were later readmitted to the human race, Paul Nash's vision of Plato's regular solids standing in for megaliths against a background of Wiltshire wilderness . . . these, almost alone of the abstract aesthetic remain real. And to see Nash's precise geometry given physical existence, even if the background is the empurpled moors, not Wiltshire, can still set ancient atavisms jangling.

The Thunderbirds-are-go response of the kids may appear more superficial, but is probably much more complicated and lavish. It does not depend on a simple contrast between the poverty of platonic aesthetics and the riches of untamed nature. It is rich in itself; in relations between objects of opposite curvature, for in this vision the concavities of the square antenna-dishes are as important as the convexities of the domes, not just as a contrast of abstract shapes, but because they express, however obtusely, the differing functions of communications and surveillance. A high monument of their world-around culture of electronic contact, but not solemn because the Ministry of Defence has unwittingly joked up the whole scene with No Entry signs headed MoD PROPERTY.

Further, and irrespective of generation, the objects themselves are visually rich, whoever the observer. This is partly due to their setting in a well-creased landscape that reveals them unexpectedly in many distant prospects across the moors, so that there is a constant element of surprise in one's perception of them, but much more due to the material of which they are made. Any old-time snob who insists that plastics are 'lifeless, soul-less' materials had better avoid Fylingdales if he treasures his illusions, for the three domes are bafflingly responsive to incident light.

They take, at all times, slight reflected colour from the sky and the heather, so that they are a cooler tint above than below; in strong sunlight they jump up in crisp modelling, lurk in grey obscurity when the clouds are zapped in solid; appear to glow with an internal radiance (maybe there were actual lights on inside) when the sun is low and the air misty. Picture postcards by three different publishers, bought in Whitby, show the radomes as three different shades of pale. None of the shades is any more convincing than any colours on picture postcards, but the variation is entirely justified.

Also, the heather deserves a word of congratulation. It is a marvellous background for geometrical effects of any sort. Not because it is untamed nature; it isn't anything of the sort. The local shootocracy keep it under very careful control both as grouse moor and sheep ranch; it is a managed ecology if not an artificial environment, and should be regarded less as a shallow jungle than as a deep pile carpet, in whose purple fuzz the eye falls, unfocusable, away from any hard-edged forms (distance judgement can be very difficult, for instance). It's like the velvet behind the pearl, exaggerating whatever virtue is there.

At one distant viewpoint for Fylingdales, rejoicing in the name of Murk Mire Moor, there is a shooting lodge: two large rooms under a common roof, a stable sticking out the back, and an unroofed stable yard wrapped in an L-shaped wall. At its exposed end, the wall reveals that it has been built with a slight but precise batter (upward taper) that reduces its thickness by about three inches in a height of eight feet.

Now, that batter is not there for the giggle or by accident. It is a very sound usage in an un-buttressed wall, giving it an inherent stability that is probably a necessity in such an exposed location. It's an easily comprehended necessity, a self-explanatory form. But the necessity adds authority to the form; and quite often the mere knowledge of the necessity, however difficult to comprehend, can still confer that kind of authority to forms. One knows that the radomes are there for a reason; some military necessity determines their location, function and form. The function may be repugnant, their internal workings incomprehensible, but the authority persists.

No such authority subsists in most works of art that are supposed to have it, like Henry Moore sculptures. Dragged out of the art gallery or Battersea Park, and located in landscape, they dwindle. They lack the authority of necessity because they exist only at the whim (however profound) of one man and have nothing to do beyond the gratification of that whim. Even the 'necessities' of the material have become pretty inoperative in Henry Moore's recent work. But the existence of such necessity, however ill comprehended, adds another dimension of richness to the aesthetic of Fylingdales, another grain of explanation of their durability as affective images. In the Harvardese of one of my students, they are 'resilient to repeated interrogation' – a singularly apt phrase because 'interrogate' is what you do to stray satellites – and even well-behaved ones, if they are the sort that only deliver information on demand. Fylingdales can't be caught out; however you sneak up on them, the radomes have something new to tell.

And they tell it to everybody. The most sensational piece of information about them as aesthetic objects appears five paragraphs above – the words 'picture postcards'. It has been granted to few monuments of technology to get into that league recently, or so quickly. The Post Office Tower is the only one that comes handily to mind, and that has certain obvious margins as a symbol of swinging London and something you can go inside. But Fylingdales is a purely visual experience, you can't go inside, because it's MoD property, and it doesn't symbolize anything. NATO is too remote and moribund a concept to give the equivalent of, say, Union Jack or Spitfire status. Any symbolism that Fylingdales carries is something that people have wished on it privately, perhaps even below the threshold of consciously knowing what they symbolize by it.

But the long-term consequences are pretty alarming-looking. If it has already achieved pop-postcard status at sufficiently profitable level for three different publishers to put out their own versions, then it must be in the same league as Anne Hathaway's cottage or Buckingham Palace. And you realize what that means? It means that there will be an outcry against any attempt to pull it down. From unwanted intrusion to ancient monument in four years flat! Don't ask me to form a preservation group, however. I *want* to see it fall down, because it will be our first major plastic ruin, and for that I can't wait.

Reyner Banham
Arts in Society, ed. Paul Barker
(New Society)

THE TRAINING OF A CRITIC/READER

It starts when the child is as young as five or six, when he arrives at school. It starts with marks, rewards, 'places', 'streams', stars – and still in many places, stripes. This horserace mentality, the victor and loser way of thinking, leads to 'Writer X is, is not, a few paces ahead of Writer Y. Writer Y has fallen behind. In his last book Writer Z has shown himself as better than Writer A.' From the very beginning the child is trained to think in this way: always in terms of comparison, of success, and of failure. It is a weeding-out system: the weaker get discouraged and fall out; a system designed to produce a few winners who are always in competition with each other. It is my belief – though this is not the place to develop this – that the talents every child has, regardless of his official 'I.Q.', could stay with him through life, to enrich him and everybody else, if these talents were not regarded as commodities with a value in the success-stakes.

The other thing taught from the start is to distrust one's own judgement. Children are taught submission to authority, how to search for other people's opinions and decisions, and how to quote and comply.

As in the political sphere, the child is taught that he is free, a democrat, with a free will and a free mind, lives in a free country, makes his own decisions. At the same time he is a prisoner of the assumptions and dogmas of his time, which he does not question, because he has never been told they exist. By the time a young person has reached the age when he has to choose (we still take it for granted that a choice is inevitable) between the arts and the sciences, he often chooses the arts because he feels that here is humanity, freedom, choice. He does not know that he is already moulded by a system: he does not know that the choice itself is the result of a false dichotomy rooted in the heart of our culture. Those who do sense this, and who don't wish to subject themselves to further moulding, tend to leave, in a half-unconscious, instinctive attempt to find work where they won't be divided against themselves. With all our institutions, from the police force to academia, from medicine to politics, we give little attention to the people who leave – that process of elimination that goes on all the time and which excludes, very early, those likely to be original and reforming, leaving those attracted to a thing because that is what they are already like. A young policeman leaves the Forces saying he doesn't like what he has to do. A young teacher leaves teaching, her idealism snubbed. This social mechanism goes almost unnoticed – yet it is as powerful as any in keeping our institutions rigid and oppressive.

These children who have spent years inside the training system become critics and reviewers, and cannot give what the author, the artist, so foolishly looks for – imaginative and original judgement. What they can do, and what they do very well, is to tell the writer how the book or play accords with current patterns of feeling and thinking – the climate of opinion. They are like litmus paper. They are wind gauges – invaluable. They are the most sensitive of barometers of public opinion. You can see changes of mood and opinion here sooner than anywhere except in the political field – it is because these are people whose whole education has been just that – to look outside themselves for their opinions, to adapt themselves to authority figures, to 'received opinion' – a marvellously revealing phrase.

It may be that there is no other way of educating people. Possibly, but I don't believe it. In the meantime it would be a help at least to describe things properly, to call things by their right names. Ideally, what should be said to every child, repeatedly, throughout his or her school life is something like this:

'You are in the process of being indoctrinated. We have not yet evolved a system of education that is not a system of indoctrination. We are sorry, but it is the best we can do. What you are being taught here is an amalgam of current prejudice and the choices of this particular culture. The slightest look at history will show how impermanent these must be. You are being taught by people who have been able to accommodate themselves to a regime of thought laid down by their predecessors. It is a self-perpetuating system. Those of you who are more robust and individual than others, will be encouraged to leave and find ways of educating yourself – educating your own judgement. Those that stay must remember, always and all the time, that they are being moulded and patterned to fit into the narrow and particular needs of this particular society.'

Like every other writer I get letters all the time from young people who are about to write theses and essays about my books in various countries – but particularly in the United States. They all say: 'Please give me a list of the articles about your work, the critics who have written about you, the authorities.' They also ask for a thousand details of total irrelevance, but which they have been taught to consider important, amounting to a dossier, like an immigration department's. These requests I answer as follows: 'Dear student. You are mad. Why spend months and years writing thousands of words about one book, or even one writer, when there are hundreds of books waiting to be read. You don't see that you are the victim of a pernicious system. And if you have yourself chosen my work as your subject, and if you do have to write a thesis – and believe me I am very grateful that what I've written is being found useful by you – then why don't you read what I have written and make up your own mind about what you think, testing it against your own life, your own experience. Never mind about Professors White and Black.'

'Dear Writer' – they reply. 'But I have to know what the authorities say, because if I don't quote them, my professor won't give me any marks.'

This is an international system, absolutely identical from the Urals to Yugoslavia, from Minnesota to Manchester.

The point is, we are all so used to it, we no longer see how bad it is.

I am not used to it, because I left school when I was fourteen. There was a time I was sorry about this, and believed I had missed out on something valuable. Now I am grateful for a lucky escape. After the publication of *The Golden Notebook,* I made it my business to find out something about the literary machinery, to examine the process which made a critic, or a reviewer. I looked at innumerable examination papers – and couldn't believe my eyes; sat in on classes for teaching literature, and couldn't believe my ears.

You might be saying: That is an exaggerated reaction, and you have no right to it, because you say you have never been part of the system. But I think it is not at all exaggerated, and that the reaction of someone from outside is valuable simply because it is fresh and not biased by allegiance to a particular education.

But after this investigation, I had no difficulty in answering my own questions: Why are they so parochial, so personal, so small-minded? Why do they always atomise, and belittle, why are they so fascinated by detail, and uninterested in the whole? Why is their interpretation of the word *critic* always to find fault? Why are they always seeing writers as in conflict with each other, rather than complementing each other . . . simple, this is how they are trained to think. That valuable person who understands what you are doing, what you are aiming for, and can give you advice and real criticism, is nearly always someone right outside the literary machine, even outside the university system; it may be a student just beginning, and still in love with literature, or perhaps it may be a thoughtful person who reads a great deal, following his own instinct.

I say to these students who have to spend a year, two years, writing theses about one book: 'There is only one way to read, which is to browse in libraries and bookshops, picking up books that attract you, reading only those, dropping them when they bore you, skipping the parts that drag – and never, never reading anything because you feel you ought, or because it is part of a trend or a movement. Remember that the book which bores you when you are twenty or thirty will open doors for you when you are forty or fifty – and vice versa. Don't read a book out of its right time for you. Remember that for all the books we have in print, are as many that have never reached print, have never been written down – even now, in this age of compulsive reverence for the written word, history, even social ethic, are taught by means of stories, and the people who have been conditioned into thinking only in terms of what is written – and unfortunately nearly all the products of our educational system can do no more than this – are missing what is before their eyes. For instance, the real history of Africa is still in the custody of black storytellers and wise men, black historians, medicine men: it is a verbal history, still kept safe from the white man and his predations. Everywhere, if you keep your mind open, you will find the truth in words *not* written down. So never let the printed page be your master. Above all, you should know that the fact that you have to spend one year, or two years, on one book, or one author means that you are badly taught – you should have been taught to read your way from one sympathy to another, you should be learning to follow your own intuitive feeling about what you need: that is what you should have been developing, not the way to quote from other people.'

But unfortunately it is nearly always too late.

It did look for a while as if the recent student rebellions might change things, as if their impatience with the dead stuff they are taught might be strong enough to substitute something more fresh and useful. But it seems as if the rebellion is over. Sad. During the lively time in the States, I had letters with accounts of how classes of students had refused their syllabuses, and were bringing to class their own choice of books, those that they had found relevant to their lives. The classes were emotional, sometimes violent, angry, exciting, sizzling with life. Of course this only happened with teachers who were sympathetic, and prepared to stand with the students against authority – prepared for the consequences. There are teachers who know that the way they have to teach is bad and boring – luckily there are still enough, with a bit of luck, to overthrow what is wrong, even if the students themselves have lost impetus.

Meanwhile there is a country where . . .

Thirty or forty years ago, a critic made a private list of writers and poets which he, personally, considered made up what was valuable in literature, dismissing all others. This list he defended lengthily in print, for The List instantly became a subject for much debate. Millions of words were written for and against – schools and sects, for and against, came into being. The argument, all these years later, still continues . . . no one finds this state of affairs sad or ridiculous . . .

Where there are critical books of immense complexity and learning, dealing, but often at second or thirdhand, with original work – novels, plays, stories. The people who write these books form a stratum in universities across the world – they are an international phenomenon, the top layer of literary academia. Their lives are spent in criticising, and in criticising each other's criticism. They at least regard this activity as more important than the original work. It is possible for literary students to spend more time reading criticism and criticism of criticism than they spend reading poetry, novels, biography, stories. A great many people regard this state of affairs as quite normal, and not sad and ridiculous . . .

I recently read an essay about *Antony and Cleopatra* by a boy shortly to take A levels. It was full of originality and excitement about the play, the feeling that any real teaching about literature aims to produce. The essay was returned by the teacher like this: I cannot mark this essay, you haven't quoted from the authorities. Few teachers would regard this as sad and ridiculous . . .

Where people who consider themselves educated, and indeed as superior to and more refined than ordinary non-reading people, will come up to a writer and congratulate him or her on getting a good review somewhere – but will not consider it necessary to read the book in question, or ever to think that what they are interested in is success . . .

Where when a book comes out on a certain subject, let's say star-gazing, instantly a dozen colleges, societies, television programmes, write to the author asking him to come and speak about star-gazing. The last thing it occurs to them to do is to read the book. This behaviour is considered quite normal, and not ridiculous at all . . .

Where a young man or woman, reviewer or critic, who has not read more of a writer's work than the book in front of him, will write patronisingly, or as if rather bored with the whole business, or as if considering how many marks to give an essay, about the writer in question – who might have written fifteen books, and have been writing for twenty or thirty years – giving the said writer instruction on what to write next, and how. No one thinks this is absurd, certainly not the young person, critic or reviewer, who has been taught to patronise and itemise everyone for years, from Shakespeare downwards.

Where a Professor of Archaeology can write of a South American tribe which has advanced knowledge of plants, and of medicine and of psychological methods: 'The astonishing thing is that these people have no written language . . .' And no one thinks him absurd.

Where, on the occasion of a centenary of Shelley, in the same week and in three different literary periodicals, three young men, of identical education, from our identical universities, can write critical pieces about Shelley, damning him with the faintest possible praise, and in identically the same tone, as if they were doing Shelley a great favour to mention him at all – and no one seems to think that such a thing can indicate that there is something seriously wrong with our literary system.

Doris Lessing
Preface to *The Golden Notebook*
(Panther)

STAGES OF RESPONSE TO SEAMUS HEANEY AT 16–19

Blackberry picking

Late August, given heavy rain and sun
For a full week, the blackberries would ripen.
At first, just one, a glossy purple clot
Among others, red, green, hard as a knot.
You ate that first one and its flesh was sweet
Like thickened wine: summer's blood was in it
Leaving stains upon the tongue and lust for
Picking. Then red ones inked up and that hunger
Sent us out with milk-cans, pea-tins, jam-pots

Where briars scratched and wet grass bleached our boots.
Round hayfields, cornfields and potato-drills
We trekked and picked until the cans were full,
Until the tinkling bottom had been covered
With green ones, and on top big dark blobs burned
Like a plate of eyes. Our hands were peppered
With thorn pricks, our palms sticky as Bluebeard's.

We hoarded the fresh berries in the byre.
But when the bath was filled we found a fur,
A rat-grey fungus, glutting on our cache.
The juice was stinking too. Once off the bush
The fruit fermented, the sweet flesh would turn sour.
I always felt like crying. It wasn't fair
That all the lovely canfuls smelt of rot.
Each year I hoped they'd keep, knew they would not.

Seamus Heaney

A   First impression jottings in a journal

Ripe blackberries, one by one, a clump of blackberries, some ripe, some unripe, soft, juicy, sweet and purple, surrounded by hard, sour green and choking, and not ready for another week. You eat one, and you're caught, addicted to pick more. 'Then red ones inked up' — red ones popped up, the red juice was summer's blood, the red ones, discharging red juice which tastes so sweet. Briars snagging on clothes as you lean over to pull them off stalks. Thorns catching on sleeves, and wet grass, and damp socks. Filling the cans, the hard green ones pinging and bouncing into the bottom of the bucket. The dark blobs bulging like staring eyeballs. Pricked hands, blue sticky fingers (and mouths!) Saving all the black-berries, but a fungus settles on them — 'glutting on our cache' — what's a cache? — A place where you hide something, a fungus stealing into the hidden store. The purple beauty turns sour, and rotten, they've been picked again, and they don't last long.

Fiona Boyne

B   Sharing and modifying first impressions through small group talk

* A = Adrian, P = Pat, M = Mandy, D = David

A: I think it's quite good but he seems to be a bit of a sadist though, doesn't he?

P & M: Why?

D: Because he, you know, he . . .

A: He was talking about Bluebeard and he said he murdered his wife and he keeps going on about 'summer's blood was in it' didn't he?

M: Yes, but you know when you've been blackberry picking you get all the juice all over your hands. Well it's just the same as him killing his . . . all his wives off.

D: Yes he must be, must be . . . it it, it's not a masochist it's a sadist isn't it? Yes. But, you know 'I always felt like crying' like he says, at the end he says, 'each year I hoped they'd keep, knew they would not' well, why the hell did he bother then?

M: Because of the enjoyment he gets out of it.

P: Well, no, no.

D: No, no can you see any sense in picking blackberries and leaving them in a bathtub or something and then leaving them to rot? 'Cause that's what happens.

M: No, but the actual picking of the blackberries . . .

P: No, no it's not that . . .

D: What's the point of picking blackberries if you're not going to eat the damn things?

A: Shh, Big Pat's got a word to say.

P: No, it's not that. It's just that . . . he doesn't think . . . I mean, people go and they see all these big bushes of blackberries and they think, 'Oh great!' You know, so they fill cans and cans of them but they don't . . .

A: I mean, it's pointless, isn't it?

P: But they don't think of what's going to happen after that.

A: No, and another thing, look it says,
    'At first just one,
    a glossy purple clot
    among others red, green hard as a knot.
    You ate the first one and its flesh was sweet.'
    You don't really, you don't really, you just eat it for the sake of eating it, don't you?

P: No but the first black . . . (long giggles) the first blackberry of the season, you don't.

M: You don't just eat it.

P: You always, you don't think, oh, you know . . .

D: I've got the first blackberry of the season, let me have it!

A: You eat 'em for the sake of 'em, don't you? You're working away . . .

P: It proves that I don't think he's right because you pick them for the sake of them, you don't think of what's going to happen after, afterwards. You'll pick the same amount next year no matter that you know that they're going to go exactly the same . . . and as a little kid, which I think they are . . . I think he's talking about when he was a little kid . . .

M: He is.

A: Yeah.

P: Well, they'll think 'Oh, maybe this year they'll keep.' You know, because they don't think about that they're going to go rotten. Do they?

M: No, they don't learn by what happens every year.

D:	Sh, no, even little kids have sense, don't they?
P:	No, but no, they don't. Not for things like that. They see these big bushes of blackberries, blackberries, you know, well . . .
D:	Well if they'd got any sense they'd have a damn freezer.
M:	Oh, Fletcher, you spoil it.
P:	Oh don't talk so bloody stupid.
M:	It's not right!
P:	That really is daft!
A:	Just like him . . .
P:	Bloody freezer!
M:	You think back to when you were a kid and you went picking something. You don't think that they're going to go bad or whatever, do you? Or do you?
P:	Well, well you do now, I mean, you would do now.
M:	You would do now.
P:	But when you're a little kid it's the same with everything.
M:	Yes.
P:	You see these great, big bars of chocolate so you buy one and you make yourself sick 'cos you eat it all . . .
M:	But you don't learn by that.
P:	But you don't learn 'cos you'll go and do it again.
M:	And again and again and again.
P:	You're just looking at it from your point of view. Yes, we're not daft enough to go and pick cans and cans, 'cos we'll put them in the fridge or we'll put them . . .
M:	Or we'll eat them then and there.
P:	But to them it's a treasure. It's their treasure.
M:	Yes!
P:	It's something that they did. They got the milk cans and everything or maybe there was a group of little kids that went out on their own and did it.
M:	Yes . . .
P:	And they wouldn't go and say, 'Mummy, mummy, will you put these in the freezer so they'll keep?' They think, 'It's our treasure. We don't want to lose it.' Now that's very ironic but it's what little kids do.
D:	Yeah, I agree with you.
PAUSE	
P:	Right! The second bit . . .
D:	It's minute . . .
P:	Yes, it's minute but it's er . . .
M:	It doesn't need to be a long one, does it?
P:	No, because . . .
D:	I think the first verse is the good side and the second verse is the bad side . . .
P:	Yes, well it is. It is the stark opposite to the first verse . . . because the first verse was full of words like er . . . 'summer's blood was in it' and

there's always these bright colourful words but then there's all these words of decay and things.

M: It's the juice, it's really flowing in the first one but it suddenly starts . . .

P: There's a . . . the inevitability there that in the back of their minds they know the fruit's going to spoil if they leave it there, but they think well, that one year it might not, you know.

C Personal writing: double perspective

Playing in the sand

Plonking down on the wet shiny surface,
Scooping up handfuls, and smearing its wet grittiness over her face,
Slapping the sand down, and clawing white fingers across the surface
gathering up handfuls of sludge,
Smoothing it over arms and legs like a paste,
Flicking it up, smuts flying about,
carving and moulding it into pies,
Sandy soles and oozing in between toes.

From a different corner, a spy thinks —
Dirty face,
Dirty hands,
Sticky fingers
Extra washing
Another bath,
Sand in the car,
Fingerprints on the windows,
A better idea?
— Staying at home.

Fiona Boyne

Lost in Woolworths — 1968

Wandering around — the droning of fans and the buzz of fluorescent lights,
Slapped in the face by coats and dresses,
stockinged legs that form bars on a cage,
Nobody notices one so small,
shopping baskets and handbags merge into a foliage above,
— can't even see their faces,
no reassuring hand to cling to, no one around to sweep you away,
A maze of stands all clicking with static,
Being buried alive with no way out.

A lost child – 'Mrs Davies, have you seen my little girl?
She was holding my hand a minute ago,
I should have left her by the escalator,
You lose little ones so easily in here –
She's only tiny you see,
– She could be over there somewhere,
Or perhaps she is near the jumpers,
– Anyway I'll find her – maybe she's outside.'

Fiona Boyne

Follower

My father worked with a horse plough,
His shoulders globed like a full sail strung
Between the shafts and the furrow.
The horses strained at his clicking tongue.

An expert. He would set the wing
And fit the bright steel-pointed sock.
The sod rolled over without breaking.
At the headrig, with a single pluck

Of reins, the sweating team turned round
And back into the land. His eye
Narrowed and angled at the ground,
Mapping the furrow exactly.

I stumbled in his hob-nailed wake,
Fell sometimes on the polished sod;
Sometimes he rode me on his back
Dipping and rising to his plod.

I wanted to grow up and plough,
To close one eye, stiffen my arm.
All I ever did was follow
In his broad shadow round the farm.

I was a nuisance, tripping, falling,
Yapping always. But today
It is my father who keeps stumbling
Behind me, and will not go away.

Seamus Heaney

210

D   Making a statement for a wider audience

'I suppose I was stranded with myself and began taking stock (of myself and of my childhood) in the poems.'

Show how Seamus Heaney 'takes stock' of his earlier experiences and understands what they mean to him now through the writing of at least two poems from the 'Death of a Naturalist'.

Seamus Heaney was stranded with himself, he was young, he had left home to go to University, leaving behind him a destined life on the land, and many questioning sceptical and possibly even blameful faces. He came from a farming background in Ireland where he had felt secure within the family, and the community in which he lived. When he was sent to University, his neighbours whispered wisely, 'the pen's lighter than the spade', was there a trace of hostility in that comment? Were they blaming Seamus? Or simply thinking him a thin-blooded weakling that they didn't really need in their community? Either way Seamus found himself in an unstable position, he had to come to terms with life the way he had chosen it, and at university he found himself wavering uncertainly. He was unsure of himself, all his family and neighbours had watched him go but it was up to him to prove that it was a worthwhile move.

He was also in the midst of a small private battle, and he had to prove that in fact measure for measure, the pen equalled, if not outweighed the spade. To find his feet was difficult, as shown by the fact that at first he could not establish an identity of his own as a poet, and he could not develop an individual style. He just splashed about at the shallow end 'desperately' imitating other people's styles. The very fact that Seamus wrote for the student magazine under the pseudonym – 'incertus' meaning uncertain, demonstrates clearly his state of mind at the time. He was not sure whether he could capably write a poem – he was not sure of his capabilities – or for that matter whether he could even write a poem at all. Undecisiveness and doubts must have crossed the mind of this poor, struggling undergraduate. Was it the right decision to pull up his roots and choose a different way of life to the one that was comfortably destined for him? If there was guilt about leaving in his mind he had to overcome it, and moreover he had to prove to the people he left that the writing of poetry was a justified reason, not just a poor man's excuse for having an easy, lazy life.

Poetry was a skill that could be compared on equal terms with digging or carpentry, it had to be considered on the same level. When he read other contemporary poets, Seamus was able to start finding his own identity, and to 'take stock' of himself was of prime importance to him.

An interesting angle is Seamus's attitude to childhood and looking back: the way he uses the 'double-perspective' idea. Two poems, 'The Follower' and 'Blackberry picking' will be used to investigate this. It has already been established why Seamus Heaney feels the need to 'take stock' of himself through poetry, but why does he use this method of looking back through the eyes of a child, and then through the eyes of an adult?

First of all he feels the need to look back and see at which point the change occurred, the change when he realised the need to express himself in poetry. Also when did he summon up the courage to accept poetry and discard a life in farming which everyone expected him to do? He has to see himself from two points of view, his own and that of his friends 'taking stock' by looking at himself as a child, how he felt, and how he was regarded by other people close to him – recapping them on the past.

Looking back from an older age at the innocent child he once was, Seamus probably feels 'set' a firmer more mature character, not so bothered about justifying his actions and proving himself to everybody. It is necessary for him to establish though how and when he turned into that person. For me it was necessary to think about that point also, when did I get 'too old' to play with dolls? And why was it that Grandma's house and garden had shrunk in size? – They always seemed so massive before. When did I stop being mad on ponies? When did I become interested in clothes and make-up? – This may all seem part of growing up, but it relates to Seamus's life – when did he start being different? Or why was it him that turned to poetry and not one of his brothers? Seamus could blame poetry on the changes from childhood to adulthood, nature, it was a natural thing that he turned to poetry.

The main thing is that Seamus is trying to take stock of himself by seeing how he changes from an inadequate, diminished kid to a mature adult.

It is one of the initial processes really, taking stock of one's childhood, but one of the things that really bridges a gap between parents and children are qualities like being practical and sensible that develop as one gets older, but in looking back they diminish finally into obscurity. In 'Blackberry picking' I think Seamus achieves this idea very well whereby some qualities are more important to adults than children, the latter who consider them irrelevant. Picking black-berries to a young mind is a wonderful process – the stains on one's clothes and the scratches on the hands are insignificant, but to pick and pick and pick till dusk, and then hoard them is a magical experience. The fact that the adult would not understand forms that bridge between youth and old age. Taking the fun out of it with practical details like damp boots or phrases such as, 'It's a waste to pick so many', or 'why didn't you tell me you'd picked them, I could have frozen them and made blackberry pie.'

It ruins the mystery to utter such realistic phrases as 'You should have known they wouldn't keep – of course they'd turn bad.' A child would not think of being sensible and freeze them. He just goes out expectantly to pick berries and then hoards them always believing that one year they would not go bad. I discovered that thread of hope when I was a child, simply reading through a fairytale. I put dolls furniture at the bottom of the garden with liquorice cakes on the table and hoped that the fairies would come. An awful uncle informed me with harsh shattering, down to earth, finality that fairies did not exist – all that was left for me was shattered dreams and furniture warped by the rain. I suppose one could say that adults hurt children more than they realise. My own experience of being lost in Woolworths when I was very young will stay with me forever. As I said in my poem I felt like I was being buried alive, it was terrifying at the time, but when I look back to try and capture the feeling, I find it difficult for me to describe how I felt, since I cannot imagine the situation as it was.

This really leads on to relations between people, which Seamus tries to analyse for himself through his poems. In particular, a touchy subject perhaps, is Seamus's attitude towards his father, his father's attitude towards him and the relationship that results. 'Follower' is a poem Seamus wrote which demonstrates that relationship. There is no doubt that as a boy Seamus was very much in awe of his father physically.

> His shoulders globed like a full sail strung
> Between the shafts and the furrow.

– His father appeared larger than life, a huge dominant figure, a master, an expert of the land. He had a masterful control of his animals – . . . with a single pluck

> Of reins, the sweating team turned round
> And back into the land . . .

– He did not need to shout at the animals to turn, they obeyed him, similarly with the soil.

> The sod rolled over without breaking.

The land was so well ploughed, the sod would not break (it wouldn't dare to). Seamus regarded his father from an almost idolic angle, watching him expertly work the land, his own boss and master. At the same time though this aura of strength and power, even brutal massiveness that radiated from his father made the child feel diminished, put down, inadequate. Of course perspective comes into it again, from down near the ground Seamus would view his father with this kind of hero worship – he would literally 'look up' to him. Yet he could never catch up with his father, he was always tripping and falling behind, stumbling to keep up, climbing over each furrow took such an effort. It would seem endless, as if he could never get to his father. The poem reads,

> All I ever did was follow
> In his broad shadow round the farm.
> I was a nuisance, tripping, falling,
> Yapping, always . . .

– A feeling of uselessness and desperation – Seamus could never achieve anything constructive. His father was unreachable as a person. Seamus must have felt pretty hurt and put down, but he might have had a complex about this inadequacy he felt. He could never achieve anything to capture his father's admiration – all he could ever do is follow like a lost sheep, rather pathetically after him in his 'hob-nailed wake'. Seamus possibly felt the same feelings in relation to his brothers with all their farming interests. Pride must have been the emotion he felt when his father gave him responsibility on the farm. For instance – 'If he could do this well – maybe his dad would think more of him.' In A Poet's Childhood by Seamus there is a scene whereby the family are trying to get cattle out of a truck.

His father says to Seamus simply 'Seamus, you stand at the shed door' — not much, but to the boy it is the responsibility if only in a small measure that his father gives him which makes him feel needed.

Looking back from an adult point of view it must have all seemed so out of proportion to Seamus, the magnificence of a man who after all was only his father. Maybe his father was channelled into farming himself (this could explain his being narrow-minded). He might not have wanted to do it either, but having had no choice himself, he perhaps despised Seamus for being a poet and not carrying on the family tradition of working on the land.

It is obvious that Seamus writes 'Follower' from a more mature point of view, as he 'takes stock' of his childhood, from an age old enough to analyse the relationship fairly. At the end of the poem, it takes an interesting turn:

> I was a nuisance, tripping, falling,
> Yapping always, but today
> It is my father who keeps stumbling
> Behind me, and will not go away.

That last line — the very example of the double-perspective idea, the reverse view point. Seamus grows into a successful poet — he is good, his books sell and he earns a lot of money. As a person he carries the image of a successful writer, coming from such humble beginnings — very creditable. His father grows old, too old to work the land, he takes on the role of spectator (as Seamus once did). He watches Seamus and his success from the position of an onlooker, helpless, unable to take part, or be involved. He is looking at Seamus with the feeling of being inadequate or no use to anybody. His days, once full with work on the fields are now empty. In other words, Seamus is now looking at his father from the superior position. It is a worthwhile point to note here though, that despite the fact that Seamus did reach the superior position, an equilibrium was never reached between father and son. On swapping roles they bypassed each other, and did not get as close as they could have done.

'Taking stock' of one's childhood through looking back by the idea of double-perspective is important, but it was particularly so for Seamus. I feel he must have been very satisfied after he had written 'Follower' and 'Blackberry picking' as a way of getting into this idea. However, there was a purpose since there are vital links joining taking stock of childhood experiences, and looking at those experiences through the eyes of a child, and then through the eyes of an adult. For Seamus it was three links, and first of all he can understand why he is 'taking stock' in the first place. In other words, he sees that the reasons why he built up this great image of his father, was that he was seeing him from a child's point of view. Now he can conclude that because he held his parents and neighbours in awe, he feels the need to prove to them that poetry is a worthwhile occupation (so he can gain their approval and favour maybe). Secondly, he can establish that then, he was merely an immature, inadequate, diminished little kid, but now is in a position whereby he is old enough to look back and be able to judge fairly what happened in his youth. Thirdly (as demonstrated in 'Follower') he

is proving that the hero-worship concept can come to people in all walks of life —
farming, carpentry, poetry, they are all equal in worth.

Fiona Boyne

ON REVIEWING

In my reckless way I would suggest all reviews were signed and all were put into
the first person. I think that would give the whole paper an amazing lift-up. A
paper that length must be *definite, personal,* or die. It can't afford the 'we' —
'in our opinion'. To sign reviews, to put them in the 1st person stimulates curiosity,
makes for correspondence, gives it (to be 19-eleventyish) *GUTS.* You see it's a
case of leaning out of the window with a board and a nail, *or* a bouquet, *or* a
flag — administering whichever it is and retiring *sharp.* This seems to me essential.
Signed reviews are tonic: the time has gone by for any others. I do wish you could
work this. I am sure it would attract the public. And there's rather a 'trop de
livres, trop de livres' faint cry in it. I read the first par of about 4 reviews and I
begin to whimper faintly.

You're all right, but the others are not. A letter ought to be drafted to your
regular contributors asking them, now that the reviews are to be signed (supposing
that were to happen) — asking them to pull themselves together and make their
attack stronger. Do you know what I mean? I feel inclined to say to them, as
if I were taking their photographs: *'Look Fearless'.* They are huddled up.

Katherine Mansfield
Letters and Journals, ed. C.K. Stead
(Penguin)

REVIEWS

Nicaragua by Susan Meiselas

Nicaragua is a stunning visual document of the people's struggle to rid themselves
of the Somoza dictatorship. It is one of the rare war documentary books which
is committed to a liberation struggle. It is, therefore, very unfortunate that the
commitment is not carried through in the presentation of the book. The book
was intended to be produced in several languages so all the colour printing was
done on pages with no text, only numbers. This means that the first impression
of the book is completely misleading: one thinks that what one has in one's hands
is a glossy art catalogue about a faraway country. The jacket photograph does
nothing to negate that impression.

The reader is invited to look at 71 photographs without commentary or guidance. The photographs are grouped chronologically and in terms of Susan Meiselas' own experience. This produces the effect of a war reportage composed of glimpses. The first photographs go through the shock of arriving in a foreign country and becoming aware of its culture. Pictures of Somoza and a country club evoke the small-town atmosphere of a 'banana republic'. The most shocking image in the book, a grizzly corpse with only arms, legs and spinal chord remaining, jolts us into the main body of the photographs, that documenting the Sandinastas' fighting and the people's experience of war. The pictures of the September 1978 insurrection show familiar images of people fleeing, house-to-house searches and bombs exploding. But there are also pictures taken from behind the barricades clearly demonstrating on whose side Susan Meiselas is. The last section is devoted to the June/July 1979 final offensive and is also taken from behind the lines. There is urgency and tension in all of these pictures except the two photographs of the National Guardsmen pressing forward which curiously say very little about what it is like to face and fight a well-armed enemy. They fall within the classic war photography tradition: the cool observer documenting soldiers and arms from a distance, lending dignity to their mundane and horrifying activities. These photographs contradict the mood and feelings of all the pictures in that section. The concluding pictures in the book are of the victory celebration on 20 July 1979 which are punctuated by another grizzly reminder of suffering as a father picks up the remains of his son, charred beyond recognition. These last images do not allow us as readers to be disengaged: we have to commit ourselves.

The 71 photographs are followed by a text of first-hand accounts by Nicaraguans, quotes and extracts from the media and an excellent chronology. Although the reasons for leaving the text at the end of the book were economic, to reduce the printing bill, the book's commercial success must have been damaged by not integrating the text and photographs. The book has become a 'mere' photography book. The reliance on a narrative of single-page, mainly landscape, colour images has also weakened the photographic discourse. The pictures have become a constant flow of images without emphases or subtleties. These single-page images give the book a very staid and conventional feel which is at odds with the photographs and goes against Meiselas' intentions in producing the book. What is missing is the sense of discovery and growing awareness of the photographer, who learnt important political lessons from her experience. We are left to judge the photographs simply as photographs well within the tradition of art photography. Publishers have yet to learn what makes a photography-based book work. In its present format the book has only a limited appeal to those interested in Nicaragua because of the lack of information alongside the pictures.

Meiselas' use of colour has been criticised perhaps because it challenges one's expectations to see war photographs which are not black and white. In fact Meiselas' photographs are brilliantly effective largely because of her intelligent use of colour, which is a dramatic advance in political photography. It also raises critical questions. The colours in *Nicaragua* are mainly rich greens, dirty brown backgrounds and overcast, whiteish washed-out skies, faintly reminiscent of Vietnam. The only splashes of colour are on the clothes, the improvised uniforms and masks of the Sandinastas, blood, fire and graffiti. While heightening the drama of individual moments, this does not show the collective nature of the struggle. This drama, in the absence of accompanying text, makes it very difficult to see beyond the photographs, outside their frames. Had the text been alongside the photographs there would have been some explanation of who was in the photographs and why they were united in fighting a corrupt dictator supported by American capital. This comes out in the words, for example of Omar Cabenas, 'Whenever we took a town, the whole population came out to watch. Then we called for new recruits . . . We never lacked people. Only arms.'

Meiselas' commitment to Nicaragua is still strong but she is now documenting the equally desperate struggle against dictatorship in El Salvador. When she went to Nicaragua she knew little about Latin America. She now has an impressive knowledge and first-hand experience of struggle behind her. Let us hope that any book she produces on El Salvador will combine that knowledge with her superb eye.

Catherine Bradley
Camerawork March 1982

Extracts from an interview with Susan Meiselas

Why and how did you choose the photographs in the book?
The book is chronological because it seemed comprehensible to do it that way. I was impressed by the revolutionary process in Nicaragua. I hoped people who were not sympathetic to armed struggle could at least understand how it came to be inevitable there. Now it seems to me there are some inherent problems in the book. Firstly, it is not the 'history of the Nicaraguan revolution.' The chronology traces my experience. It is a record of the events and everyday I happened to observe and came to perceive as significant. When I look at the first picture in the book, the pig in the street, that was how crudely I comprehended Latin America.

In making a book of 70 images, a number determined by the publisher, often the less dramatic but no less important moments are eliminated. In the September insurrection it would never have occurred to me to photograph the woman making coffee for the kids behind the barricades. I could not have focussed on her because I was so amazed at the sight of the kids with pistols. Nine months later in the last offensive I do photograph those women, in that sense the book is a document of a process as I came to understand it. A book is a limited form. It can create a sense of continuity through sequencing photographs on pages to be turned. However the effect is to isolate rather than reveal the complexity of the moments from which they are 'taken'. In the light of a moment evolving it is difficult to interpret the life of one person within it.

In the States all the criticism has been about the captions not being with the pictures. The critics do not see the need for any text. The pain for me is that the texts are not with the pictures. The texts recreate the situation from which the moments are isolated. The texts are what the people said when they saw the pictures. Their words create the frame around the frame — the context from which the photographs have come. The captions are not very elaborate so as not to become a crutch for the readers. People want to be told what to see, I want them to feel. They have to dig for information in the pictures. Captions like 'Sandinistas behind the barricades' do not say much. The readers hopefully have to engage with the people in the picture.

How much does the book reflect your experience?
You come out of a year of that intensity and it is very hard to have a perspective on how to make something which is not just an abstraction. There was also the question of whether or not the book should be a more direct translation of my experience in comprehending their revolutionary process. I felt that was inappropriate. The pictures are mine, seen through my eyes and my preoccupations. The text was intended to be theirs as much as it could be, edited according to what I thought was interesting and culturally relevant to 'my people'. Strange how 'my people' does not have the same power as 'muy pueblo'. There are a lot of cultural gaps. At best one can get traces of that experience and maybe lay the ground for someone who wants to know more. Maybe that is all one can do.

Shirley Read and Megan Martin

MEN WHO MARCH AWAY

Poems of the First World War, ed. I. M. Parsons

The first world war goes on getting stronger, our number one national ghost. It's still everywhere, molesting everybody. It's still politically alive, too, in an underground way. On those battlefields the main English social issues surfaced and showed their colours. An English social revolution was fought out in the trenches.

The poetry of the war certainly suggests this. Sassoon's and Owen's poems were shaped and directed by ideas that were ultimately revolutionary in a political sense, no less than the more evidently committed poetry of the 'thirties. The enemy was not German. For four years, France was like England's dream world, a previously unguessed fantasy dimension, where the social oppressions and corruptions slipped into nightmare gear. Men had to act out the roles and undergo the extremes normally suffered only by dream shadows, but under just the same kind of sleep. If the poetry has one guiding theme it is: 'Wake up, we are what is really happening'. Or, perhaps: 'This is what you are doing to us'. The next step, logical but unimaginable, would have been a rising of the ranks, a purging of the mechanical generals, the politicians, the war-profiteers, everything brass-hat and jingoistic both civilian and military. The only German in Owen's poems is the ghost of one he has bayoneted and who calls him 'friend'. But France remained a dream-world, where everything could be suffered but no decision put into effect. In so far as the decisions made there have still not been put into effect, we are possessed by the dream and find a special relevance in the poetry.

An extra fascination, that may well have disappeared in twenty years' time, radiates from the memories of the survivors. They gave their brain-scarred accounts, and every generation since has grown up under their huge first-hand fairy-tale. And somewhere in the nervous system of each survivor the underworld of perpetual Somme rages on unabated, ready to reabsorb the man completely at the right moment of alcohol or drug. We are still in the living thick of it, as well as being far out of it; so all the poems in this anthology have a circumstantial hold on us.

But on the whole, apart from Owen and Sassoon, the poets lost that war. Perhaps Georgian language wouldn't look nearly so bad if it hadn't been put to such a test. It was the worst equipment they could have had – the language of the very state of mind that belied and concealed the possibility of the nightmare that now had to be expressed. Yet these poems are evidence, in one way, of what one important aspect of the war was like, in that they record – as we find hardly anywhere else – the prevailing feeling of being, at that moment, well-educated, English, and conscripted. This collection is really an anthology of those typical feelings, rather than of objective re-creations of the war. Those feelings changed, as the editor points out, during the four years, from 'Now God be thanked Who has matched us with His hour' to 'What more fitting memorial for the fallen/Than that their children/Should fall for the same cause?' They are stereotyped, familiar patterns, but it's these poems that have made them familiar.

After the first flush, the pattern settles to variations of the contrast between the battle-field in France and the rural beauties of England. Owen, Sassoon, Graves, and Thomas all use this in some of their best pieces. This simple strategy sharpens to something more serious later on, a bitter contrast between the landscape of dead bodies and the English-in-England complacency, which engages more urgent and more national feelings, and produces some of Owen's and Sassoon's best work. It might be said to have created Owen. We know that he intended his poems – as he intended those photographs of the trenches, emergency operations, and the like, which he wanted to magnify and display in London – to drive the actuality of the front-line sufferings into the faces of those safe in England. His poems are partly substitutes or verbal parallels for those photographs. The main thing was that they could never be vivid or terrible enough. This immediate journalistic purpose was just what was needed to focus and mobilize his genius for absorbing suffering. Perhaps what he called 'Pity' gave the depth, and the painful tenderness, to his experience, but it was indignation that turned it into poems – poems that were meant to frighten people, and to incite political action.

The war provided Owen and Sassoon with material their special gifts might not have found elsewhere, but it was disastrous for most of the others. Rosenberg seems grotesquely out of place in uniform. His imagination was bound to inner struggle, and seems to have found it hard to connect with the war, though 'Break of Day in the Trenches' is one of the best poems here. Two interesting survivors are Ivor Gurney and Osbert Sitwell. Both of them used a plain unpoetic language, which makes an impressive lesson in preservation among the other tainted fruit.

Perhaps what we would like from these poets is fuller descriptive and objective evidence. Except for Owen's pieces (of which the editor excludes half the best and perhaps the most graphic) there is very little. We have to remember how they were taken by surprise. It's that surprise which makes all the difference between the human measure of the first world war and of the second. Four years was not long enough, nor Edwardian and Georgian England the right training, nor stunned, somnambulist exhaustion the right condition, for digesting the shock of machine guns, armies of millions, and the plunge into the new dimension, where suddenly and for the first time Adam's descendants found themselves meaningless. All that had to wait for later embodiment in the prose of Henry Williamson, and in David Jones's 'In Parenthesis'.

Ted Hughes
Listener 5.8.65

ON COBBETT'S STYLE

His [Cobbett's] style, with all its open-air virility, is yet lean and hard and undecorated, in accordance with his shrewd puritanism . . . It is like watching a man, a confident, free-speaking man, with a fine head, a thick neck, and a voice and gestures peculiarly his own, standing up in a crowd, a head taller than the rest, talking democracy despotically. He comes to us offering, as only a few other men do, the pleasure of watching a fighter whose brain and voice are, as it were, part of his physical and muscular development. The movement of his prose is a bodily thing. His sentences do not precisely suggest the swing of an arm or a leg, but they have something in common with it. His style is perhaps the nearest to speech that has really survived.

Edward Thomas
Introduction to Cobbett's *Rural Rides*
(1912 edition)

GREEN BEEF

Unlike Bionic Woman or Six Million Dollar Man *The Incredible Hulk* (ITV) is not a rebuild but a true mutant. Bionic and Six used to be ordinary human beings but were transformed by engineering. Hulk remains an ordinary human being who can't help turning into an extraordinary one every time he gets angry. An 'overdose of gamma radiation' has altered 'his body chemistry' so that in vexing moments he becomes the physical expression of his own fury.

'The creature', it is explained, 'is driven by rage.' A combination of Clark Kent and Dr Jekyll, 'mild-mannered' David Banner falls first into a sweat, then into a trance, and finally into a metamorphosis. In the same time that it takes to wheel a small actor off and a large one on, a weedy schnurk like you and me is transmogrified into seven feet of green beef.

Hulk has the standard body-builder's physique, with two sets of shoulders one on top of the other and wings of lateral muscle that hold his arms out from his sides as if his armpits had piles. He is made remarkable by his avocado complexion, eyes like plover's eggs and the same permanently exposed lower teeth displayed by Richard Harris when he is acting determined, or indeed just acting.

Given a flying start by the shock effect of his personal appearance, Hulk goes into action against the heavies, flinging them about in slow motion. Like Bionic, Six and Wonder-woman, Hulk does his action numbers at glacial speed. Emitting slow roars of rage, Hulk runs very slowly towards the enemy, who slowly attempt to make their escape. But no matter how slowly they run, Hulk runs more slowly. Slowly he picks them up, gradually bangs their heads together, and with a supreme burst of lethargy throws them through the side of a building.

Hardly have the bricks floated to the ground before Hulk is changing back into spindly David, with a sad cello weeping on the sound-track. One thinks of Frankenstein's monster or the Hunchback of Notre Dame. One thinks of King Kong. One thinks one is being had. Why can't the soft twit cut the soul-searching and just enjoy his ability to swell up and clobber the foe? But David is in quest of 'a way to control the raging spirit that dwells within him'. Since the series could hardly continue if he finds it, presumably he will be a long time on the trail.

If you took the violence out of American television there wouldn't be much left, and if you took the American television out of British television there wouldn't be much left of that either. Without imported series, our programme planners couldn't fill the schedules. Whether schedules ought to be filled is another question. As things stand, American series have to be bought in. Nearly all of them are violent to some degree. But those who believe that violence on television causes violence in real life should take consolation from the fact that most of the violence in American series is on a par with the Incredible Hulk torpidly jumping up and down on the langorously writhing opponents of freedom and justice.

Clive James
The Crystal Bucket (Picador)

WHY 'THE DEER HUNTER' IS A LIE

Eleven years ago I went to the movies in Montgomery, Alabama. It was a Saturday night and the local fleapalace was packed, mostly with 'good ole boys' who, in those days, hung about gas stations and giggled menacingly at the occupants of any car with out-of-Dixie plates. This was the summer of 1968; children had died in the firebombing of a black church in Montgomery, Richard Nixon was making his comeback and the American war in Vietnam was at its peak. The movie was *The Green Berets,* starring John Wayne.

From scene one they cheered. They threw their beer cans and yelped and when 'The Duke' dealt single-handedly with an entire regiment of gooks, a Buddha shape in front of me, hoarse with adulation, stood and saluted.

Like a fool, I laughed through it all, and therefore found myself having to exit well before the credits, and smartly. It didn't matter that I knew Vietnam and the war; this was such a *bad* movie – badly put together, badly acted – and so unwittingly silly that it was funny. And although it was hailed in towns like Montgomery, where John Wayne is part of the weaning process, it was generally dismissed as crude Hollywood stuff, whose antics by no stretch of the imagination tallied with the nightly television images of napalmed civilians and the greatest military machine in history going nowhere.

The other night I saw *The Deer Hunter,* which, as almost everybody must know by now, is about Vietnam, plus nice pictures of small-town America, a wedding and mountains. This film has been nominated for so many awards that only the Congressional Medal of Honour appears to be missing and the bestowal of that appropriate gong might well be a possibility if the relentless eulogising continues, here and in America. So finely orchestrated has been the pre-publicity for this film that 'Have you seen *The Deer Hunter?'* has become a breathless catch cry of one-upmanship. Indeed, it is difficult to get seats for a film which Derek Malcolm in the *Guardian* insists we should see 'at all costs', and which the *Daily Mail* describes as 'the story they never dared to tell before . . . the film that could purge a nation's guilt!' and which left Milton Shulman 'quivering and shattered' and which, according to Alexander Walker in the *Evening Standard,* 'says things that needed saying'. And so on, and so on. Lady Delfont, wife of one of the backers apparently wept openly.

There is much to weep about. The backers and makers of this film are reported to have spent fourteen million dollars on sifting the ashes of one of history's most documented atrocities – in order to re-package it and re-sell it as a Hollywood 'smash' that will, and probably already has, made them fortunes; to reincarnate the triumphant Batman-jawed Caucasian warrior and to present a suffering, courageous people as sub-human Oriental brutes and dolts; to convert truth into lie. And, as I say, if the queues and touts at the box office are any indication, they are getting away with it.

Compared with *The Deer Hunter, The Green Berets* was an honest film; its B-movie fantasy was discernible to all but the most evangelical 'patriot'. *The Deer Hunter* is technically slick, and perhaps its documentary and *verité* effects are even brilliant; *something* must have prompted usually discriminating critics to opt for unction and naïvete.

And, I suppose, for those who have forgotten what Vietnam was really about, or would wish to forget, or are too young to remember, or are truly naïve, the slickness is persuasive; the wedding guests act like wedding guests, the blood gushes, the bullets thud and the rotors of helicopters make the sound that is forever embedded in my brain, from years of attending the reality. Otherwise, the symbolism is leaden (one shot for the proud stag etc.) the *schmaltz* elongated and the sadism utterly gratuitious: the kind of sadism that packs 'em in.

There are times when, even by the film's own standards, the slick runs precariously thin; the strong, silent Batman-jawed Robert DeNiro and the brave, sensitive, baby-faced Boy Wonder Christopher Walken could not merely suffer in captivity as soldiers; no, the Dynamic Duo get away by wiping out a house-full of their barbaric captors, mighty M-16s rotating from their hips. Pow! Wham! Rat-tat-tat! 'C'mon, letzgetouttahere!' *ad nauseam.* Big John would have shown them how it's really done.

This is how Hollywood created the myth of the Wild West, which was harmless enough unless you happened to be an American Indian, and how World War Two and the Korean War were absorbed into box office folklore, which was harmless enough unless you happened to be a dumb Kraut or an unspeakable Nip or a Commie chink, or one of a malleable generation and liable to be conditioned by endless, bragging, simplistic good guy/bad guy images of war. And of course, *The Deer Hunter* is harmless enough unless you happen to be a gook, Commie or otherwise, or of a generation too young to remember genocidal 'free fire zones' and towns and villages that 'had to be destroyed to save them'.

That the same cynical mythmaking is now being applied to Vietnam (there'll be *Deer Hunter 2,* I bet) induces more melancholy than anger in those like myself, who saw whole Vietnamese communities used as guinea pigs for the testing of a range of 'anti-personnel' military technology, and who saw demoralised, brutalised, often mutinous and doped American teenagers lying in their own blood and shit, for the purposes of some pointless, sacrificial siege staged in the cause of nothing, except the gratification of inept brass in their air-conditioned bubbles.

There is not a passing hint in *The Deer Hunter* that Vietnam was, above all, a war of rampant technology against human beings. There are, however, heavenly violins.

Richard Grenier, the New York critic, tells me that the director of *The Deer Hunter,* Michael Cimino, is being hailed in America as the champion of the 'new patriotism'. Linda Christmas of the *Guardian* reported Cimino as saying

> During the making of the film, I certainly had a sense that we were doing something special. It was such an agonising experience both emotionally, physically – the tropics, the heat, the humidity. I can't shake off *The Deer Hunter* even now. I have this insane feeling that I was there, in Vietnam. Somehow the fine wires have got really crossed and the line between reality and fiction has become blurred.

The above is how you 'sell' and justify a myth. Cimino is an expert salesman. He sold *The Deer Hunter* without a script. Originally, it was to be the recollections of a group of former GIs, but what helped to convince the major backers that they were on to a winner were the orgiastic Russian roulette scenes that recur throughout the film and leave an audience with the impression that the Vietnamese gamble on human life as casually as the British gamble on the pools.

How odd: in Vietnam, I never heard about this game. I have asked other correspondents and they have never heard about this game. And interviews with POWs never mentioned this game; but much of Cimino's picture is given over to this 'meaningful horror', which he insists happened and which is meant to be somehow redemptive.

There is another problem. Although Cimino says he has 'this insane feeling that I was there, in Vietnam', he was never there. He told Linda Christmas, and Leticia Kent of the *New York Times*, that he was called up shortly after the *Tet* offensive in 1968 and was a medic attached to the Green Berets. He 'missed' Vietnam because, he says, he had a job 'involved in defence and classified. Something to do with that . . .'

The Pentagon's records tell a different story. He was in the army reserve before draftees were sent to Vietnam and was pursuing a career in advertising at the time of *Tet*. These minor discrepancies would matter little, except that they may help to explain something about the source of *The Deer Hunter's* mythmaking.

The timing of *The Deer Hunter* is perfect. The 'new patriotism' and the mood of national redemption decree that it is time the American conscience was salved and the Vietnamese 'punished' for defeating and humiliating the greatest power on earth. In February 1979, Vietnam was attacked by America's new ally, China, on the pretext that the Vietnamese were the stooges of Moscow. The American Government condemned the Chinese action with all the force of a verbal leg-slap, while linking it, astutely, to a condemnation of Hanoi's overthrow of the genocidal regime in Cambodia; there was no mention that Cambodia had attacked Vietnam in 1977.

During these past weeks of 'punishment' — when the Vietnamese, by most accounts, stopped their latest invader — official Washington statements neglected to mention that the Vietnamese had been pleading for diplomatic ties with America with such desperation that they had dropped all previous demands for reparations; that for two years the Vietnamese, having maintained their independence from both Russia and China during the war years, had resisted Russian pressure to sign a 'friendship treaty', until they had no choice; that the Americans ignored these overtures and used their influence to prevent Asian Development Bank funds going to Vietnam for desperately needed reconstruction aid.

And who now is vocal in backing China's 'punishment' of Vietnam, and China's ambition to 'smash the myth of Vietnam's invincibility? William C. Westmoreland, one of the chief architects of American vandalism (and defeat) in Vietnam; Senator John Tower, hero of the far right; Nguyen Ky, former President of South Vietnam (now in the liquor business in California); patriots all.

I was in Vietnam last year. It seems incredible that there is still need to offer reminders of what was done to that nation. But, with Hollywood now re-making history, and with current events being reported so as to make the Vietnamese appear as Oriental Prussians, such reminders are necessary.

Much of North Vietnam is a moonscape, from which visible signs of life — houses, factories, schools, hospitals, pagodas, churches — have been obliterated. Forty-four per cent of the forests have been destroyed; in many of those still standing there are no longer birds and animals; and there are lorry drivers who will not respond to the hooting of a horn because they are deaf from the incessant sound of bombs; and there are some 30 000 children in Hanoi and Haiphong alone who are permanently deaf as a result of the American bombing at Christmas 1972.

The B52s spared the spacious French-built centre of the cities and laid 'carpets' of bombs down such crowded arteries as Kham Thiem Street in Hanoi, where today an old nicotine-stained figure with a wispy beard keeps a vigil at a gap where 283 people died. 'It was a block of flats', he told me, 'we were mostly the old, women and children. There was no time to reach the shelters, and we sang as the bombs came down . . . singing is louder than bombs'. Such dignity, out of horror, is representative of the Vietnamese and differs sharply from Mr Cimino's fantasies. (More bombs were dropped on Vietnam than ever dropped during all of World War Two and Korea combined: the greatest aerial onslaught ever.)

In Hanoi's Bach Mai Hospital, doctors have discovered that 'Napalm B', which the Dow Chemical Company created especially for Vietnam, continues to smoulder under the skin's tissues through the lifetime of its victims. People continue to die from the effects of plastic needles which were sprayed by bombs created especially for Vietnam and designed so that the needles moved through human organs and escape detection, even under X-ray.

Places called Ham Long and Dong Loc ought to be as well known as Dresden, but they are not. Ham Long, like so many towns in the north, was bombed literally back to the Stone Age: every day for four years, from five in the morning till two in the afternoon, the planes came in low from carriers in the South China Sea. At Cu Chi, in the south, an horizon that was once thick vegetation now shimmers in the heat, laid completely to waste 'for maybe half a century or more', according to the report of one member of an American Academy of Science team. This is the result of 'Operation Hades' (later Hollywoodised to 'Operation Ranch Hand'): the defoliation and poisoning of the landscape and crops, and the sowing of the seeds of human mutations for generations. In 1970 I wrote about a 'foetal disaster' at the Tu Duc Hospital in Saigon where deformed babies were beginning to arrive by the dozen: the result, said American doctors at the time, of an aerial spray called 245-T, which is banned in the United States.

That is enough, I suppose. There are the tens of thousands of heroin addicts, and a strain of VD for which there is no certain cure. There are the permanently dislocated and the insane, who ran from General Westmoreland's 'free fire zones'. And there are the thousands of American-fathered children; several of them were singing a song when I visited a Saigon orphanage. I wrote these words in the *New Statesman* in 1978 and I believe they are worth repeating. 'The war is gone . . . planes come no more . . . do not weep for those just born . . . the human being is evergreen'. If you see *The Deer Hunter*, you may like to remember these lines.

John Pilger
Aftermath: the struggle of Cambodia and Vietnam
(New Statesman)

WRITING IN THE STYLE OF
'ONE FLEW OVER THE CUCKOO'S NEST'

I can see by the clock on the wall it's gone three but my legs just too tired to move over to the table with Will and the others. I've been like this since they caught me – can't figure just how long ago it was. I quit thinking and let them watch me as I shrunk and shrunk and the man in the spectacles curled over my head.

I could of run, but what's the use? They gets you in the end, in or out. I knew soon as I saw the dam: I knew when I saw the insects crawling over, white helmets like it was some kind of party, laughing and joking. Not twenty thousand could of knocked that dam over a crazy injun would never get near. And it will dance down the generations, like that old bluetick dog, running on from its own life and makin' its future like it was making its own fear – don't need to look back 'cos it's light with papa's face, glowing like a pinhead.

Over the room Kesey is plugging in the first of the patients. He moves like he was scared of something, fumbling the plug and smiling quickly at the visitors. He smiles funny – like that PR man back at the hospital, but he's not the same. His neck's drained white as a fish and his cheeks so thin and yellow you could peel them off and write on them.

Kesey turns round and plugs the next patient in, and the next, until there's more'n twenty pink young faces staring pop-eyed at us through the glass.

'Ready nurse? . . . switch on.'

The wires fizz and pop a while before settling down to a steady hum as the tragedies of the others' lives seep into the patients. There's one on his own at the end, and I can see he's meant for me. Kesey walks over and stretches out his rough, calloused hand – so rough and cracked it might be older'n the fish mountain. As he touches my shoulder I can see the owner where the plastic's wearing off, and wonder if McMurphy's raw hands were like that.

'Come on, chief,' he says kindly, like papa talked to mother the day the Government Men came: 'Let's go to the table and tell these people about the *horrible* hospital.' His voice is empty, cold as the frosty air over the valley.

Just then Willy starts strugglin' more'n he ought. I can see Kesey's annoyed and I figure he's gonna tie Willy down.

'Come on, now, William. These people are here to be educated; helped to realise what a *terrible* monster Modern Western Society is. You've got to help them by letting them know all the *terrible* things they did to you in that *horrible* hospital.'

He's walkin' all the time he talks and fetches up against Willy's chair just's he finishes. Willy turns to see him and his eyes pop up white like a frightened skunk's.

'Nuh nuh nuh nn No! Please!'

Kesey's got a sock full o' bird shot he lifted from some black boy at the hospital, and Willy quits fighting. I can see Kesey's madder'n a bull and his thin smile's stretched like a mountain stream 'cross the rocks as he turns to me.

'Now chief. Hurry – we're all waiting.'

I watch him walk towards me again, this time gently swinging the sock; his eyes full of high-tension electric, colour of carbon. I figure if I get near enough he'll short out and kill me, and I try to push more'n more into the chair. I can hear him speaking, saying as I ought to be grateful that I can help rid the world of Modern Western Society and it's going to be hard on me if I *don't* tell 'em 'bout EST and the rest, but it's like watching TV through shop windows: he's remote, like a wolf barking in the hills. I keep telling myself I gotta move, an' scrabblin' to get away from him as he reaches his hand out to catch me again.

'It's for your own good.' He's straining hard to smile, like it hurts him but he gotta keep going.

'Come on, now. How would you like to be back in that *nasty* hospital?'

There's no fog to hide in, no comfort in the oily new leather of the chair.

'Do you want to go back? Well . . . ?'

I been awake only a few days. I'm in a ward, but I can tell it's not back at the asylum 'cos of the beds. They're cold grey with no sheets or blankets or nothing. It's different here – no OD cards so I figure they just got one they use alla time. Kesey don't mess with the docs like Big Nurse used to and it's always goin' like it oughta.

Since I woke up this time I've been thinking a lot about Kesey. They can't get at you when you think if you're still mostly asleep, and I'm more'n half asleep most of the time I'm awake: that sounds stupid, don't it? You're maybe right.

It's true what he says: I hated the hospital pretty much – but he don't understand: it's the *Combine* I gotta fight.

Papa whistled to the dog, and the whistle echoed so clear and loud I figure it reached the city. One day Papa and me are going into the city and papa says it's full of palefaces.

When I'm a big Indian chief Papa says I can have a bow and arrow and a horse and a fish spear and everybody in the *whole world* will have to do as I say.

'Goodnight, my little chief.'

'G' night, mama.'

The warm crept down from my stomach and filled my toes and I wriggled them up and down over the buffalo hide, soft and furry like a caterpillar. It was good to be warm: the white man came in the morning.

Elizabeth Gladwin
(Sixth-form student)

HALS AND BANKRUPTCY

In my mind's eye I see the story of Frans Hals in theatrical terms.

The first act opens with a banquet that has already been going on for several hours. (In reality these banquets often continued for several days.) It is a banquet

Frans Hals, *Banquet of the Offices of St George Civic Guard Company*

for the officers of one of the civic guard companies of Haarlem – let us say the St George's Company of 1627. I choose this one because Hals's painted record of the occasion is the greatest of his civic guard group portraits.

The officers are gay, noisy and emphatic. Their soldierly air has more to do with the absence of women and with their uniforms than with their faces or gestures, which are too bland for campaigning soldiers. And on second thoughts even their uniforms seem curiously unworn. The toasts which they drink to one another are to eternal friendship and trust. May all prosper together!

One of the most animated is Captain Michiel de Wael – down-stage wearing a yellow jerkin. The look on his face is the look of a man certain that he is as young as the night and certain that all his companions can see it. It is a look that you can find at a certain moment at most tables in any night-club. But before Hals it had never been recorded. We watch Captain de Wael as the sober always watch a man getting tipsy – coldly and very aware of being an outsider. It is like watching a departure for a journey we haven't the means to make. Twelve years later Hals painted the same man wearing the same chamois jerkin at another banquet. The stare, the look, has become fixed and the eyes wetter. If he can, he now spends the afternoons drinking at club bars. And his throaty voice as he talks and tells stories has a kind of urgency which hints that once, a long way back when he was young, he lived as we have never done.

Hals is at the banquet – though not in the painting. He is a man of nearly fifty, also drinking heavily. He is at the height of his success. He has the reputation of being wilful and alternately lethargic and violent. (Twenty years ago there was

228

a scandal because they said he beat his wife to death when drunk. Afterwards he married again and had eight children.) He is a man of very considerable intelligence. We have no evidence about his conversation but I am certain that it was quick, epigrammatic, critical. Part of his attraction must have lain in the fact that he behaved as though he actually enjoyed the freedom which his companions believed in in principle. His even greater attraction was in his incomparable ability as a painter. Only he could paint his companions as they wished. Only he could bridge the contradiction in their wish. Each must be painted as a distinct individual and, at the same time, as a spontaneous natural member of the group.

Who are these men? As we sensed, they are not soldiers. The civic guards, although originally formed for active service, have long since become purely ceremonial clubs. These men come from the richest and most powerful merchant families in Haarlem, which is a textile-manufacturing centre.

Haarlem is only eleven miles from Amsterdam and twenty years before, Amsterdam had suddenly and spectacularly become the financial capital of the entire world. Speculation concerning grain, precious metals, currencies, slaves, spices and commodities of every kind is being pursued on a scale and with a success that leaves the rest of Europe not only amazed but dependent on Dutch capital.

A new energy has been released and a kind of metaphysic of money is being born. Money acquires its own virtue — and, on its own terms, demonstrates its

own tolerance. (Holland is the only state in Europe without religious persecution.) All traditional values are being either superseded or placed within limits and so robbed of their absolutism. The States of Holland have officially declared that the Church has no concern with questions of usury within the world of banking. Dutch arms-merchants consistently sell arms, not only to every contestant in Europe, but also, during the cruellest wars, to their own enemies.

The officers of the St George's Company of the Haarlem Civic Guard belong to the first generation of the modern spirit of Free Enterprise. A little later Hals painted a portrait which seems to me to depict this spirit more vividly than any other painting or photograph I have ever seen. It is of Willem van Heythuyzen.

Willem Van Heythuzen

What distinguishes this portrait from all earlier portraits of wealthy or powerful men is its instability. Nothing is secure in its place. You have the feeling of looking at a man in a ship's cabin during a gale. The table will slide across the floor. The book will fall off the table. The curtain will tumble down.

Furthermore, to emphasize and make a virtue out of this precariousness, the man leans back on his chair to the maximum angle of possible balance, and tenses the switch which he is holding in his hands so as almost to make it snap. And it is the same with his face and expression. His glance is a momentary one, and around his eyes you see the tiredness which is the consequence of having always, at each moment, to calculate afresh.

At the same time the portrait in no way suggests decay or disintegration. There may be a gale but the ship is sailing fast and confidently. Today van Heythuyzen would doubtless be described by his associates as being 'electric', and there are millions who model themselves — though not necessarily consciously — on the bearing of such men.

Put van Heythuyzen in a swivel chair, without altering his posture, pull the desk up in front of him, change the switch in his hands to a ruler or an aluminium rod, and he becomes a typical modern executive, sparing a few moments of his time to listen to your case.

But to return to the banquet. All the men are now somewhat drunk. The hands that previously balanced a knife, held a glass between two fingers, or squeezed a lemon over the oysters, now fumble a little. At the same time their gestures become more exaggerated — and more directed towards us, the imaginary audience. There is nothing like alcohol for making one believe that the self one is presenting is one's true, up to now always hidden, self.

They interrupt each other and talk at cross-purposes. The less they communicate by thought, the more they put their arms round each other. From time to time they sing, content that at last they are acting in unison, for each, half lost in his own fantasy of self-presentation, wishes to prove to himself and to the others only one thing — that he is the truest friend there.

Hals is more often than not a little apart from the group. And he appears to be watching them as we are watching them.

The second act opens on the same set with the same banqueting table, but now Hals sits alone at the end of it. He is in his late sixties or early seventies, but still very much in possession of his faculties. The passing of the intervening years has, however, considerably changed the atmosphere of the scene. It has acquired a curiously mid-nineteenth-century air. Hals is dressed in a black cloak, with a black hat somewhat like a nineteenth-century top hat. The bottle in front of him is black. The only relief to the blackness is his loose white collar and the white page of the book open on the table.

The turning point occurred in 1645. For several years before that, Hals had it. We think of Baudelaire. We begin to understand why Courbet and Manet admired Hals so much.

The turning point occurred in 1645. For several years before that, Hals had received fewer and fewer commissions. The spontaneity of his portraits which had so pleased his contemporaries became unfashionable with the next generation, who already wanted portraits which were more morally reassuring – who demanded in fact the prototypes of that official bourgeois hypocritical portraiture which has gone on ever since.

In 1645 Hals painted a portrait of a man in black looking over the back of a chair. Probably the sitter was a friend. His expression is another one that Hals was the first to record. It is the look of a man who does not believe in the life he witnesses, yet can see no alternative. He has considered, quite impersonally, the possibility that life may be absurd. He is by no means desperate. He is interested. But his intelligence isolates him from the current purpose of men and the supposed purpose of God. A few years later Hals painted a self-portrait displaying a different character but the same expression.

As he sits at the table it is reasonable to suppose that he reflects on his situation. Now that he receives so few commissions, he is in severe financial difficulties. But his financial crisis is secondary in his own mind to his doubts about the meaning of his work.

When he does paint, he does so with even greater mastery than previously. But his mastery has itself become a problem. Nobody before Hals painted portraits of greater dignity and greater sympathy, implying greater performance. But nobody before seized upon the momentary personality of the sitter as Hals has done. It is with him that the notion of 'the speaking likeness' is born. Everything is sacrificed to the demands of the sitter's immediate presence.

Or almost everything, for the painter needs a defence against the threat of becoming the mere medium through whom the sitter presents himself. In Hals's portraits his brushmarks increasingly acquire a life of their own. By no means all of their energy is absorbed by their descriptive function. We are not only made acutely aware of the subject of the painting, but also of *how* it has been painted. With 'the speaking likeness' of the sitter is also born the notion of the virtuoso performance by the painter, the latter being the artist's protection against the former.

Yet it is a protection that offers little consolation, for the virtuoso performance only satisfies the performer for the duration of the performance. Whilst he is painting, it is as though the rendering of each face or hand by Hals is a colossal gamble for which all the sharp, rapid brushstrokes are the stakes. But when the painting is finished, what remains? The record of a passing personality and the record of a performance which is over. There are no real stakes. There are only careers. And with these – making a virtue of necessity – he has no truck.

Whilst he sits there, people – whose seventeenth-century Dutch costumes by now surprise us – come to the other end of the table and pause there. Some are friends, some are patrons. They ask to be painted. In most cases Hals declines. His lethargic manner is an aid. And perhaps his age as well. But there is also a certain defiance about his attitude. He makes it clear, that whatever may have happened when he was younger, he no longer shares their illusions.

Occasionally he agrees to paint a portrait. His method of selection seems arbitrary: sometimes it is because the man is a friend: sometimes because the face interests him. (It must be made clear that this second act covers a period of several years.) When a face interests him, we perhaps gather from the conver-

Portrait of a Seated Man Holding a Branch

sation that it is because in some way or another the character of the sitter is related to the problem that preoccupies Hals, the problem of what it is that is changing so fundamentally during his lifetime.

It is in this spirit that he paints Descartes, that he paints the new, ineffective professor of theology, that he paints the minister Herman Langelius who 'fought with the help of God's words, as with an iron sword, against atheism', that he paints the twin portraits of Alderman Geraerdts and his wife.

233

The wife in her canvas is standing, turned to the right and offering a rose in her outstretched hand. On her face is a compliant smile. The husband in his canvas is seated, one hand limply held up to receive the rose. His expression is simultaneously lascivious and appraising. He has no need to make the effort of any pretence. It is as though he is holding out his hand to take a bill of credit that is owing to him.

At the end of the second act a baker claims a debt of 200 florins from Hals. His property and his paintings are seized and he is declared bankrupt.

The third act is set in the men's almshouse of Haarlem. It is the almshouse whose men and women governors Hals was commissioned to paint in 1664. The two resulting paintings are among the greatest he ever painted.

After he went bankrupt, Hals had to apply for municipal aid. For a long while it was thought that he was actually an inmate of the almshouse – which today is the Frans Hals Museum – but apparently this was not the case. He experienced, however, both extreme poverty and the flavour of official charity.

In the centre of the stage the old men who are inmates sit at the same banqueting table, as featured in the first act, with bowls of soup before them. Again it strikes us as a nineteenth-century scene – Dickensian. Behind the old men at the table, Hals, facing us, is between two canvases on easels. He is now in his eighties. Throughout the act he peers and paints on both canvases, totally without regard to what is going on elsewhere. He has become thinner as very old men can.

On the left on a raised platform are the men governors whom he is painting on

Regentesses of the Old Man's Alms House

234

one canvas; on the right, on a similar platform, are the women governors whom he is painting on the other canvas.

The inmates between each slow spoonful stare fixedly at us or at one of the two groups. Occasionally a quarrel breaks out between a pair of them.

The men governors discuss private and city business. But whenever they sense that they are being stared at, they stop talking and take up the positions in which Hals painted them, each lost in his own fantasy of morality, their hands fluttering like broken wings. Only the drunk with the large tilted hat goes on reminiscing and occasionally proposing a mock banquet toast. Once he tries to engage Hals in conversation.

(I should point out here that this is a theatrical image; in fact the governors and governesses posed singly for these group portraits.)

The women discuss the character of the inmates and offer explanations for their lack of enterprise or moral rectitude. When they sense that they are being stared at, the woman on the extreme right brings down her merciless hand on her thigh and this is a sign for the others to stare back at the old men eating their soup.

The hypocrisy of these women is not that they give while feeling nothing, but that they never admit to the hate now lodged permanently under their black clothes. Each is secretly obsessed with her own hate. She puts out crumbs for it

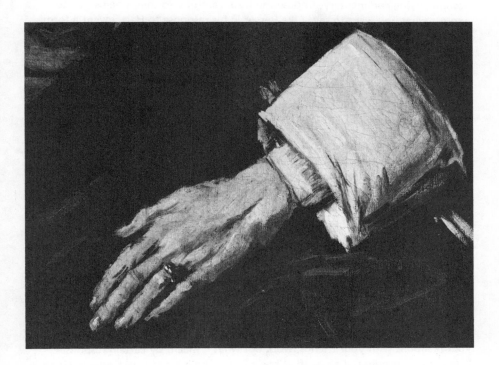

every morning of the endless winter until finally it is tame enough to tap on the glass of her bedroom window and wake her at dawn.

Darkness. Only the two paintings remain – two of the most severe indictments ever painted. They are projected side by side to fill a screen across the whole stage.

Offstage there is the sound of banqueting. Then a voice announces: He was eighty-four and he had lost his touch. He could no longer control his hands. The result is crude and, considering what he once was, pathetic.

John Berger
About Looking
(Writers and Readers Cooperative)

WAYS OF WORKING

● Try out new forms of response to what you are reading, watching, or listening to. For example, prepare a taped programme with selected extracts, interviews, characters being questioned about motives and behaviour, sound effects; collage work; answering in role; improvised drama; strip cartoons; illustrations with accompanying commentary. Choose the form carefully so that it helps you to express what you want to say. Like Berger in his response to Hals, invent a form that gives your imagination a great deal of scope.

● Probe the early reading experiences that stay in the mind; collect memories and accounts from friends or adults either on tape or in written form. Investigate the reasons for that early influence and what possible results came out of them. Share your findings with other members of your group. (Read Fred Inglis on his early enthusiasm for comics.)

● Keep a reading log or journal throughout your course and record your first impression jottings on what you read. Allow the first encounter to sink in and then swap your impressions with other members of the group. Come back to what you have read and written later on in the course and reflect and comment on the change in your reactions. (Look at Fiona Boyne's impressions as precise examples of this kind of developing response.)

● In small groups read what Katherine Mansfield has to say on reviewing and decide which of the reviews (Ted Hughes, Edward Thomas, Camerawork) you like most. Decide what makes an effective review. Then prepare a group review on a recent play you've seen, television programme or film, putting into practice your agreed approach to reviewing.

● Read or watch John Berger's *Ways of Seeing* (Penguin). After talking through your reactions with your friends, work out what is meant by certain responses being seen as product of a specific time, a way of seeing and a particular position. Record and comment on your responses to jokes, cartoons, situation comedies on television. (Read Trevor Griffiths' *Comedians* (Faber) for a penetrating light on this.)

● Do different kinds of media produce different kinds of response? Explore how audio-visual media, with their much more intense and immediate use of sound, image and colour often affect people in different ways than do reading experiences. Decide where you stand in relation to John Pilger's attack on *The Deer Hunter* for cynical, technical slickness.

● Make attempts to cross boundaries in the expressive arts; share what you mean by response in English studies with other insights from music, visual arts, drama, photography, sculpture, etc. Can you understand each other? If you can't, what are the snags? Can you find a common meeting-ground in the languages you use?

FURTHER REFERENCES

Two Worlds of Andrew Wyeth: A conversation with Andrew Wyeth Thomas Hoving, Houghton Mifflin Press, Boston
Ways of Seeing John Berger, Penguin (and film)
Preoccupations Seamus Heaney, Faber
Living With a Text: some examples of written encounters with texts at 'A' level Northern English Group (AEB Mode 3). Copies available from Bernard Harrison, Dept. of Education, University of Sheffield.
Deeper into Movies Pauline Kael, Calder Boyars
Letters and Journals Katherine Mansfield, ed. C.K. Stead, Penguin
Arts in Society ed. Paul Barker, Fontana
The Golden Notebook (Preface) Doris Lessing, Panther
The Promise of Happiness: Value and meaning in children's fiction Fred Inglis, CUP
Camerawork: a journal of the politics of photography. Available from 121 Roman Road, London EE2 OQNN.
Edward Weston: The Flame of Recognition; his photographs accompanied by excerpts from the Daybooks and Letters ed. Nancy Newhall, Gordon Fraser
Ian Nairn's architectural criticism e.g. *Nairn's London,* Penguin (now out of print)
About Looking John Berger, Writers and Readers Cooperative
Theatre Poems from *Poems 1913–1956,* Bertolt Brecht, Eyre Methuen
Fenimore Cooper's Literary Offenses Mark Twain from *A Mark Twain Reader,* Penguin/Doubleday Anchor
The Crystal Bucket – TV Criticism from 1976–78 Clive James, Picador
'Looking', 'Screen and Dream' and 'Books and Bookpersons' from *Nothing Sacred* Angela Carter, Virago

Acknowledgements

The authors and publishers wish to thank the following who have kindly given permission for the use of copyright material:

Gillon Aitken on behalf of Paul Theroux for an extract from *The Great Railway Bazaar*; Allison and Busby Ltd for the poem 'Dry River Bed' from *Away* by Andrew Salkey; Basil Blackwell Publishers Ltd for an extract from *Hooligans or Rebels* by Stephen Humphries; Marion Boyars Publishers Ltd for an extract from 'On Peter Brook's Film of King Lear' by Pauline Kael in *Deeper into the Movies*; Curtis Brown Ltd on behalf of the Estates of W. H. Auden and Louis MacNeice for an extract from *Letter to Iceland*; Cambridge University Press for an extract from *The Promise of Happiness* by Fred Inglis; Camerawork for extracts from *A Seventh Man—Theory in Practice* and *The Process of Documentary* by John Berger, a review of *Nicaragua* by Susan Meiselas, and an extract from an interview with Susan Meiselas by Shirley Read and Megan Martin; Cameron Books for 'St Helens in the 1920s—Work and Play' from *Industrial Town* by Charles Forman; Jonathan Cape Ltd on behalf of Clive James for an extract from *The Crystal Bucket*; an extract from *Tristes Tropiques* by Claude Lévi-Strauss, translated by John and Doreen Weightman, and on behalf of the Estate of Robert Frost for an extract from *The Selected Letters of Robert Frost* edited by Lawrence Thompson; Carcanet Press Ltd for 'Grierson' from 'Five Poems on Film Directors' by Edwin Morgan in *Poems of Thirty Years*; Centerprise Trust Ltd for an extract from 'Mortuary Technician' by George Wood from *Working Lives*; Jonathan Clowes Ltd on behalf of Doris Lessing for an extract from *The Golden Notebook*; David & Charles Publishers, for two letters from *A Place Called Armageddon: Letters from The Great War*; Andre Deutsch Ltd for an extract from *I Can't Stay Long* by Laurie Lee, and 'Letter to his Mother' by e. e. cummings from *Selected Letters of e. e. cummings* edited by F. Dupee and George Stade; The English Centre (ILEA) for 'Me and My History' by Anna Leitrim from *Our Lives—Young People's Autobiography*; Faber and Faber Ltd for 'Portrait Photograph, 1915' from *Barbarians* by Douglas Dunn, and 'Deceased Effects' from *A State of Justice* by Tom Paulin; Granta Publications Ltd for an extract from 'The Other Argentina' by Daniel Kon; Harper & Row, Publishers, Inc. for an extract from 'The Ethics

of Living Jim Crow: An Autobiographical Sketch' in *Uncle Tom's Children* by
Richard Wright. Copyright 1937 by Richard Wright; William Heinemann Ltd for
an extract from *Going Back* by Penelope Lively; David Higham Associates Ltd on
behalf of Keith Waterhouse for 'Writing for the *Daily Mirror*' in *The Mirror's Way
with Words* and an extract from *Rhubarb, Rhubarb*; The Hogarth Press Ltd for a
letter from *Selected Letters of Edwin Muir*, edited by P. H. Butler; Michael Joseph
Ltd for an extract from *The Fire Next Time* by James Baldwin; Little, Brown
and Company for an extract from *The Complete Letters of Vincent van Gogh*, New
York Graphic Society Books, 1958, 1978; London Magazine Editions for 'Writing
of the Past' from *Notes from Another Country* by Julian Symons; Manchester
University Press for 'The Piano' from *A Ragged Schooling* by Robert Roberts;
John Murray (Publishers) Ltd for an extract from *A Place Apart* by Dervla Murphy;
New Society for the articles 'The Concrete Elephant' by Andrea Waind and 'On
a Distant Prospect ... Arts in Society' by Reyner Banham; The New Statesman
for 'Heroes' and 'Why *The Deer Hunter* is a Lie' by John Pilger from *Aftermath:
The Struggle of Cambodia and Vietnam*; Peter Owen Ltd for an extract from *Let
us Now Praise Famous Men* by James Agee and Walker Evans; Oxford University
Press for Part 1 from 'Ancestors' in *Islands* by Edward Kamau Brathwaite, 1969;
'Black Mountains' by Raymond Williams from *Places* edited by Ronald Blythe,
1981, and two letters from Wilfred Owen's *Collected Letters* edited by Harold
Owen and John Bell, 1967; Oxford University Press Inc. for extracts from *Abroad:
British Literary Travelling Between the Wars* by Paul Fussell. Copyright © 1980
by Paul Fussell; Lawrence Pollinger Ltd on behalf of the Estate of Frieda Lawrence
Ravagli for two letters from *The Letters of D. H. Lawrence* published by Cambridge
University Press, and on behalf of Graham Greene for an extract from *A Sort
of Life*, published by The Bodley Head; Penguin Books Ltd for poems 'Passengers',
'Rio de Janeiro' and 'Sunsets' by Blaise Cendrars from *Selected Poems* by Blaise
Cendrars, translated by Peter Hoida (Penguin Modern European Poets 1979).
Translation copyright © Peter Hoida 1979; an extract from *The View in Winter*
by Ronald Blythe (Penguin Books 1981). Copyright © Ronald Blythe 1979, and an
extract from *Hiroshima* by John Hersey (Penguin Modern Classics, 1972), copyright
© John Hersey, 1966; A. D. Peters & Co Ltd on behalf of Arthur Koestler for an
extract from *Arrow in the Blue*, published by Hutchinson Publishing Group;
Quartet Books Ltd for extracts from *Unemployment* by Jeremy Seabrook, and
Down and Out by Tony Wilkinson; Douglas Rae (Management) Ltd on behalf
of Martha Gellhorn for an extract from *Travels With Myself and Another*,
published by Eland Books, Copyright © Martha Gellhorn 1978; Anthony Sheil
Associates Ltd on behalf of George Jackson for an extract from *Soledad Brother:
Letters from Prison*, published by Jonathan Cape Ltd. Copyright © 1970 by World
Entertainers Ltd; Robson Books Ltd for extracts from *Related Twilights* by Josef
Herman and *The Rhinestone as Big as the Ritz* by Alan Coren; Routledge & Kegan
Paul PLC for an extract from the article 'The Seamen's Strike, Liverpool, 1966'
in *History Workshop Journal*, Issue 5, Spring 1978; Dr Jan van Loewen Ltd for an
extract from *Pebbles from my Skull* by Stuart Hood.

The author and publishers wish to acknowledge the following photograph sources:

J. Allan Cash Ltd p. 68; John Cornwall p. 84; Daily Mirror/British Museum Newspaper Library p. 166; Frans Halsmuseum pp. 228, 229, 234, 235; Musée Royaux Des Beaux Arts, Brussels p. 230; Jean Mohr p. 127; National Gallery of Canada, Ottawa — *Portrait d'un homme assis* (Adrian van Ostade?); National Museum Vincent Van Gogh, Amsterdam p. 139; Letter to Frieda Weekley 7.5.1912. Reproduced in the letters of D.H. Lawrence Volume 1, Cambridge University Press p. 134.